"After I followed Matt Bird's writing advice, I received an offer of representation from an agent who called my manuscript 'masterfully structured.' It's a testament to how helpful Bird's advice has been— I've learned more from him than from any other book about writing, and certainly more than from taking any writing class." **—PARKER PEEVYHOUSE, AUTHOR OF *WHERE FUTURES END***

. . . .

"Matt Bird's blog is possibly my favorite resource on storytelling, maybe even more than Robert McKee's *Story*. It-'s really insightful on story structure—detailed without being too rigid, and with a keen appreciation for both big blockbusters and smaller stories." **—EMILY HORNER, AUTHOR OF *A LOVE STORY STARRING MY DEAD BEST FRIEND***

THE SECRETS OF STORY

WRITER'S DIGEST
BOOKS

An imprint of Penguin Random House LLC
penguinrandomhouse.com

ISBN 978-1-4403-4823-5

Printed in the United States of America

Edited by Chelsea Plunkett
Designed by Alexis Estoye

ABOUT THE AUTHOR

DEDICATION

To Betsy

ACKNOWLEDGMENTS

I want to acknowledge the indefatigable assistance of many blog commenters who helped me develop this advice over several years, especially Jacob Snyder.

ABOUT THE AUTHOR

Matt Bird has an MFA in screenwriting from Columbia University. He developed these ideas on his popular blog, *Cockeyed Caravan*. He works as a screenwriter in Chicago, where he and his wife, Betsy, are raising two delightful little kids.

TABLE  CONTENTS

Preface.. 1

PART I

Writing for Strangers

1: George Clooney and Me 6

2: The Thirteen Essential Laws of Writing for Strangers......................... 15

PART II

The Ultimate Story Checklist

3: Concocting an Intriguing Concept 42

4: Creating Compelling Characters 81

5: Shaping a Resonant Structure... 128

6: Staging Strategic Scene Work 157

7: Drafting Electric Dialogue 196

8: Maintaining a Meticulous Tone 241

9: Interweaving an Irreconcilable Theme 266

PART III

Getting from Good to "Good Lord, This Is Amazing!"

10: Don't Revise, Rewrite! 299

11: When It's Finally Time to Fine-Tune 317

12: Now Cut Another 10 Percent 322

13: The Final Rule 331

Conclusion: Tell Great Stories Or Die! 334

Afterword 337

Appendix: The Ultimate Story Checklist 338

Index 351

PREFACE

You've just boarded a plane. Your iPhone is loaded with all your favorite podcasts, but before you can get your earbuds in, disaster strikes: The guy in the next seat starts telling you all about something crazy that happened to him—in great detail. This guy is an *unwelcome storyteller* trying to convince an extremely reluctant audience to care about his story. We all hate that guy, right?

But any time you write a story for strangers (*any* kind of story: novel, memoir, screenplay, comic, even just a cover letter), *you* become that unwelcome storyteller, desperately trying to make a connection before those earbuds pop in.

Twenty-first-century culture moves fast, and there's an endless amount of content bombarding us at all times. What are the new rules for succeeding as a writer in this oversaturated environment? The answer is simple: If you want to write for strangers, you have to remember what it feels like to *be* that jaded audience.

When that guy next to you starts talking, do you just assume he's got a good story to tell? No, you don't. Do you *automatically* care about what he has to say? Certainly not. But wait … could you ever *possibly* care? Yes, but only if he swiftly wins you over:

- How quickly do you want that chatty passenger's story to become interesting? *Right away!*
- Do you want him to start with a lot of background information about where he was born and what childhood traumas he had? *No! You want him to skip over all that.*

- Do you want him to tell you about a bunch of unrelated things that happened this week? *No! You want him to tell you a focused story about one unique and interesting thing that happened to him.*
- Do you want him to go on and on about what a pitiful, inactive, incapable failure he is? *No! If you're going to care about him, he'd better be worth caring about.*

It's that simple. Tell the story that would win *you* over, even if you didn't want to hear it. This is the heart of *The Secrets of Story*.

Of course, there are thousands of other writing guides, so what makes this one unique (and uniquely necessary)? The advice in this book is …

IRREVERENT: Writers are snarky people, but too many writing books are burdened by a grandiosity and solemnity that seem totally alien to a writer's day-to-day experience. I love writing, and I'm in awe of great stories, but the best way to write those stories is to never lose your perspective or sense of humor.

COMPREHENSIVE: Too many writing books fall into the category of "Here are a few pointers I picked up over the course of my career." That's great if those pointers happen to be the ones you need right now, but these books offer no place to begin, and they make no attempt to systematically cover each step of the process. This book has a step-by-step, concept-by-concept approach that examines just about everything that goes into writing a great story.

PRACTICAL: My focus is less on "What does it all mean?" and more on accumulating surgical instruments for specific situations you'll encounter. The hope is that the next time you're laboring over some poor patient and desperately hold out your hand for the next tool, it will be within reach. Consider me your operating room nurse.

COUNTERINTUITIVE: Too many books fill their pages with common sense or easy wisdom, confirming the certainties that readers brought with them. I try to limit myself to counterintuitive insights I never would have guessed when I started. This book strips away the easy assumptions that struggling writers fall prey to and replaces them with less-than-obvious solutions.

BASED ON HUMAN NATURE: Why do stories from all over the world have so much in common with each other? Is it because the authors are all following the same rule book? No, it's because they're all describing the same thing: human nature. Too many books say, "This is the way you have to do it because Aristotle said so," or because Hollywood says so, or because a market analysis says so, etc. This book rejects all of that in favor of natural, organic rules.

FOCUSED ON AUDIENCE IDENTIFICATION: And now we get to the big one. This is the essential quality of this book. I just can't find another book that puts the audience's satisfaction above your own or your professors'. If you really value your audience, you'll never have to choose between audience satisfaction and writing from the heart, because the two will be one and the same.

You have to embrace your audience. They are the *only* reason to write anything, and once you start listening to what they need, your writing will improve by leaps and bounds.

This is a book for anyone who tries to sell a narrative to a weary public: novelists, screenwriters, playwrights, creative nonfiction writers, journalists, marketers, speechwriters, and résumé writers. This book will show you how to create powerful audience identification, which is the heart of good storytelling.

I'm gratified that this advice has been embraced by many types of writers over my years of online pontificating (in fact, my top followers have always been novelists), but I should warn you up front: I won't be able to hide very well that my background is in film and TV writing, so the majority of the examples I give are taken from those two media. I've found that this actually works best for all writers because movies and TV, more than novels and plays, are the cultural currency we all share. And when a novel is adapted for the screen, it's boiled down to its essence, and the essence of writing is what we're talking about here. Rest assured, I use these examples in universal ways, so the lessons drawn from them are applicable to all types of writing.

So here we go! I hope this book will be for you what I wish I'd gotten when I started out: useful, illuminating, and, most of all, fun.

PART I
Writing for Strangers

GEORGE CLOONEY AND ME

The CAA agent was getting excited: "Great! Do you think you could make these changes in two weeks?"

"Of course!" I responded, trying to sound healthy. I was excited, too, but I was worried about whether I could pull this off without having to reveal my little secret.

After all, most of the people on this conference call didn't know about my diagnosis.

A year earlier, I had graduated from Columbia University with an MFA in screenwriting. I had won some awards there, so I was part of a group that got flown to L.A. to meet with agents and managers. I wound up signing with a fantastic young go-getter who worked for one of the highest-profile managers in the country, and they both promised me big things.

Soon afterward, I had been through a whirlwind of meetings with production companies, both in New York and Los Angeles, and now here I was on the phone with my manager, her boss, and the big-time agent they wanted to partner with on this project. They all loved my pitch for an hour-long period-piece spy show, and they wanted to set it up using the agent's deal at HBO.

Unfortunately, throughout the whole round of meetings, I was getting sicker. At first, my doctors couldn't figure out why. By the time they finally detected the cancer, it had metastasized into multiple systems and spread to both halves of my body. That's called "stage 4B." There is no stage 5.

The only *good* news was it was Hodgkin's lymphoma. Though Hodgkin's is swiftly fatal without treatment, it responds to chemotherapy relatively well. Even though we'd caught mine very late, there was still a 75 percent chance it could be permanently beaten within a year. I just had to make it through that year without wrecking my career.

When I told my industry friends about my diagnosis, they all said the same thing: "Don't tell your managers—they'll drop you." But I didn't have a lot of choice. If I didn't tell them, then someone else would. I was getting chemo every other Monday, and for a week afterward, I would stumble around semiconscious from toxic shock. At first, I simply arranged to have my studio meetings on the off weeks so that nobody would notice, but then my hair started falling out, and I was losing weight. I couldn't keep it a secret for long. It was time to come clean.

I called the manager who signed me and told her the truth, making sure to "joke" about the fact that everyone had said she'd drop me. She was aghast: "What a horrible thing to say! How could anybody think that? Of course we'll support you as you go through this." I told her how relieved I was. Then, without missing a beat, she said that we shouldn't tell her boss. "He's so excited by this new project, and we don't want him to lose interest." Um, okay. So now it was *our* secret.

Luckily, the conference call was scheduled for the Friday at the end of my off week, so most of the chemicals were out of my system and I was feeling spry. I was ready for whatever they might throw at me.

I'd sent in the pilot script a few weeks before. The purpose of the call was to get "notes," which is always a nerve-racking process. You're afraid you'll get hit with suggestions that make no sense whatsoever. It's a crapshoot: Will the note giver be a glad-handing boob who blundered into the business or a thoughtful professional who really cares about the work?

Fortunately, the CAA guy was *great*, and he gave me some of the best notes I've ever gotten, but, of course, the best notes are often the *toughest*. He loved the pilot, but he focused in like a laser on my greatest weakness: character creation. He said we needed all-new introductions for every character. I needed to make each member of the ensemble "pop" right away.

Luckily, he gave me a great example: George Clooney's introduction in the pilot for *ER*: A pediatrician stumbles into the hospital after a night of partying. His exasperated colleagues forcibly hook him up to a saline drip to get him sober, and he promptly falls asleep. When incoming patients jolt him awake, he leaps up and flies into action, saving lives.

I instantly saw what the agent meant. That's the kind of introduction that lets you know right away that this is going to be a rich, deep character with eight seasons of conflict built into his DNA.

The CAA guy asked if I could come up with introductions that good for *all* of my characters in two weeks. It was a tall order, but I said I could do it. What I didn't say, of course, was that I was about to be pumped full of poison, and I wouldn't be able to start until that dose wore off. Oh, and there was one more problem: The effects of chemo were cumulative, so I was now recovering less and less every time. My off weeks were getting shorter.

Still, my career momentum was on the line, so I told him it would be no problem. As we got off the phone, everybody engaged in some virtual backslapping, assuring each other this thing was going all the way to the top.

That Monday, I got my dose. A week later, I was becoming lucid again. I tried to use my impending deadline to snap my mind back into line and start writing. (*But in the meantime, maybe I should take another nap.*) And so went the week.

Whenever I could stay awake, I tried to force myself to come up with character introductions as good as Clooney's and then berated myself when I couldn't. My professors and managers told me I was such a great writer, so why was this so hard? Why couldn't I do this? Why didn't I have these skills?

Then Friday arrived, and I had nothing.

As it happened, Friday was also the day I was supposed to get my blood tested to ensure I had recovered enough to prepare for the *next* batch of poison. I was reluctant to tear myself away from my writing desk, but I finally shambled over to the hospital.

Once there, I asked my wonderfully maternal nurse, Joy, for a "stat" on the blood tests so I could get back to the writing as quickly as possible. Unfortunately, Joy ran my blood work and didn't like what she saw. Yes, my white blood cell count was high enough to prepare for the next round of chemo, but the rest of my levels were so low she couldn't believe I was able to stand. Joy ordered me to lie down for an hour of saline drip before I went home.

As I lay there, the saline worked wonders. I started feeling better and thinking more clearly. Eventually, the humor of the situation occurred to me: I had been studying that *ER* intro so long that I'd started to *live* it.

Just like Clooney, I leapt up afterward, rejuvenated. I went home and wrote all night. In the morning I sent off four strong intro scenes to my managers and the CAA guy. I could only hope that they wouldn't respond with any immediate notes, since I was about to go out of commission again for another agonizing week.

That was a few years ago. The good news is the chemo eventually worked, and it looks like the cancer's never coming back. The bad news is, like most projects, the TV show eventually stalled out. It's never died completely—in fact, it recently came back to life—but I've learned not to get too excited about these things.

But what really stuck with me from this incident was the harrowing realization that, despite my pricey education and all that praise I'd racked up, I didn't actually know what I was doing. At all.

When asked to write those introductions, I realized, to my horror, that no one had ever asked me to do *anything* like that before. I'd developed a lot of screenplays and TV scripts at Columbia, but most of the notes I'd received were about the work as a whole: The professors always wanted to talk about my ideas and introduce some even bigger ideas of their own. Never in a million years would they say, "Here's a popular TV show; write something as good as that." We were supposed to be *better* than the knuckle draggers writing Hollywood movies or network TV. We were supposed to be *artists*. As a result, I had learned the art but not the craft. When push came to shove, I simply didn't have the necessary tools I needed to do the job.

As bad as the cancer and chemo felt, this realization felt worse. I had just plunged myself (and my lovely new wife) into $150,000 worth of debt, only to discover I was totally unprepared for my profession.

This was *real* trouble. And the chances of recovery were a lot less than 75 percent.

THE POISONOUS CINDERELLA STORY

Up until that week, I was still clinging to my personal version of the Cinderella story: I was convinced I could go to a top MFA program, impress my professors, get whisked into a job in the industry, start at the top by selling a show to HBO, and begin a life of fame, fortune, and acclaim. So far, everything had *seemed* to work out (CAA liked the new intros, after all), but I began to feel a sense of dread: This was all an illusion. I didn't really "have it" yet.

Looking back, this was the time I began to see that Columbia had been run like a fantasy camp. We were encouraged to dabble in everything and specialize in nothing, to follow our muse wherever it led us, content in the knowledge that we were in a "safe space." We got tons of praise and very little criticism.

In fact, there was only one guaranteed way to get chewed out. More than once, when I hesitantly proposed to fellow students that they may need to reconceive some aspect of a project, my professors would bring the class to an abrupt halt and tear into me: How dare I imply that there was a "right way" or a "wrong way" to write? Students were free to follow their pure unadulterated visions, and nobody had any right to interfere in that process. Chastened, I would meekly reassure my fellow students that they should stick to their original vision, no matter what. That was the gospel.

In the end, the message of my program could be summarized in two words: *Never compromise.* Or to put it another way: *Never fix your story.*

Why did they insulate us from criticism? Why didn't they load us up with useful tools? Why didn't they teach us to satisfy an audience? I realized I had been scammed. They wanted us to feel as good as possible for as long as possible in order to get as much money out of us as they could. The way to do that was to assure us we were already geniuses.

But could we blame them for that? After all, why were we *really* there? To get our asses kicked? To have cold water thrown on us? Of course not. We were paying them a fortune to tell us we were great and about to become creative royalty. We had enrolled ourselves in fantasy camp, and it was their job to sell us the fantasy.

But it's not just MFA programs. Writers are plied with Cinderella stories from every direction, and particularly from book promoters. If a writer produces a hit after years of less-successful books (as was the case with Suzanne Collins), then her personal story is downplayed, but if the writer has a hugely successful debut (as was the case with J.K. Rowling and Stephenie Meyer), then her story is constantly trumpeted. Audiences love Cinderella stories, and promoting an author's rags-to-riches ordeal will sell more books.

The problem is, writers get fooled. We think instant success is the norm, not the exception. We expect million-dollar stories to appear to us in our dreams, fully formed, and all we have to do is write them down. This makes it painfully disappointing when we fail to achieve overnight success, and it also makes it hard *to learn* to write, because we think that great writers shouldn't need to learn.

As I was finally coming down from my own Cinderella story, I noticed two different news reports that perfectly encapsulated the myth and the reality of making your first sale.

The first was about a first-time novelist who bragged that fifty-four agents rejected his novel, but he stubbornly kept sending it out until the fifty-fifth took a chance on him and got it published. Press releases like this are very common, but they always leave out one *huge* detail: *Was he revising his manuscript the whole time, or not?*

These stories always imply that the early rejecters were abject fools who failed to see the author's inherent brilliance, but the author stuck to his guns and refused to listen to the naysayers. Finally, one brave agent and/or publisher saw the value that everybody else missed, proving the author had been right all along. But isn't there another possibility? Surely, by the time you've been rejected by ten agents, much less fifty-four, you should start *eagerly* listening to the naysayers, pumping them for notes, and rewriting your text to satisfy the most persistent objections.

Isn't it possible that agent fifty-five *didn't* prove the previous fifty-four wrong? What if that last agent proved the others *right*? Isn't it more likely those rejections provided the impetus the author needed to fix his manuscript? Why can't the press release be honest and admit that?

I was gratified a few months later to read a far more humble and honest interview. Unlike the writer profiled in the earlier article, this novelist's debut book was a huge success—but this was no Cinderella story. Read how Kathryn Stockett, author of *The Help*, describes what she went through in her attempts to get her book to market:

> By rejection number forty-five, I was truly neurotic. It was all I could think about—revising the book, making it better, getting an agent, getting it published. I insisted on rewriting the last chapter an hour before I was due at the hospital to give birth to my daughter. I would not go to the hospital until I'd typed "The End."

That's the reality of writing. It doesn't spring from your genius, fully formed—you cobble it into shape with a lot of sweat and elbow grease. You take those rejections seriously and rewrite it over and over until you finally figure out how to overcome the most persistent objections. Writing is a process of trial and error, trial and error, trial and error.

WE CAN REBUILD HIM

So there I was, reeling from my newfound realizations. My MFA program had left me without the skills I needed; it had also given me exactly the wrong attitude toward writing. It was time to reject every lofty theory I had been taught and learn the nuts and bolts of real writing.

As I slowly recovered from the chemo, I started working on new and better manuscripts, but I also started a daily blog called *Cockeyed Caravan*. At first, it was just an excuse to rewatch and write about my favorite movies and TV shows, but then it became something else entirely. I was reapproaching these stories with new eyes, and I began to see many of the things I'd missed before.

I had borrowed the name of the blog from one of my favorite old movies, *Sullivan's Travels*. Though I didn't realize it at the time, this quote presaged my growing realization of the importance of audience identification for writers.

In the movie, Joel McCrea plays a pretentious Hollywood writer/director who refuses to make a studio assignment called *Ants in Your Pants of 1939* until his studio releases his previous movie, a grim allegory for modern America called *O Brother, Where Art Thou?* (Of course, there would later be a *real* movie made with that title, in tribute to this one.)

Everyone who sees McCrea's ponderous epic tells him that he just doesn't understand poverty, so he leaves all of his possessions behind and goes on the bum, riding the rails like a real hobo. Unfortunately, McCrea still can't entirely connect to his poor compatriots because he always knows that his butler is just a phone call away. It's only when he gets mugged and falsely arrested for murder that he comes to understand the true nature of poverty. His fellow chain gang members are not moved by his lofty rhetoric, but when they're shown silly cartoons on movie night, they finally rise above their miserable situation and feel human again for a moment.

After McCrea manages to free himself, he happily signs up to direct the comedy, saying, "There's a lot to be said for making people laugh. Did you know that's all that some people have? It isn't much, but it's better than nothing in this cockeyed caravan!"

I gradually came to realize that there was a deeper resonance to my choice of a title: More and more, I was using the blog to create a new model of writing advice, one focused on satisfying an audience rather than merely satisfying yourself.

With the help of many amazing blog commenters that became my collaborators, I picked apart my favorite stories and then put them back together, carefully cataloging what *really* made each one work.

What I ended up with was a long list of counterintuitive realizations about storytelling that were entirely the opposite of what I'd been taught in school and quite different from the advice in the most popular writing books as well. This was the *true* nature of story, which was hiding just below the surface.

And so, once I fully recovered my health, I dived back into my career with what I'd learned in exile, and I've had far more financial success. Now I understand how to write those killer character introductions producers demand, how to invisibly structure like a pro, and how to make something meaningful.

Meanwhile, unexpectedly, the advice took on a life of its own, which is what led to this book. With the invaluable contribution of my commenters, I ended up with a comprehensive list of incisive questions that provide new insight into every step of the writing process.

Those questions will form the heart of this book, but before I get to them, I need to melt down your brain a little bit so that it'll be easier for me to reshape it according to my fiendish whims. Let's start with the thirteen big game-changing breakthroughs that led to everything else.

THE THIRTEEN ESSENTIAL LAWS
OF WRITING FOR STRANGERS

Let me preface this by saying that I'm not claiming to be Edmund Hillary, reaching a peak that has never been glimpsed before—hopefully you're a lot smarter than me and this stuff has always been perfectly obvious to you. Primarily, these laws are intended as a sort of antivenom. I use them to flush poison out of my veins, and I offer them up to you in case you need the same cure.

You have to ask yourself *why* you're doing this. If you're only doing it to please yourself, then you're guaranteed to succeed *and* guaranteed to fail. I promise that you *will* eventually satisfy yourself, but your end product will never satisfy anybody else. You may think you're capable of holding yourself to a high standard, but that almost certainly isn't true.

The problem is that you *already know* how to identify with yourself, so achieving self-satisfaction will be way too easy. What you don't know how to do is make *strangers* identify with the heroes you create. That's much harder, and a much more ambitious goal.

When you look at your manuscript, you see a shiny gem that you lovingly cut and polished. Strangers just see a pile of paper. Eventually, you realize it's not that gratifying to say, "I love my shiny gem!" but it's *very* gratifying to say, "A stranger loves my pile of paper!" The first is easy to achieve, and therefore worthless. The second is extremely difficult, which makes it priceless.

1. YOU MUST WRITE FOR AN AUDIENCE, NOT JUST YOURSELF

This is the big one. And it's also the biggest hurdle for some writers.

Many writers fear that if they try to write for an audience they'll end up "pandering" or "chasing the market." Indeed, both of those are bad, because the audience doesn't want to control your narrative. They want *you* to control *their* experience. They want you to set, upset, and reset their expectations. They'll never admit it, but they want you to masterfully manipulate their emotional experience every step of the way. Figuring out how to do that is the number one goal for any writer.

If you feel you have to choose between writing for an audience and writing from the heart, then you're in big trouble, because to become a great writer, the two must be the same thing.

In the 1970s, Francis Ford Coppola turned out a remarkable string of masterpieces (*The Godfather, The Conversation, The Godfather: Part II, Apocalypse Now*) because he respected himself *and* his public at the same time. He wasn't *chasing* an audience but was skillfully *enticing* them to chase after him. He didn't give his audience exactly what they wanted, but he did tune into their wavelength to find stories that resonated with them.

But by the time Coppola got to the nineties, he had a total disconnect: He gave several interviews in which he explained that his goal was to make "one for them" followed by "one for me." But it was kind of hard to tell which was which, because none of his movies from that period (*The Godfather: Part III, Bram Stoker's Dracula, The Rainmaker, Jack*) were any good. As soon as you make the distinction, you've sabotaged yourself.

Now, of course, you might be thinking, *Don't audiences get it wrong all the time? Don't they embrace crap? Why should I trust their taste more than my own?* But this sort of antagonistic thinking will cripple your artistic growth. Do audiences get browbeaten into consuming and even "liking" bad stories? Yes, but in most cases they feel guilty about it before too long. Ultimately, they know a truly great story when they see it, and those are the stories that stay with them. That's the story you want to write.

2. AUDIENCES *PURCHASE* YOUR WORK BECAUSE OF YOUR CONCEPT, BUT THEY *EMBRACE* IT BECAUSE OF YOUR CHARACTERS

Writers get a lot of mixed messages about the value of their ideas. Beginners, believing their ideas are valuable, will protect them with secrecy and copyright symbols on the title page, while professionals know that ideas are a dime a dozen and nobody wants to steal them. It's only the unique expression of an idea that's valuable. They calmly explain that beginners should stop worrying about protecting their "unique idea" and instead disseminate their work as widely as possible.

For the most part, that's true. But consider this: Each week, producers and publishers announce new acquisitions with much fanfare, and never once has anyone said they've purchased "a standard story with exceptionally rich characters." Instead, acquisitions are almost always accompanied by a one-line description of the brand-new "high-concept" idea they've just snatched up.

So which is it? Are ideas cheap or valuable? Are writers in the concept or the execution business? It's true that ideas are ephemeral and the only marketable *skill* is good writing, but those who buy your work can't boast to their colleagues about your skill. They can't impress anybody with their *opinion* that the story they bought is well written. They can only boast about the *fact* that it has a unique concept. So that's what they do.

And this carries over to marketing: When it's time to release the final product, they can't say, "I know it doesn't sound interesting, but trust us—it's really well written." To market your work, it has to have a unique, appealing concept.

But, then, a funny thing happens: Audiences have their interest piqued by your concept, and that's what gets them to put their money down. But as soon as your audience steps into your story, they lose all interest in your concept. Now all they care about is your story's *hero*.

But wait, you say, what if my story isn't about a hero?

3. AUDIENCES WILL ALWAYS CHOOSE ONE CHARACTER TO BE *THEIR* HERO

Throughout this book, I'll be using the word *hero* a lot, but it's a word some writers resist. What if you don't want your main character to be heroic? For that matter, what if you don't even want to *have* a main character? What if you don't want to celebrate an *individual* hero?

Well, I've got some bad news for you: Audiences will *always* choose one character to represent their point of view and interests. This is their hero. (According to this definition, the term is gender neutral and morally neutral. A hero can be male or female, good or evil, or anywhere in between.)

But what if your story is about an ensemble? It doesn't matter. Your audience will choose *one* member of the ensemble to be the anchor for their identification, and you can't stop them from doing that. When we watch the pilot for *Lost*, we don't identify with each member of the ensemble equally; we only identify with Jack. In later episodes we have other heroes, but we intensely identify with one and only one hero per episode.

Interestingly, the hero the audience chooses may not be their favorite character in the ensemble. In the case of *Star Wars*, most of us enjoy hanging out with Han Solo more than Luke Skywalker, but when Han abandons the rebel cause, we would be upset if the story followed him and left the others behind. Luke may not be our favorite, but he's our hero. He's the character we identify with and the one whose goals we share.

So you need to ask yourself: Which character will my audience choose to be *their* hero?

Audiences have a remarkable willingness to root for heroes with ambiguous or even downright rotten morality, but there are some heroes they will never accept. Two things must be true of a character if the audience is going to choose that character for their hero: Every hero must be *active* and *resourceful*.

Some writers think they can simply place a passive character up front in every scene and the audience will have no choice but to accept that character as their hero. But audiences will inevitably reject these would-be heroes and search the story for someone else, *anyone* else, to care about.

In the case of *Paradise Lost*, the Renaissance poet John Milton was incensed to discover that many people identified Satan as the hero, simply because he was active, resourceful, clever, and powerfully motivated, while Adam just kind of sat around. But the decision wasn't up to the author. The audience chose their own hero, and the choice was fairly obvious. The wonderful thing is that even if you root for the villain (Satan himself in this case) it's still a great work of literature. Milton made exactly the opposite point of what he intended, but the result was still powerful.

The same cannot be said, unfortunately, for more modern examples of this problem. Let's look at *Superman Returns*. The supposed hero is such a passive, morose, flying lump that viewers have no choice but to choose a different hero. They need look no further than Lois Lane's *other* suitor, an active, resourceful, smart, funny, courageous everyday guy. He has no powers, but when he finds out that Superman is in trouble, he runs out of his house, jumps in a (convenient) seaplane, and flies toward the middle of the ocean to fish him out of the drink! Now *that's* a hero.

This is one of the big problems with stories where the "good guy" is suddenly revealed to be the bad guy more than halfway through. The writers of these types of stories labor under a fundamental misconception. They think the audience assumes the main character is the good guy until told otherwise. But the opposite is actually true: The audience will automatically *distrust* your main characters and will only invest in them if they are sufficiently compelling early in your story. Your audience will be watching your heroes intensely, and they'll know your heroes aren't *really* heroic long before the "big reveal."

So what are the consequences if the audience *doesn't* care about your hero? Let's just say that you're in a *lot* of trouble, because ...

4. AUDIENCES DON'T REALLY CARE ABOUT STORIES; THEY CARE ABOUT CHARACTERS

This is probably the most shocking of all of the laws. Could this really be true? Yes, it can, and once you notice it, you see it *everywhere*. That's when so many things start to make sense.

Two of the worst box office flops of this century are *John Carter* and *Green Lantern*. In both cases, audiences immediately knew they were in for an epic disaster because the movies begin with a long, ponderous voice-over and special-effects montage showing us the entire history of an alien civilization. This is almost always a sign you're watching a flop.

These montages represent a fundamental misunderstanding of how stories work: They assume the audience is going to care about the plot. The fact is that audiences, no matter how much they love the story, can't really care about the plot; they can only really care about the hero.

Two weeks before *John Carter* opened, a profile of director Andrew Stanton ran in *The New Yorker*. Writer Tad Friend portrays Stanton as a frantic micromanager who is belatedly coming to suspect that his movie doesn't work. Nevertheless, he's still unwilling to compromise, despite the best efforts of his colleagues to set him straight. Here's how Friend describes the problem:

> At most studios, filmmakers try to keep the execs at bay, but at Pixar the Brain Trust of six to twelve story gurus is intimately involved in revising every movie—"plussing" it, in Pixar's term. They were confused by the film's beginning, in which Princess Dejah delivered a lecture about the state of the Barsoomian wars, and they found her arch and stony. John Lasseter asked Stanton, "What are people going to hang on to and care about?"

Stanton is famously candid in other people's Brain Trust sessions, and famously prickly in his own. The Brain Trust suggested a fix for the opening: Why don't we discover Mars through John Carter's eyes, when he arrives? "That's lazy thinking, guys," Stanton replied. "If I do that, then thirty minutes in I'm going to have to stop the film to explain the war, and Dejah, and who everyone is, and we're going to have even bigger problems."

But the Brain Trust was right. When the movie was released, audiences laughed it off the screen. Nobody cared about the history of Mars. Stanton had it backward.

It may seem sad to hear the audience will never care about your story, but it's actually great news, since it makes your job a lot easier. While it's insanely hard to get an audience to truly care about your hero, the upside is that it's all you have to do.

Stanton put himself in an impossible position: His movie had *five* unrelated framing sequences, and he expected his audience to find a new way to care about each one. But we weren't going to care about Mars until *John* cared about Mars.

Indeed, this is exactly how author Edgar Rice Burroughs arranged it in the movie's excellent source novel, *A Princess of Mars*. First, we invest ourselves in John's journey, and then we see how Mars affects that journey. Burroughs was a grand master of creating wild worlds, but he first created compelling characters. Once we were invested, he knew we would follow them anywhere.

5. THE BEST WAY TO INTRODUCE EVERY ELEMENT OF YOUR STORY IS FROM YOUR HERO'S POINT OF VIEW

Once you've gotten us to care about the hero, you've got a huge resource: We'll care about *anything* the hero cares about. Writers are smart to maximize this resource to its full potential by introducing almost every story element from the hero's point of view.

Don't get me wrong: Certainly a lot of great stories have been written where we meet several different elements separately, but their authors are choosing to run uphill. If you want to make things easier on your audience, let the hero be their guide.

The Harry Potter novels and the TV series *The Sopranos* are two very different sagas, but they benefit greatly by obeying this law. In both cases, each character is first defined by our hero's feelings. The hero is not just one of many characters we meet all at once; he's our point of view, our guide to this universe.

In time, these sagas became wildly complex, with a lot of fully rounded characters and satisfying subplots. And crucially, in both cases, the audience *eventually* breaks away from the hero's point of view. At first, all we understand about each character is what the hero understands, and we share the hero's prejudices about each character. (We initially share Tony's belief that his wife is unreasonable and Harry's belief that Professor Snape is a villain.) But once the world is established, we begin to see complexities in these characters that the hero *can't*.

In each case, these character complexities *gradually* emerge. Both J.K. Rowling and David Chase knew it would be too ambitious to present several coequal points of view right from the beginning. The best way to introduce these two worlds is from one point of view. Then, *only* once we're situated, show that the hero's perspective is actually limited and his world is more complex than he (or *we*) first perceived.

You always risk stopping a story dead when you cut away to a dramatic, quirky introduction of a secondary character who doesn't yet have any obvious connection to the hero. In most cases, it's too much to ask us to *separately* identify and care about an endless stream of new characters.

Even if we're switching to villains your hero isn't aware of yet, they should still be defined by their relationship to your hero, either as the unseen obstacle to the hero's goal or as the negation of the hero's philosophy.

This makes writing much easier because you don't have to make the audience care about every person, place, and thing individually. The audience only cares about seeing the hero tackle this challenge. Since everything else in the story is defined in relationship to that challenge, the audience will naturally care about each of these things, too, simply by caring about that *one* thing.

But, of course, all of this depends on your ability to get people to invest in your hero.

6. IT'S VERY HARD TO GET AUDIENCES TO CARE ABOUT *ANY* HERO BECAUSE THEY'RE AFRAID OF BEING *HURT*

This is a bit of a paradox. As I said, your audience will insist on choosing one character from your story to be their hero. But that doesn't mean they'll choose to *root* for that character. What it means is they're going to warily *place their expectations* on that character. And those expectations are *huge*.

Once we tentatively identify with your heroes, we begin to demand a lot from them—and swiftly reject them if they fail to deliver. This is why character creation is the hardest and most vital part of a writer's job.

For beginning writers, it can be shocking to realize that audiences absolutely will *not* give their characters the benefit of the doubt. Why can't the audience just meet the hero halfway, no matter how passive or indecisive or downright useless that hero might be? Why does the writer have to *make* them care? Why does the audience need to be seduced *every time*?

There's actually a very good reason for this. You need to realize you're asking the audience to do three things:

1. Believe in the reality of the story you're telling.
2. Fall in love with your hero.
3. Invest in the outcome of the story.

In other words, you're asking your audience to become *emotionally involved*, and that's always an uncomfortable request. Every time your audience members become emotionally invested in a person, even a fictional person, they run the risk of getting *hurt*.

- How do *you* feel when you fall for a lie? You feel like a fool.
- How do *you* feel when you fall in love with someone who is ultimately not worth caring about? You feel heartbroken.
- What happens when *you* invest your hopes and dreams in a cause, only to find out you've been led into a bottomless quagmire? You feel betrayed.

Yes, it sucks to toss aside a book you just bought or to suffer through a play or movie you've paid a lot to see. From an economic point of view, you're better off simply choosing to enjoy your purchase. But as much as it hurts to lose that money, it feels worse to make yourself emotionally vulnerable to a bad story.

This is why the job is so insanely hard. How do you reach an audience who is *afraid* of your story? Afraid that you're going to make fools of them? Afraid of having their hearts broken? Afraid of being betrayed?

How do you let them know that this time it'll be different? That this time they're in good hands? That this time it's safe to believe in your world, fall in love with your hero, and assume there will be a satisfactory emotional impact at the end?

You have to convince a hostile audience to believe in a world that they *know* is actually a lie. You have to force them to suspend their disbelief against their will. You have to trick them into falling in love with your characters despite the fact that these characters will cease to exist when the story ends. You have to get them worked up about fictional danger.

And every time an audience reads a bad book, watches a bad movie, or attends a bad play, it just gets harder for the *next* writer, because the audience is increasingly reluctant to care again.

So how do you convince an audience to go against their better judgment and care about your hero? It sounds like you need a really likable hero, right? Well, not so fast.

7. YOUR AUDIENCE NEED NOT ALWAYS SYMPATHIZE WITH YOUR HERO, BUT THEY MUST EMPATHIZE WITH YOUR HERO

In my television writing classes, my fellow students and I dreamed of writing tough, challenging, brutally smart series like *The Sopranos*, *Mad Men*, or *Breaking Bad*. We were drawn to these shows because we *thought* they had broken free of the shackles of the "likable protagonist." We thought they had made our jobs a lot easier because they proved you didn't need "sympathetic characters" anymore. It seemed to us that these shows enjoyed a greater freedom than everything else on TV. And now *we* were going to be the beneficiaries of that freedom.

In our pilots, we gleefully created antiheroes who out-monstered Tony Soprano, Don Draper, and Walter White combined. And why not? There were no rules now! But we were shocked to find that everybody *hated* our antiheroes. Even *we* hated them. We were baffled: Tony, Don, and Walter got away with so much bad behavior, and yet everybody still loved them. Why didn't anybody love *our* morally murky characters?

We had totally misunderstood the appeal of those shows. We thought those writers had liberated themselves from false limitations, but the opposite was true: They had *constrained* themselves by accepting *additional* limitations. They had set the difficulty level at maximum.

If we had checked IMDb (the Internet Movie Database), we would have seen that the brilliant creators of those shows had spent years mastering the art of writing *likable* characters. Before he created *The*

Sopranos, David Chase had written for *The Rockford Files*; *Mad Men* creator Matthew Weiner had written for a lot of sitcoms, such as *The Naked Truth*, *Baby Blues*, and *Becker*; and *Breaking Bad* creator Vince Gilligan had been one of the head writers for *The X-Files*. These writers had gotten so good at making traditional heroes likable that they decided to set a bigger challenge for themselves: Could they somehow get their audiences to love *rotten* guys?

Sympathy is great, but it's not as important as *empathy*. Tony Soprano, Don Draper, and Walter White are less sympathetic than most heroes, and to make up for it, the writers generate *twice as much empathy*. We *intensely* feel for these antiheroes, sharing their frustrations and anguish, though not their hates. We are privileged with an intimate understanding of their raw hopes and fears, even if we never sympathize with their goals. But that's okay, because …

8. MOST IMPORTANT, YOUR AUDIENCE MUST *IDENTIFY* WITH YOUR HERO

Bad stories will often feature an over-the-top moment at the beginning in which the meek hero suddenly thwarts a mugging, punches out a bully, or stops a car from hitting a potential love interest.

This is sometimes known as the "Save the Cat" moment, so named by the late Blake Snyder in his best-selling book series. Snyder's books are full of smart writing tips, and they're well worth reading, but the titular piece of advice has led a lot of writers astray.

Don't get me wrong—I agree with Snyder's basic point. He starts off by talking about Angelina Jolie's god-awful *Tomb Raider* movies, which embody the foolish Hollywood idea that audiences merely want their heroes to be strutting badasses who blow stuff up, mutter sarcastic one-liners, and expect everyone to fall in love with them. Snyder correctly pointed out that audiences actually have a limited tolerance for badassery. The whole idea behind "Save the Cat" was that heroes have to go back to *earning* an audience's goodwill by doing sympathetic actions like saving cats. To a certain extent, he was right. After all, would Jolie's character have been more likable if she'd saved a few cats? Definitely.

But that only goes so far. It's nice if your audience admires your hero, but it's far more important that they *identify* with your hero. Heroic actions, like saving cats, generate sympathy for your hero, but what you really want to do is generate identification. The two are not identical. In fact, they're often at odds with each other. The more "heroically" your hero acts, the *harder* it can be to identify with that hero, because most of us *aren't* very heroic.

After all, when was the last time you saved a cat?

Let's look at the opening of two of the most beloved novels of all time. Both Elizabeth Bennet in *Pride and Prejudice* and Jane in *Jane Eyre* are somewhat prickly heroines, but the authors generate our identification with them right away by using a ridiculously simple trick. Here's one of Elizabeth's first scenes:

> On entering the drawing-room she found the whole party at loo, and was immediately invited to join them; but suspecting them to be playing high she declined it, and making her sister the excuse, said she would amuse herself for the short time she could stay below, with a book. Mr. Hurst looked at her with astonishment.
>
> "Do you prefer reading to cards?" said he; "that is rather singular."
>
> "Miss Eliza Bennet," said Miss Bingley, "despises cards. She is a great reader, and has no pleasure in anything else."

And here's the introduction of *Jane Eyre*:

> "Jane, I don't like cavillers or questioners; besides, there is something truly forbidding in a child taking up her elders in that manner. Be seated somewhere; and until you can speak pleasantly, remain silent."
>
> A breakfast-room adjoined the drawing-room, I slipped in there. It contained a bookcase: I soon possessed myself of a volume, taking care that it should be one stored with pictures. I mounted into the window-seat: gathering up my feet, I sat cross-

legged, like a Turk; and, having drawn the red moreen curtain nearly close, I was shrined in double retirement. …

With Bewick on my knee, I was then happy: happy at least in my way. I feared nothing but interruption, and that came too soon. The breakfast-room door opened.

While your audience is reading your book, there's no better way to create instant identification with your heroine than by having a mean character *interrupt* her reading and criticize her for having such a useless hobby! This is better than a dozen saved cats.

What you're looking for is the moment of shared *humanity*. As C.S. Lewis said, "Friendship is born at the moment when one person says to another, 'What! You too? I thought I was the only one!'"

But you need not have your hero or heroine do the exact same thing the reader is doing. Instead, you can just follow this general rule …

9. THE BEST WAY TO CREATE IDENTIFICATION IS FOR A CHARACTER TO BE MISUNDERSTOOD

Some people try to be heroes, while others prefer to be scoundrels. Some feel like winners; others feel like losers. Some are naturally happy, and others are perpetually gloomy. But there's *one* thing each of us feels, *one* universal human emotion.

Everyone feels *misunderstood*.

Most of the time, we feel unfairly condemned or underestimated, but sometimes we feel like we're *worse* than anyone suspects. As Bob Dylan says, "If my thought-dreams could be seen, they'd probably put my head in a guillotine." But either way, we feel misunderstood.

Audiences love to get to know heroes intimately. We love to see actions no one else is watching and then feel sudden umbrage when others, who haven't shared our intimacy, make false assumptions about them. We love to see heroes' true motivation established in one scene and then see others unfairly ascribe false motives to them in the next scene. This truly bonds us to a character.

Let's look at a great moment of audience identification in the movie that made Amy Adams a star: *Junebug*. Ben McKenzie plays a lout who pays no attention to his pregnant wife, played by Adams. McKenzie gets banished to the basement during the baby shower because the family is sure he'll be an embarrassment to everybody. But then a TV special comes on about Adams's favorite animal, the meerkat. McKenzie desperately tries to find a blank VHS tape to record the special. When he can't find one, he runs upstairs to ask his wife for one. She's normally very patient with him, but this time she finally decides to stand up to him and not let him interrupt the shower. He slinks away and apologizes without ever letting on that he was trying to do something nice for her.

Suddenly we *love* this guy, not so much because he tried, in his own incompetent way, to do something nice for his fiancée, but because his actions were unfairly judged and misunderstood. We've been through something with him. We've seen his secret honor.

Once we identify with the heroes, we'll go almost anywhere with them—but that doesn't mean you get to waste your audience's time …

10. YOUR STORY IS NOT ABOUT YOUR HERO'S LIFE; IT'S ABOUT YOUR HERO'S PROBLEM

We've already limited your story to one hero, but now let's limit it a lot more. You're not writing about your hero's *life*; you're writing about your hero's *problem*.

Most successful stories are structured around one and *only* one problem. It begins or becomes undeniable in the first scene, and ends (or is peacefully accepted) in the last scene. The problem should have multiple levels, with internal and external aspects, and a sprawling series of consequences and mini-conflicts that spiral out of it, but it should still basically be *one* problem. Even if you're writing about a broad societal problem, you should probably focus on how it manifests itself in the life of one hero.

So you have to cut out all of the material that doesn't relate to the hero's problem, but this can be surprisingly hard to do. Sometimes, this means that you have to cut out *great* material.

The Iliad is not about *everything* that happened in the Trojan War, nor is it about several unrelated incidents in the life of its hero, Achilles. It's about one problem: Homer has come to sing of the wrath of Achilles and the various conflicts that occur because of his wrath. That's it. Even though we cut away from Achilles, we are seeing story elements that will (eventually) directly engage his wrath.

One of the most shocking things about the epic is that it ends just *before* the story of the Trojan Horse. We find out about that part of the story in other epics, but Homer never mentions it in *The Iliad*. Why? Because that incident happens after the wrath of Achilles *ends*. In fact, it happens *because* the wrath of Achilles has ended: He's gotten over himself, and he's ready to lead the final battle.

Homer can't include that part of the story because it falls outside the realm of his dramatic question. If he had tacked it onto the end, it would have made for a great spectacle, but it would have felt empty. By the end, Achilles' feud with Agamemnon has already resolved itself, and we are no longer emotionally invested in the story.

Like *The Iliad*, David O. Russell's 2010 biopic, *The Fighter*, is careful to avoid tacked-on scenes. Here's the funny thing about that movie: Micky Ward is actually most famous for the three knock-down, dragout, never-say-die title fights he fought against boxer Arturo Gatti in the nineties. Go watch them on YouTube—they're astonishing. But those legendary fights are *not* in the movie.

The writers took a good look at Ward's life and decided that the *best* story was Ward's struggle with his family. Once they made that choice, they ruthlessly pared down that story to its essence. The story begins when Ward finally becomes aware that his family is his real problem, and it ends when that problem is ultimately resolved.

The writers must have been hugely tempted to tack on the stunning Gatti fights at the end of the movie, but, as with Achilles, the whole reason those fights came about was because Ward had *solved* the problems outside the ring that had been holding him back. And if his big problem is over, then the story's over, even if it means leaving out some wildly entertaining scenes.

But it's easy to fall into the trap of covering a character's whole life, as was the case with the 2004 biopic *The Aviator*. Over the years, a lot of writers thought a Howard Hughes biopic would be a sure bet. After all, the guy did so many interesting things! He invented some famous airplanes, produced some famous movies, dated some famous actresses, helped de-monopolize Atlantic air travel, bought up a lot of Vegas real estate, and went crazy. That's a pretty easy way to fill up two hours, right?

But a biopic isn't a comprehensive biography or an exhaustive catalog of great deeds. It's a *story*. And most good stories are about *one* problem. Hughes's tendency to flit from project to project actually makes him a *terrible* candidate for a biopic.

The filmmakers tried their hardest, but their Hughes biopic fell flat. Like its hero, it jumped around without committing to any one story. We see Leonardo DiCaprio make an expensive movie, outfox a crooked senator, and bottle his pee, but none of these scenes have any connection to each other.

Cramming a lot of Hughes's various accomplishments into one story was self-defeating. It was impossible to care about all those little things. The audience wants to care about one big problem and follow it to its natural climax.

So how do you structure your story around one big problem?

11. STORY STRUCTURE IS JUST A LIST OF THE STEPS AND MISSTEPS MOST PEOPLE GO THROUGH WHEN SOLVING A LARGE PROBLEM IN REAL LIFE

There's no more controversial topic for writers than story structure. We become instantly dubious when we're told that most stories have a similar underlying structure. *That's true for mediocre stories, maybe, but not mine. I'm not going to give in to the structure Nazis!* Only after we've been at it for a while, and have written a lot of unsatisfying stories, do we begin to suspect there's something happening here, and what it is ain't exactly clear.

We are sometimes ordered to read and memorize books that dictate certain structures. Often, we're told, like math students, that wise gray-haired old men have figured this stuff out and we should merely plug in their formulas. This is unsatisfying, and we naturally rebel. After all, isn't it wrong to write something formulaic?

Every year, some new article appears blaming Snyder's *Save the Cat* for the decline of movies. These critics have decided that today's movies seem too "by the book," and sure enough, here's the book! They've found their culprit. But when we look into the past, we discover something peculiar: The structure always *predates* the gurus.

Snyder and all of his fellow gurus are tweaking Joseph Campbell's *The Hero with a Thousand Faces*, but Campbell didn't make up these rules, either. He discovered them by distilling the essence of myths from different cultures, all of which turned out to have strikingly similar plot turns, even though many of those ancient scribes had no idea that those other stories existed.

Gurus don't dictate the structure. They discover it.

The *real* problem with most structure gurus is that they describe their structures *externally*. They say, "These are the rules, as determined by important men, so who are you to question why?" This attitude makes it easy for writers to reject these books and easy for critics to go on the attack.

But structure isn't a set of external rules. Gurus are wrong to take an antagonistic attitude toward their readers, angrily demanding that they defer to their betters. Instead of laying down the law, they should invite authors to do what Campbell did: explore many different journeys, both real and imagined, and see what they discover.

Inevitably, what writers find is that a certain type of structure tends to *naturally* be more powerful than others. Lo and behold, most good stories *do* share a similar underlying structure, *not* because authors have been forced to adopt it but because the heroes, if left on their own, will naturally make a similar sequence of choices.

Why is this? Where does this natural structure come from? Why do most heroes follow a similar sequence of choices, resulting in a similar series of ups and downs?

The answer is simple: No matter what your deconstructionist professors told you, there *is* such a thing as human nature. People know how people are. Human nature dictates that most of us will tend to follow the same steps and missteps when solving a large problem. Therefore, stories will feel more natural if *heroes* tend to follow those same steps and missteps.

If someone says your story has a structure problem, it doesn't mean you broke some arbitrary rules. It means your writing doesn't ring true because some of the natural steps or missteps are missing.

Now don't get me wrong—your story will indeed feel formulaic if you start with an artificial structure and work *backward*, painting by numbers. But if you start by afflicting your hero with a large problem and work *forward* from there, you will find yourself rediscovering the most common structure from scratch.

You shouldn't use a guru's structure to answer the question "What should happen next?" but you might want to consult it if you find yourself asking, "My hero's arc seems unconvincing—which natural steps am I missing here?"

But if my characters make a familiar series of choices, you may ask, then how can I defy expectations? Well, rest assured …

12. FIRST AND FOREMOST, AUDIENCES DON'T WANT YOU TO DEFY EXPECTATIONS; THEY WANT YOU TO *CREATE* THEM

When I started out, I had one overriding goal: I wanted to defy expectations. I knew that most scripts were boring and clichéd, so I was determined to write stories that were amazing and unpredictable.

To my pleasant surprise, I discovered this was an easy way to write. It was fun and exciting to write something that lurched in a different direction every twenty pages. I started asking myself, "Why doesn't everybody do this?"

Then, I discovered that nobody liked those scripts because they couldn't connect with my characters. Those out-of-nowhere left turns were actually alienating my readers. What's up with that? Do people crave clichés?

It turns out that people don't actually want to say, "I had no idea that was going to happen!" In fact, they're often delighted to say, "I *knew* that was going to happen!" People love to get to know characters, and they feel clever when they can predict those characters' reactions.

Defying expectations is easy. Creating expectations is hard. To create expectations, you have to write consistent, believable, well-defined characters. Will your heroes change in the end? Yes, certainly. But first, as the saying goes, they have to *want* to change. More important, the *audience* has to want your hero to change.

Your audience will only feel that way if you first write scene after scene in which your heroes act consistently, and consistently *fail* to change. These scenes are frustrating to write. You know what's wrong with your characters, and you want them to figure it out for themselves, but you have to hold back as long as possible. Creating expectations is hard work because you're rolling the rock uphill, creating kinetic energy, creating *value*.

When you finally let the character *defy* expectations, the writing becomes a lot more fun: It's a release of energy, a cashing in of the value you've accumulated. But like any investment, if you remove the value too early, it's worthless.

This is especially clear in character studies, which lack authenticity if the character wants to change too soon. In the 2004 film *Garden State*, the hero decides to change at the very beginning of the story. He *tells* the audience he's tired of being neurotic and quickly starts a redemptive journey. But we haven't seen enough self-destructive behavior to feel involved, so the journey feels unearned.

It's tricky though, because some stories go too far in the other direction. Many independent films from the same decade feature mopey, twitchy characters who change too little, too late, after being way too annoying.

One novel-turned-movie that got the balance just right was *Sideways*. When our hero, Miles, finally makes progress at the end of the story, it's an enormous payoff because, by that point, we have wanted him to change so much for so long. The novel/movie rolled the rock way uphill before finally letting it go, whereupon it successfully knocked the audience flat.

But why put all this work into manipulating your audience? Isn't it rude? After all, no audience ever asked an author to manipulate them. In fact, they get offended if they catch you doing it. Isn't it better to just leave well enough alone?

No. Setting expectations is your job. Your audience may not want it, but they most certainly *need* it. In fact, they subconsciously *crave* it because once you've created expectations, you have control of irony, and that's great, because …

13. IRONY IS THE SOURCE OF ALL MEANING

Once you've learned to set and reset your audience's expectations, you can control the relationship between expectation and outcome, and that means that you can generate irony. That's good, because irony is the heart of meaning.

Irony can have many different definitions, but the best overall definition I've come up with is this: Irony is any meaningful gap between expectation and reality.

The tricky part is that word *meaningful*. Why are some gaps ironic, while others are merely unexpected? It's hard to define, but true irony usually includes an element of *mortification*. In truly ironic situations, characters are trying to preserve a false expectation or prevent an unwanted outcome, and then reality upsets their expectations or efforts.

Ironic story elements create meaning because they lure the audience into expecting a certain outcome and then *upset* that expectation in more ways than one. This not only piques the audience's interest, but it also upsets their certainties. It lets them know you're going to do things they don't expect in ways they haven't seen before, and ultimately show them things they don't already know. This is why almost every element of your writing should be packed with irony.

An ironic difference between expectation and outcome can be comedic (expected a kiss but got a pie in the face, or vice versa) or it can be dramatic (sought justice but found injustice, or vice versa). Either way, the greater the gulf between expectation and outcome, the more meaning the story will have. Likewise, the smaller the gap, the less meaningful it will be, no matter how well you write it.

When stories seem meaningless, it is usually because they lack irony. When stories are especially powerful, you can be certain the author has packed it full of many different types of irony. Learning to recognize and control irony in your story is one of the most important skills a writer can have.

In this book, we'll encounter *many* different types of irony. Here's a preview (which also introduces the seven skills that will organize the next section of this book):

1. Your story will be more meaningful if you present a fundamentally ironic concept (which will sometimes be encapsulated by an ironic title).
2. There are three big ways to have ironic characterization: Your heroes will be more compelling if they have an ironic backstory, an ironic contrast between their exterior and interior, and a great flaw that's the ironic flip side of a great strength.
3. Our examination of structure will center around another great irony: Though your heroes might initially perceive this challenge as an unwelcome crisis, it will often prove to be a crisis that ironically provides just the opportunity your heroes need, directly or indirectly, to address their longstanding social problems and/or internal flaws.

4. Each scene will be more meaningful if the hero encounters a turn of events that upsets some pre-established ironic presumptions about what would happen. Likewise, the conclusion of each scene will be more meaningful if the character's actions result in an ironic scene outcome in which the events of the scene ironically flip the original intention, even if things turn out well for the hero.

5. We'll look at several types of ironic dialogue: On the one hand, we'll look at intentionally ironic dialogue, such as sarcasm. On the other hand, we'll explore unintentionally ironic dialogue, such as when there's an ironic contrast between word and deed or an ironic contrast between what the character says and what the audience knows.

6. We'll discuss the pros and (potentially big) cons of having an ironic tone, which is the one type of irony that most stories *shouldn't* have, although it can be a useful tool for certain very specific types of stories.

7. Finally, we'll look at the thematic ironies that every story should have: The story's *ironic thematic dilemma*, in which the story's overall dilemma comes down to a choice of good versus good (or bad versus bad), as well as *several smaller ironic dilemmas* along the way, in which your characters must consistently choose between goods, or between evils, throughout your story. This will culminate in an *ironic final outcome* separate from the ironic concept and the thematic dilemma.

Each of these ironies can be tremendously powerful, and throughout this book we'll explore each one in depth.

The thirteen laws we've discussed in this chapter lead to the rest of this book. So why is there so much book left? Because these laws interact with each other in a lot of surprising ways, and they've generated hundreds of insights I never dreamed of before I started reevaluating story from this point of view. The result is a rigorous and illuminating set of questions that can make any story stronger.

PART II
The Ultimate Story Checklist

True story: On the first day of my MFA program, a scowling professor walked in and announced, "I don't know what the point of this is. I can't teach you any of this stuff. Either you have talent or you don't." Unfortunately, we were paying him a fortune to teach us everything we needed to know. It was not money well spent.

And he was dead wrong.

Of course talent can be taught. Not easily, no, but nothing valuable is easy, or else we'd all be rich. You most certainly can be taught how to develop talents you don't have. Or, even better, you can teach yourself.

How can you be sure that this is true? Because otherwise nothing good would ever get written. Every writer learns to write. Nobody relies entirely on natural talent.

Now don't get me wrong. If you have no natural talent for any aspect of the writing process, you've got a lot of work ahead of you. By the time you've learned it all, you might be eighty years old. But most people choose to write because they have a natural talent for at least one part of the process. Maybe they have a natural ear for dialogue, or they can dream up thrilling plot twists, or they effortlessly know how to convert their own life experience into meaningful metaphor. And so they think, *Hey, why don't I use this skill to get rich? Easy-peasy!*

But then they discover that one skill is not enough.

Writers have to be great at dialogue *and* plot twists *and* thematic metaphors, all at the same time. Great writing requires an almost ludicrous range of skills. And no matter how good you are at some of them, nobody is naturally good at *all* of them.

So you have to learn the skills you lack, sometimes from scratch. And since everybody has to learn *different* skills, then *every* skill has to be teachable. There are people who naturally write terrible dialogue but then teach themselves to write great dialogue. It happens all the time.

And once you feel you've finally mastered every skill, guess what happens? That one skill you had a natural talent for is now your weakest area, because you've been doing it instinctively rather than intentionally. Instinct isn't reliable, but well-learned tools are. By the time you're done, you jettison your "talents" altogether, and you end up learning *every* skill, even if it means relearning the stuff you already knew.

Writing is not one big talent. It is a *discipline* consisting of several distinct skills, each of which must be *individually* mastered by writing every day, day after day, for years, as you slowly get better.

For the purposes of this book, we're going to talk about seven skills, and, even though there's overlap between them, we're going to try to discuss them *separately*.

WHY IT'S USEFUL TO CONSIDER SKILLS SEPARATELY

So you're finally ready to show off your manuscript. You send it out to trusted friends, and you wait on pins and needles. Friend number one calls back and says, "It's really good!" Your first inclination is to say, "Great!" and hang up. Lock that praise away. Put it in the bank. Let it appreciate.

But then you call friend number two, who hems and haws but finally comes clean: "Honestly, it kind of sucked." Now you want to hang up even quicker and never call back.

But both conversations are just beginning. The good/bad report is somewhat interesting, but it's not exactly news you can use. It's nice to know what overall impression your readers are getting from your story at this stage, but it doesn't mean very much, because every reader has different priorities.

Those qualities that ring the "good" bell for one reader may not be appreciated by another, and vice versa. If you have friends who are nice enough to read your stuff and let you know what they think, see if you can't push them a little further and figure out what they *really* meant by "It's great!" or "It sucks!"

There's nothing more frustrating than lovingly crafting your first manuscript, masterfully showing off your natural talent for dialogue, only to be told, "It sucks," by a reader who thought it had a lousy concept. You mutter to yourself, "That jerk didn't even say *anything* about the dialogue!"

The problem is that, all too often, writers and their early readers are totally miscommunicating, because they're each referring to a *different* skill when they talk about "good writing." To figure out how good your work really is, it's far more useful to separately evaluate the specific skills involved and develop them one at a time.

Now let me be clear: This is my personal list. Unless this book becomes wildly popular, and I become a household name ("Get out of here with your silly Birdisms," they'll say), then you don't want to brag to an agent about how good you are at the "seven skills."

But whether improving my work or evaluating others', I've found this breakdown to be very useful:

- Concept
- Character
- Structure
- Scene Work
- Dialogue
- Tone
- Theme

In the chapters that follow, I'll define each skill, tackle common misconceptions that keep you from developing it, and list the questions you need to ask yourself to perfect it.

3

CONCOCTING AN
INTRIGUING CONCEPT

. . . .

WHAT IS CONCEPT?

We're going to start at the beginning, with the core idea that forms the basis of your story. Ultimately, concept is far less important than character when it comes to determining the overall quality of your story, but your audience is *attracted* to your story based on your concept alone. Does your concept have what it takes to draw people in, at least long enough to introduce them to your wonderful characters?

As with each chapter in this section, the key here is to picture strangers. They have enough stories already, thanks, and they don't need a new one. What concept will win them over despite their apathy?

MISCONCEPTIONS ABOUT CONCEPT

MISCONCEPTION: It's easy to write a simple story, but it's more ambitious to write a big, complicated story.

AU CONTRAIRE: Writing a clean, lean, simple story is one of the hardest things in the world to do.

When stories are first born, they're *always* big and complicated, but simple stories are more powerful and meaningful. Think of Blaise Pascal's famous postscript: "I'm sorry for writing such a long letter, but I didn't have the time to write a shorter one."

Writers are always inclined to make their stories bigger and more complicated than anyone else wants them to be. Luckily, there are gatekeepers to cut us off at the pass. Editors chop novels down to size. Theater directors chop out scenes that don't work. Producers slice the fat out of screenplays. They take sprawling, complicated messes and find the lean, simple story hiding inside.

Ghostbusters was sold to the studio in the form of a forty-page treatment. It was set in the future. New York had been under siege by ghosts for years. There were dozens of teams of competing ghostbusters. Our heroes were tired and bored with their job when the story began. The Marshmallow Man showed up on page 20. The budget would have been bigger than any movie ever made, and far more than anybody was willing to spend.

So why did the studio buy it? Because it liked one image: a bunch of guys who live in a firehouse slide down a pole and hop in an old-fashioned ambulance, then go out to catch ghosts. So the studio stripped away all the other stuff, put that image in the middle of the story, spent the first half gradually moving us from a normal world toward that moment, and spent the second half creating a heroic pay-off to that situation. That's it. That's all they had time to do.

A few years after the success of *Ghostbusters*, one of the writers/stars of that movie, Harold Ramis, found himself on the other side of the fence. He wanted to direct a script called *Groundhog Day*, written by first-time screenwriter Danny Rubin.

This was a very similar situation: In the first draft of that movie, the weatherman had already repeated the same day 3,650,000 times before the movie began!

Everybody loved the script, so Rubin had his pick of directors, but most of them told him up front they wanted him to rewrite the story to begin with the *origin* of the situation. Ramis won the bidding war by promising Rubin he would stick to the *in medias res* version.

Guess what happened? By the time the movie made it to the screen, Ramis had broken his promise. The final movie spends the first half getting the weatherman into the situation and the second half creating the most heroic payoff.

Can anybody dispute that the filmmakers did the right thing in both cases? Would you really like to give up the beloved finished versions of *Ghostbusters* and *Groundhog Day* for those original treatments? Clean, lean, simple stories are more meaningful than stories about permutations of permutations of permutations.

Pacific Rim is a movie that gets this spectacularly wrong: It starts with the concept of robots versus monsters and then asks, "But how do we make that *interesting*?" To answer that question, they created a vastly complicated story set fifteen years after the first monster attack, involving a pair of pilots who have to master a bizarre mind-melding process to control one of many monster-fighting robots.

But here's the problem: You don't have to *make* robots versus monsters interesting, because robots versus monsters is *already* interesting. In fact, you *cannot* make it any more interesting than it already is. Its interest level is set to maximum.

Instead of trying to make it interesting, the filmmakers needed to do the opposite: They needed to make it *sensible*. They needed to get the audience to say, "Oh yeah, it totally makes sense to fight those monsters with those robots."

The first robot-versus-monster battle in *Pacific Rim* happens way out in the middle of the ocean, far away from any civilian population, so everybody in the audience was yelling out the same question: "Why not just nuke the monster instead of using a robot?" The movie had no answer for that question. Unfortunately, it just presumed its premise instead of establishing it. The filmmakers assumed the audience would just go along for the ride.

This is why so many modern stories are impossible to care about—they aren't luring the audience into the world anymore. They aren't *building* these concepts block by block, and so they aren't building any *identification*. They're just dumping these robots and monsters on us, an act which leaves us feeling flattened. But if writers are going to rediscover how to create beloved stories from scratch, then they'll have to understand the power of a streamlined story that invites the audience along for the ride.

MISCONCEPTION: You want to write the most interesting story you can dream up.

AU CONTRAIRE: You want to write the most interesting story you can personally identify with.

These are the early steps and missteps for most writing careers:

1. I want to write! *Time to fire up my imagination.*
2. I've got a cool idea for a story, but it turns out other people have already done it better. *Time to consume a lot of classic stories.*
3. I've got another cool idea, and they've never done anything like this before! But everybody is telling me there's a good reason for that. *Time to figure out which sort of ideas work and which ones don't.*
4. I got a great idea and wrote it from start to finish! But nobody who reads it will represent me. *Time to study writing seriously: structure, character, theme, etc.*
5. I finally wrote something good enough to secure representation! But my reps couldn't sell it. *Time to consume a lot of recent stories and figure out what people are willing to buy right now.*
6. I sold my story, but audiences didn't like it. *Time to figure out how to write something that powerfully resonates with an audience.*

You have to force yourself to stop asking whether an idea could or should work and start asking the most important question of all: Do I know how to make people *identify* with this character *as the story begins*?

Once you start asking that question, all of the not-good-enough ideas begin to fall away. You may have an idea and think, *It's cool! It's commercial! It's high concept! I can see the poster! I can see the lunch box!* Or you may have another idea and think, *It's profound! It's a devastating allegory for the modern world! The ending will be gut-wrenching!* And all of these things are good. But none of them will do you any good if you can't make people identify with your main character as the story begins.

For all types of writers, it's vital to find realistic career role models who aren't overnight successes. You don't want to listen to Great Artists talking about what it all means. You want to listen to successful, everyday people telling the humbling truth about their experiences on the way to "making it."

A good example is Danny McBride. The movies and TV series McBride has co-written are unapologetically rude and crude, so his writing may not be your cup of tea, but his career path is very instructive. Plus, he's been unusually open about his process in a way that lets us see what a more typical career is like.

McBride gave a long, humble, hilarious recounting of his early career stumbles on Marc Maron's invaluable "WTF" podcast, and it provides several good examples of what to do and what not to do.

Right out of college, McBride moved from small-town southern Virginia to Hollywood, hoping to make it big. He got a job waiting tables at the Crocodile Café and started pitching screenplays during his off-hours wherever he could.

> **McBride:** A lot of the stuff I'd write was all over the place, like I'd write weird fantasy stuff, or horror stuff. Like movies about dragon hunters, weird shit.
>
> **Maron:** [*laughs*] Oh really? You got a dragon-hunter script somewhere?
>
> **McBride:** Oh yeah. *The Draven*. He's half-dragon, half-man. [*both laugh*] Pretty exciting. It's gonna be a huge franchise, of course! The guy who works at Crocodile Café wrote this! It's gonna be a huge franchise, Hollywood!
>
> **Maron:** Wow, what was the horror movie?
>
> **McBride:** It was this weird thing, which I still think is a good idea. You know back in New Orleans, back in the day, when there would be floods, the coffins would rise out of the ground, and they would hire these guys who would go out in the swamps and retrieve the coffins. So it was the really fucked-up *Apocalypse Now*-type dark horror film about these guys.

Maron: Mercenary corpse finders?

McBride: [*laughs*] In the 1800s, so it's a period piece, too. All the kind of shit that Hollywood's looking for from a nineteen-year-old kid! [*both laugh*]

The Draven just sounds terrible, of course, but the coffin story is the classic example of a "neat" idea. These ideas are very tempting: Everybody perks up when they hear them, but as McBride later realized, they actually make terrible material for first-time writers.

McBride didn't *know* these mercenary corpse finders. He didn't even know what it was like to live in Louisiana or in a swamp. He didn't know how to make these characters resonate powerfully, and certainly not in the first ten pages (which is all the professional readers are going to give you before they start skimming).

To write that script convincingly, McBride would have had to plunge himself into research about the language and the customs of nineteenth-century Louisiana, as well as the jargon and tradecraft of corpse finders, which would have taken months of library work. Was he prepared to tackle these challenges? Of course not. He just thought it was a "neat" idea, but he wasn't being honest with himself about the assets and liabilities that came with it.

Big high-concept ideas are great, but it remains absolutely essential that you do the following:

1. Choose a setting you know well, through direct experience or tons of research.
2. Create characters you can make an audience identify with as the story begins.
3. Write about problems that powerfully resonate with your own, directly or metaphorically.
4. Write dialogue in voices you know well.

Don't get me wrong—it's a huge asset to start with a cool idea. After all, if you *only* prioritize these four aspects, then you'll end up writing about you and your friends hanging out behind the Dairy Queen. You need to think bigger than that, but you can't totally abandon those relationships, those problems, and those voices you got to know behind the Dairy Queen, either.

Or, to put that another way …

> **MISCONCEPTION:** "Write what you know" means that you should write about the particulars of your life.
>
> **AU CONTRAIRE:** It means that you should write about the *emotions* you know, only you must project them onto a bigger canvas.

So let's continue with that McBride interview. Eventually, McBride gave up on selling movies like *The Draven* and moved back to his small Virginia town in defeat, where he took a humiliating job as a substitute teacher. He still dreamed of making it big, but he couldn't imagine how.

Nevertheless, before long, he found himself tossing around ideas with his friend Jody Hill. The two talked about the potential of a comedy set in the world of southern mini-mall martial arts classes. They realized this was an inherently humorous world that had never been seen onscreen before. As McBride told Maron:

> Jody had grown up doing Tae Kwon Do. He's like a black belt, and I had grown up taking karate as a kid, so it's definitely a world that we were kinda used to and we knew about. And I think at the time, too, we had—both of us really fell in love with the British *Office*, and we were obsessed with how funny it was, how awkward it was, and I think it was like, we want to make something that has that sort of tone …

For the first time, they created a character whom people could *care about*, and they did it by marrying Ricky Gervais's comic persona to that of the southern-fried Tae Kwon Do instructors they knew.

The result was a movie called *The Foot Fist Way*. They wrote it, shot it, and starred in it themselves on a miniscule budget. Against astronomical odds, the movie got into Sundance, where it found a lot of fans. By writing what they knew, they had "broken in," but they still had another hurdle to jump.

Unfortunately, like so many Sundance purchases, *The Foot Fist Way* barely got released in theaters nationwide, but it became a cult favorite on DVD. Copies of the movie started getting passed around Hollywood, and soon a lot of big names wanted to work with both Hill and McBride. McBride got a lot of acting work, and they both got opportunities to pitch writing projects.

Before long, McBride had a chance to pitch a show to HBO. He knew this was the biggest opportunity he'd ever had to reach a wider audience. What story could he tell that would connect with the greatest number of people?

McBride thought back on a particularly embarrassing incident from his first day as a substitute teacher, when he introduced himself to his class. With chagrin, he remembered how he defensively boasted to his young students that he didn't really belong there, since he was actually a big-shot screenwriter, and he was going back to Hollywood any day and he'd show them! The kids, of course, couldn't have cared less, which made the whole thing that much more embarrassing.

Even at the time, McBride had enough self-awareness to realize how vainglorious his boasting was, and his embarrassment stayed with him for years. Now, as he was searching for a pitch, he thought back to that moment. Was there a show there?

He could have taken "write what you know" literally and written about a twenty-two-year-old would-be screenwriter turned substitute teacher, but who would care about that guy? Instead, he took that situation and made it *bigger*.

In his pitch, the would-be screenwriter became a famous ex-baseball star. "Quitting the Crocodile Café" became "having an epic meltdown on national TV." Suddenly, this loser substitute boasting to his class became a much funnier character, with further to fall and further to climb back up. The resulting HBO show, *East Bound and Down*, was a big hit—the last piece of the puzzle that finally turned McBride into a household name.

Let's compare this to the first time I got a chance to pitch a show directly to HBO: I pitched a show about the Harlem Hellfighters of World War I, an all-black regiment featuring a world-class jazz band that liberated town after town and then introduced those towns to jazz for the first time.

Once again, this is a very "neat" idea, a true story that deserves to be told, but I was totally the wrong person to pitch it. It wasn't a story that powerfully resonated with *my experience* on an emotional level. I had no personal connection to the material. I'd just read about it somewhere. I'm not black, not a soldier, and not a musician. I don't even listen to old-time jazz.

McBride and I had the same big opportunity. He nailed it, but I blew it because I didn't pitch something that powerfully resonated with me, so I couldn't make it resonate with the people I was pitching to.

Part of the problem was that I was still too focused on the search for a neat idea. I still hadn't accepted that neat ideas are not all they're cracked up to be.

MISCONCEPTION: A great concept will write itself.

AU CONTRAIRE: All stories are "execution dependent."

A great idea is worth its weight in gold. There's just one problem: An idea doesn't weigh anything, so it still equals $0.

Don't get me wrong, a great concept opens a lot of doors, but you need to be aware that the potential buyer is probably overvaluing it. You can sell them the sizzle, but don't fool yourself into thinking that there's a steak underneath.

The lure of the great concept is that you can start with an initial idea so damn interesting that you can flub the execution and everybody will still love it. Publishers and Hollywood studios have been pursuing this goal for years. This is why they try more and more to presell books and movies to audiences before critics ever get to see them. Who cares what the critics say? You'll want it even if it's crappy!

But this is an impossible dream. Nothing is execution independent. No idea is good enough to factor quality out of the equation.

I read the new loglines in the trades every month. For each one, I either say, "I wish I'd thought of that!" or "That's idiotic!" (The all-time worst was "the story of a serial killer who only kills people in the eye of a tornado.") But eventually, I noticed something: Good or bad, *none* of these movies ever actually seemed to get made, even if the idea was great.

To understand why, I need look no further than the one exception that proved the rule. It was, hands down, the best idea I ever read about in the trades. I will paraphrase it from memory:

> **Title:** *Time Capsule*
>
> **Concept:** A kindergarten teacher and her class open a time capsule from the 1950s, where kids drew what they thought the future would look like. To the teacher's horror, one kid drew childish crayon drawings of the Kennedy assassination, the Challenger blowing up, the twin towers toppling, and a fourth disaster that has yet to happen. The cops assume this is her own sick joke, but she knows it's real, so she's got to find the grown-up kid and help him prevent the last disaster.

How can you hear that idea and not picture the trailer? A camera pans across the four crayon drawings and then lands on the last one (maybe a nuclear bomb hitting DC). Everyone in the theater would instantly say, "I gotta see that!"

For years, I wondered what ever happened to that great idea. And then, just when I'd forgotten all about it, the actual movie came out.

But the kindergarten teacher had somehow been replaced by Nicolas Cage as an alcoholic mathematician. The drawings had now become pages and pages of numbers (numbers are more cinematic than drawings?). The disaster had become unpreventable (the sun going supernova), so the premonitions were for naught anyway. The convoluted explanation involved angels *and* aliens. The title had changed from *Time Capsule* to *Knowing*. It was a huge flop.

For once, Hollywood had actually bought a once-in-a-lifetime, nobody-could-mess-this-up idea—and messed it up.

Everything is execution dependent. Yes, you need to come up with a great idea, and yes, it'll be a lot easier to sell it if it's instantly appealing, but don't kid yourself: Concept only gets you so far. You still have to write the hell out of it. On paper, *Time Capsule* sounds fantastic, but that's why they play the ball game. Execution turns out to be a lot more important than concept.

QUESTIONS TO ASK ABOUT CONCEPT

Once you rid yourself of misconceptions, it's time to consider a list of concept questions before you pitch. As you review, remember that *none* of these checkboxes is required of *every* story (even though I may sound rather insistent at times).

Concept, as I'm using the term, basically breaks down into three parts:

- **THE ELEVATOR PITCH:** This is the one-sentence version of your story that describes its uniquely appealing central idea. This is what gets your foot in the door with agents, managers, publishers, producers, and any other gatekeepers.
- **STORY FUNDAMENTALS:** Once you have the gatekeepers' attention, how will you describe your story? When you launch into your ten-minute summary, will they like what they hear? We'll ask the basic questions that will stress-test your concept and determine if it actually has the fundamental elements of a good story.
- **THE HOOK:** But, of course, those gatekeepers aren't just listening to hear if this is a good story; they're listening for the elements they'll need to sell the story to an audience.

Does it have unique imagery, buzzworthy scenes, and a few narrative surprises? Will it attract a general audience, keep their interest, and pay off that interest in a satisfactory way so it can earn the most valuable buzz of all, word of mouth?

The Elevator Pitch

☑ *Is the one-sentence description uniquely appealing?*

Right here at the beginning, I want to emphasize that great stories need not answer yes to every question, and this first one is a great example. As you'll see below, it's great to answer yes to this question but by no means essential.

So how do you boil your big, beautiful story down to just one line? It sounds impossible. In fact, it sounds insulting! Your story is large. It contains multitudes! But let's say that you have twenty seconds to pitch it to someone. Can you do it? Of course you can. Because every great story grows from one simple idea.

This is the usual layout for a one-sentence summary, which is also called a "logline":

> A [adjective indicating longstanding social problem] [profession or social role] must [goal, sometimes including the ticking clock and stakes].

This can work for many different types of stories:

- The movie *Casablanca*: An amoral American nightclub owner must decide between joining the fight against the Nazis or pursuing his true love.
- The novel and movie *Beloved*: A guilt-wracked ex-slave must confront the vengeful ghost of the daughter she killed.
- The novel and movie *Silence of the Lambs*: An underestimated FBI rookie must work with a devious imprisoned serial killer to rescue a senator's daughter.
- The movie *Groundhog Day*: A selfish weatherman must repeat the same day over and over until he achieves personal growth.
- The novel and movie *Harry Potter and the Philosopher's Stone*: A mistreated boy gets a chance to go to wizard school, where he must defeat the evil wizard who killed his parents.

- The comic series and movie *Iron Man*: An arrogant arms dealer must build a suit of armor to free himself from a warlord and then perfect his suit to deal with related menaces at home.

But wait, there are two more examples we'll keep returning to that don't exactly fit this model:

- The memoir and movie *An Education*: A clever-but-bored schoolgirl in pre-Beatles London puts her Oxford dreams on hold when she meets a devilishly charming older man.
- The novel and movie *Sideways*: Two miserable middle-aged men romantically pursue two divorcées during a weeklong trip to wine country.

Crucially, there's no "must" in the last two examples, which inherently makes them a harder sell. As it turns out, both movies are wonderfully entertaining, but it's hard to know that from reading the logline. Because there's no "must," we fear that the stories will lack stakes and motivation. Because the hero is not being literally compelled to enter the world of the story, we fear that *we* will not be compelled to, either.

The first six are stories you might try out simply based on this intriguing line. Of the eight, these last two are the ones you're more likely to try only if you've read good reviews or you've heard good things about the author of the novel or the director of the movie. As it happened, both movies got great reviews, and so people checked them out and discovered they *were* compelling.

So every great story *doesn't* need a uniquely appealing logline, but it definitely *helps*, both in selling your work to a buyer and eventually to an audience. As mentioned in chapter two, publishers and producers hate to say to the public, "I know it doesn't sound interesting, but trust us—it's really well written." In order for them to market your work, they prefer to have a unique, appealing concept.

A sharp logline also focuses your mind as a writer: You're not feeling your way through the shapeless blob of a half-formed idea; you're starting with a unique and clever concept that automatically excites both your readers and yourself. That's a great way to start.

As you pitch concepts you'll hear the term *high concept* a lot, without explanation. It's worth noting that the term *high concept* has changed in meaning over the years. It used to refer to big, complicated, highly conceptual ideas like *2001*, but now it refers to the opposite: a concept that is uniquely *simple*.

- *Limitless* (and the novel it's based on, *The Dark Fields*) is high concept because you instantly understand the appeal of the premise: What if a pill could make you rich and powerful?
- But it can also apply to movies without any science fiction elements. *The Hangover* was also high concept: Three groomsmen can't remember their wild bachelor party or find the missing groom.
- For that matter, *Wedding Crashers* is the *ultimate* high-concept story because you got the unique appeal of it as soon as you heard the title, no poster or tagline necessary.

High concept now refers to a simple one-sentence premise that makes everybody say, "Oooh, that sounds fun!" High-concept ideas are easy to market. If the concept is instantly and uniquely appealing, it's an easy sell.

Of course, this doesn't mean that every story has to be high concept to work. Let's look at a movie that has an unappealing, low-concept logline (even though it does have a "must" in it). Here's the one-line summary of *The King's Speech*: "A nervous figurehead must work with a radical speech therapist to overcome his stutter and give an inspiring speech as World War II begins."

The financiers of that movie took a huge risk: Instead of starting with an asset (an appealing logline), they started with a huge liability (an *unappealing* logline). Every step of the way, they had to explain to potential directors, actors, and distributors, "We know it doesn't sound very interesting, but if we do a good job we can *make it* interesting." That took a lot of persuasion on the part of the producers.

But somehow, in the end, they did it. They convinced enough people at every step to take a chance on it, and shepherded it all the way to box office success and a Best Picture win. And guess what? The final product was a much better movie than any of the three I just listed. It can be done, *if* you're willing to run uphill.

But if you want to give yourself a big boost, both in terms of selling it *and* in terms of writing it, a uniquely appealing logline works wonders.

☑ Does the concept contain an intriguing ironic contradiction?

So I've promised you many different types of irony, and now I'm ready to deliver the first two, **ironic concept** and **ironic title**. Let's look at the ironies contained in those same example stories:

- *Casablanca*: The least patriotic American has to save the Allied cause.
- *Beloved*: A mother kills her daughter to ensure her freedom.
- *Silence of the Lambs*: The only way to catch one serial killer is to work with another serial killer.
- *Groundhog Day*: A man who just wants to get his least favorite day over with has to live it again and again.
- *Harry Potter and the Philosopher's Stone*: A miserable and unfortunate kid discovers that he's secretly rich, famous, and heroic.
- *Sideways*: A man helps his friend celebrate his upcoming wedding by playing wingman for him as he pursues other women.
- *Iron Man*: An arms dealer is attacked with his own weapons and then declares war on arms dealing.
- *An Education*: A girl rejects the idea of getting "an education" but learns another meaning of the word in the process.

Because this rule is so nearly universal, it's instructive to look at an exception that proves the rule. A few years ago, Denzel Washington directed and starred in a highly fictionalized true story called *The Great Debaters* about a debate team at an all-black college that gets to challenge the Harvard team in the 1930s. As it happens, the team gets assigned to defend the proposition that civil disobedience is good. They do a good job with that and win, which is good, because otherwise what would the movie be saying?

This movie is actually worth watching, but it commits the cardinal sin of many well-meaning period pieces: It irons out the irony.

What makes this so frustrating is there is a lot of potential irony inherent in the premise, if the makers of the film had been willing to fictionalize it a little bit more. Here's why college debate teams are interesting: You don't get to choose which side you argue—it is randomly assigned. So what if the black team had been assigned the *anti*-civil rights side of the argument?

The team would balk, but then, after a few stern speeches from Washington, they would realize this was their big opportunity. They would have to create devastating anti-integration arguments, but the more they proved that blacks weren't equal in theory, the more their eloquence would prove they *were* equal in reality!

At that point you could end the movie either way and it would still be powerfully ironic. With that ending in doubt, the whole movie would come alive. Instead, with the version they made, we know the whole time that there's only one way to end it, unless they want to make it look like integration was a big mistake.

Of course, another problem is that *The Great Debaters* is a *terrible* title. You can tell right away it has no irony. It always drives me crazy when I see a fantasy novel with a title like *The Knight's Sword* or an airport paperback with a title like *Deadly Assassin*. These titles are telling you right off the bat that this book will be predictable. A good story needs conflict, and why not start with the title, which is your first opportunity to set two incongruous elements against each other?

Just glancing down the list of underrated movies I've recommended on my blog over the years, I see that these titles are inherently intriguing: *Blast of Silence*, *Dark Days*, *Killer's Kiss*, *The Little Fugitive*, *Little Murders*, *My Favorite Wife*, *Safety Last*, *Unfaithfully Yours*, and *The White Sheik*.

The Court Jester, on the other hand, is a great movie, but it has an inherently weak title, because where else would a jester be? *Shoot to Kill* could be the title of any thriller ever made. And Fritz Lang rightly complained when the studio changed the name of his movie from the ironic *The Human Beast* to *Human Desire*. Lang demanded to know,

"What other kind of desire is there?" An ironic concept is great, and an ironic title is a nice bonus on top of that.

☑ Is this a story anyone can identify with, projected onto a bigger canvas, with higher stakes?

As I said in the misconceptions at the start of this chapter, "write what you know" really means you should write the *emotions* you know, but put those emotions into a more extreme situation with a lot more at stake.

This is what it means to *dramatize*. In real life, nobody wants to have "way too much drama going on right now," but when it comes to stories, that's *exactly* what you want. The same *types* of things that happen to you are happening to them (the same universal emotions, the same universal dilemmas), but in the fictional version, the highs are higher, the lows are lower, and the potential consequences are far more life shattering.

You totally identify with the hero's situation and emotions, but you get to vicariously experience the thrill of a much bigger *transgression* than you would ever actually commit, followed by the pain of the big *consequences* you'll never have to suffer, followed by the gratification of a big *transformation* that is always out of your reach. And if, along the way, you get to inhabit a glamorous (or fascinatingly gruesome) world you would never otherwise get to visit, all the better.

Once again, of course, masterful storytellers can successfully break this rule. TV shows like *The Office* and *Parks and Recreation* excel at creating low-stakes, unglamorous worlds in which small interactions and minor complaints become just as compelling as an alien invasion. Once again, those shows are choosing to run uphill, but they prove that it can be done.

Story Fundamentals

☑ Is the concept simple enough to spend more time on character than plot?

When I started out writing screenplays, I had a weakness for overly complicated plots, because I would ask myself the wrong questions. *Is that it? Are there enough twists? Is there enough story? Does it feel big enough? Does it feel like a movie?* And so I would pile on twists, escalations, and reversals until it really felt like a movie. After all, only in a movie would all this crazy stuff happen to one person!

At first, my elephantine plots combined with my flabby scene work to create first drafts that were upward of 150 pages. Even a beginner knows he's done something wrong when that happens. (In screenwriting, every page is supposed to equal a minute of screen time, so you don't want to go over 120 pages.) Soon, I figured out how to make scenes as lean as possible and to strip away enough subplots so my screenplays were squeaking in just under the line at 119 pages.

But I gradually realized that these 119-page wonders were still not working. A lot was happening to my heroes, but they had little time to think about it or react to it. There certainly wasn't any time to pre-establish what their expectations were before a scene happened, so nothing had any irony when it hit.

I eventually realized my heroes were going on massive external journeys and teensy-weensy internal journeys. My first instinct was to add some "character scenes," but I was already out of room page-wise. Even if I shaved off another plot twist to give them some rumination downtime, it was too little, too late to create a fully realized character.

Here's the problem: When I was asking, "Does it feel like a movie?" I thought the key word was *movie*, but I should have focused on the word *feel*. If it doesn't feel like a movie, don't amplify the *movieness* of it all; amplify the *feeling*. This is the difference between complicated and complex. All the complications in the world don't add complexity, which is what makes a story great.

I suddenly realized my characters spent all their time talking about the plot, explaining it to themselves and explaining it to the audience. This is inevitable when the plot is too complicated. But a good plot should be simple enough that both the characters and the audience understand it just by looking at it.

Once I understood my characters needed to have deeper emotional stakes—and they needed to talk about something other than the plot at least once per scene—I knew my plots needed to be massively downsized. I had been so proud of myself for shrinking my three-hour plots down to two hours, but now they needed to get even leaner: I realized that a good *two-hour* movie has a *one-hour* plot.

Die Hard, for all its little twists, is a relatively simple, self-explanatory story: Gunmen have taken over a bank's headquarters and hold everybody hostage long enough to drill into the vault. The reason this fills two hours is the hero isn't only figuring out what's going on, but he's also dealing with his own personal baggage, since the villains attacked during a massive emotional crisis.

In *Die Hard 2*, the same hero has no personal baggage, no emotional crisis, and never discusses anything but the plot. The extra room this creates in the script is filled by a far more complicated plot that's not at all self-explanatory. In the first movie, you can tell what the bad guys want to do just by looking at them. In the second, both sides have to keep explaining every step of the process. *Die Hard* has a one-hour plot, stretched to two hours by John's emotional crisis. *Die Hard 2* has two hours of pure plot, which leaves us exhausted but not exhilarated.

No matter what type of fiction you're writing—a novel, a play, a TV episode, etc.—you should always try to have a plot that only fills half your pages, and then let your complex scenes expand to fill the rest with unexpectedly volatile emotional complications.

☑ Is there one character whom the audience will choose to be their hero?

As I said earlier, audiences will *always* choose *one* character to represent their point of view and their interests. This is their hero. Even in an ensemble story, or a story about various walks of life, the audience will choose one character to primarily identify with. They have to— that's how we're hardwired to process stories.

You may wish to equally privilege various characters, but the audience will usually choose only one to fully identify with. In *Traffic*, only Benicio Del Toro's story is really compelling, because he has the biggest challenge. The other stories are there to make various points, but once we've identified with Del Toro, it becomes more and more annoying to cut away from him. We know who our hero is.

So you have to acknowledge that your audience will begin your story by desperately searching for a strong character to identify with, and that they will expect the story to follow the arc of that hero's problem from beginning to end.

It's important to remember that your audience must *identify* with your hero, but they need not sympathize with the hero's larger goal. "Antihero" stories are extremely hard to write well, but they can become beloved when done right. As we watch *Breaking Bad*, we fully identify with the tragic hero Walter White, and we even get pulled into rooting for his little schemes in most episodes, but we always hope that his business will ultimately fail and that he will learn the error of his ways, before it's too late. This powerful irony fuels the show.

☑ Does the story follow the progress of the hero's problem, not the hero's daily life?

What is the worst possible way for any story to begin? "BRINGGGGG! Angie's eyes open and she looks over at her alarm clock. ..." Don't do this. Your story is not about your hero's *life*. Your story is not about your hero's *day*. Your story is about your hero's *problem*. Do not follow your hero around like a puppy, waiting for something to begin. Begin the moment the problem begins—no sooner and no later.

If you're writing a lot of scenes in which the hero wakes up in the morning or goes to bed at night, you're doing it wrong, because those scenes have nothing to do with the hero's problem. In the overstuffed fantasy novel *Eragon*, there are no fewer than nineteen scenes of the hero waking up in the morning!

Likewise, the way to get from scene to scene is not to ask, "What does the hero do next?" but rather, "What is the next step in the progression of this problem?" That next step might happen immediately after this scene, or the next day, or years later. Your audience will happily make that leap forward with you, because they are invested in this one problem, not the progress of your hero's daily life.

Let your story start at the moment the problem becomes acute, and then end at the moment the problem is solved (or succumbed to, or peaceably accepted). If you simply follow the development of that problem, then everything before it begins, everything after it's resolved, a lot of extraneous events along the way will simply fall away, and you'll find your story.

☑ Does the story present a unique central relationship?

Unique characters are overrated. Does your main character feel familiar? Good! Audiences want characters to feel familiar so they can identify with them. Besides, it's almost impossible to come up with a unique character. There have been too many stories, and we've seen them all before.

But there's an easier way to tell a unique story. You're going to have much better luck if you take two familiar characters and give them a believable but never-seen-before *relationship*.

The high school outcast is a familiar archetype, but let's put that character into a unique never-seen-in-a-story-before relationship:

- *My Bodyguard* is about a high school outcast who pays a scary bully to protect him from the other kids.
- *Rushmore* is about a high school outcast who strikes up a friendship with one of his private school's funders who feels equally alienated.
- *Election* is about a high school outcast who infuriates her teacher so much that he tries to sabotage her student government election.

If those stories had been about watching these outcasts try to get a date with the popular kid, then they would have fallen into overly familiar territory. It's the unique relationship, not the unique character, that makes the story great.

I've known a lot of strange people, but none so strange that I can't think of a preexisting character just like them. On the other hand, I've had a dozen oddball relationships in my life that I've never seen replicated: unlikely friendships, overdivulging bosses, bizarre dates, etc.

Don't force one dysfunctional character to generate conflict single-handedly. Allow two seemingly functional characters to set each other off in an unexpectedly dysfunctional way. Such things have happened to you, and if it's happened to you, then it's happened to others in the audience. They'll happily smile in identification when they see it portrayed.

It's fascinating to go back and rewatch the first few episodes of *30 Rock*. All of the *elements* of greatness are there from the beginning, but the show doesn't work yet, because the writers haven't found their focus. Tina Fey's Liz Lemon is annoyed by her boss, Jack (Alec Baldwin), and by her own employees, generating a lot of conflict, but the conflict is flat. All of the individual characters are funny, but they all have relationships we've seen before.

Then, suddenly, in episode six, everything snaps into place, and the show recenters itself on a new, never-before-seen-on-television *relationship*. In that episode, Liz reluctantly accepts an ongoing offer of mentorship from Jack, despite the fact that she's a loosey-goosey, left-wing girl-about-town and he's a type A, right-wing, ultrasexist alpha male. This odd but mutually beneficial mentor-mentee relationship quickly becomes the heart of the show, generating dozens of unique stories and conflicts we haven't seen before. The result is seven great seasons of television.

Think about times in your life when an acquaintance suddenly became your nemesis or a love affair took a strange left turn. If this was a fascinating relationship that we haven't seen portrayed before, then you'll find fresh emotions to tap into.

Can you find relationships from your life that are as incongruous as those seen in *Paper Moon* (a conman teams up with an eleven-year-old girl) or *Midnight Run* (a hard-assed bounty hunter has to escort a timid accountant)? If not, you can always invent one. Simply take two very different types of characters and force them to rely on each other in a unique way.

☑ *Is at least one actual human being opposed to what the hero is doing?*

Occasionally friends ask me to consult on reality TV series they're pitching. One was about adventure travelers who go to unsafe countries, one was about Live Action Role Players, and another was about a struggling hip-hop label. Every time, I had the same advice: Someone onscreen has to be opposed to what your subjects are doing. I implored them to shoot interviews with people who *disapproved* of this activity.

In each of the above cases, this advice met with resistance: "But I want to present what these people do in a *positive* light! I don't want to bring negativity into it." My argument was (and still is) that the *only* way to portray an activity as a positive thing is to prove your subjects are willing to overcome opposition to do it. If you just show people doing their thing and having a great time, there's no story. If you show them doing it despite opposition, then the audience can appreciate the meaning of what they do.

"Well, okay, sure, all stories need conflict," you might say, "but my fictional characters are more compelling than those would-be reality show stars. If I create a great fictional character who's *internally* conflicted, can't that create meaning on its own, without bringing any *external* conflict into it?"

It is possible to write a meaningful story in which the primary conflict is internal, not external, but it's much harder. The only form of writing that is *naturally* suited to showing internal conflict is the first-person novel, but even movies can pull it off if they work *really* hard.

For instance, *The Secret Life of Dentists*, based on the novella *The Age of Grief* by Jane Smiley, successfully dramatizes the internal conflict of a passive protagonist. Campbell Scott plays a conflicted dentist who can't bring himself to confront his wife about her infidelity. So how does the movie dramatize this internal struggle, this *lack* of action? It uses every trick in the book—voice-over, dream sequences, wish-fulfillment fantasies—but ultimately, all of these fall short, so Scott must argue with an imaginary character (Denis Leary) who represents his suppressed rage. So this movie becomes the exception that proves the rule: One way or another, conflict must be dramatized.

Even if you are writing a first-person novel, internalized stories without external conflict are hard to write well. Drama refers to interaction between characters, not conflict within a character, and drama is at the heart of great writing. Conflicted characters are great because they're volatile, but that volatility only erupts when that conflicted character meets her match and is thereby *challenged*. When we pick on ourselves, we rarely do so in a surprising way. When other people pick on us, that's when things get real.

☑ Does this challenge represent the hero's greatest hope and/or greatest fear and/or an ironic answer to the hero's question?

At the beginning of a story, all heroes must want something, but that doesn't mean they will necessarily want the opportunity they are presented with.

The relationship between what your heroes want and the actual opportunities they discover can play out in many different ways:

- Some heroes, like Luke Skywalker in *Star Wars*, get **the opportunity they've always dreamed of**: Luke always wanted to run off and become a heroic space pilot, and then that opportunity presents itself in an unexpected way.
- For other heroes, the opportunity that appears is **the *opposite* of what they've always wanted**. Brody in *Jaws* wants to prove himself as sheriff, but the opportunity to do so arrives in the form of one of his deepest fears, going into the ocean.
- For others, like Sarah Connor in *The Terminator*, it's more of **an ironic "be careful what you wish for" situation**. She drops a bunch of dishes at work and then wonders, "In a hundred years, who's gonna care?" It's just a rhetorical question, but she gets her answer in spades.
- Sometimes, the connection between the character's want and opportunity is even more abstract. Marty McFly in *Back to the Future* wants to be cooler than his lame parents. Getting sent back in time isn't something he's always wanted to do or something he's always been afraid of, but when he gets there, he stumbles upon a strange opportunity to solve his problem: First he comes to understand his parents better, and then he improves their lives retroactively, **solving his original problem in a *very* roundabout yet satisfying way**.

Beware of stories in which the character and plot arcs never intersect, because the story will never come together. This is why you need to ask yourself ...

☑ Does something inside the hero have a particularly volatile reaction to the challenge?

Heroes must have secrets or qualities that cause them to have unique reactions to challenges, some internal ionic charge that sets the compass of the story spinning—something the people sitting on the hero's right and left *don't* have. This is fairly obvious in comedies and dramas, where the volatility of the hero is front and center:

- In a romantic comedy or drama, the heroes react to each other in an unexpectedly volatile way. That's what romance is.
- In any character-driven story, the unique psychology of the hero is the main topic of the story.

Though it can be harder to remember in adventure stories or thrillers (where it's tempting to have an Everyman hero), your heroes shouldn't react to their situations in typical ways. Instead, heroes must respond to their challenge in their own unique way. That unique reaction is what makes them heroes. This is what the Everyman *wouldn't* do. This is *why* this story happens.

- In *Men in Black*, we see that Will Smith is more *clever* than all of the other applicants when he figures out that he has to drag the table over while filling out forms rather than trying to write on his lap.
- *Captain America* (who is *also* being judged by Tommy Lee Jones as he tries to join a *different* secret government agency) has more *valor* inside him than everybody else, even when he's tiny. This is revealed when Jones tosses a dummy grenade into a group of soldiers. Everybody else scatters except our scrawny hero, who jumps on the grenade.
- In *Margin Call*, Zachary Quinto's stock analyst character has more *compassion* than the others: Only he gives a heartfelt farewell to

Stanley Tucci's fired risk assessment officer, so only he gets tipped off about the doom awaiting the firm.

These are simple but powerful moments that allow the audience to *choose* this character to be *their* hero. These characters aren't just in the right place at the right time; they earn their place at the table.

In the examples I cited, the heroes had something good inside them, but sometimes a more neurotic internal contradiction causes the hero to react in an unexpectedly volatile way. In each of the following cases, it's a neurosis that ironically helps the hero succeed.

- In both *Vertigo* and *Rear Window*, only Jimmy Stewart's characters would have uncovered the crimes that are central to the story, because the natures of the crimes happen to tap into the characters' festering neuroses.
- In *The French Connection*, only Popeye, with his self-destructive "never trust anybody" ethic, could have spotted the well-hidden drug ring.
- In *Silence of the Lambs*, only Clarice, with her suppressed rural background, could have gotten this reaction out of Hannibal Lecter. That background also proves to be the key to solving the mystery, because Clarice has a unique understanding of the type of town where Bill lives.

Remember: We can only care about your hero, not your plot. If your hero is a generic everyman who exists just to introduce us to your world or dazzle us with story twists, then you'll sabotage yourself. Your story exists to serve your hero; your hero cannot exist to serve your story.

☑ Does this challenge become something that's not just hard for the hero to do (an obstacle) but also hard for the hero to want to do (a conflict)?

Obstacles are fine, but conflicts are better. An obstacle is anything that makes a task difficult to do. A conflict is anything that makes a hero not want to do it.

Amazingly, the Disney animation team had been writing and rewriting drafts of *Frozen* for two years before deciding that the two girls should be sisters. Instantly, the story came alive, and they never looked back. Defeating a random snow witch is hard to do. Defeating your sister is hard *to want* to do. That's the difference between an obstacle and a conflict.

Not all conflict is created equal. *Genuine* conflict occurs when characters don't want to do something for reasons such as these:

- **IT WOULD REQUIRE THEM TO QUESTION THEIR DEEP-SEATED ASSUMPTIONS:** *Huckleberry Finn* is convinced he'll go to hell if he helps Jim escape.
- **IT WOULD REQUIRE THEM TO OVERCOME AN INNER WEAKNESS:** Steve Carell's character has built up an extreme reluctance to mature in *The 40-Year-Old Virgin*.
- **THEY PROMISED SOMEONE THEY WOULDN'T DO IT:** Mark Wahlberg feels he cannot go on his own without betraying his family in *The Fighter*.
- **IT WOULD REVEAL THEIR PAINFUL SECRETS TO OTHERS.** Harrison Ford in *The Fugitive* cannot investigate his wife's murder without exposing himself to the police.
- **IT WOULD GET THEIR LOVE INTEREST OR A FAMILY MEMBER IN TROUBLE:** Tobey Maguire's character is constantly afraid his activities will endanger his family members in the *Spider-Man* movies.

This is a problem that plagues tons of lackluster stories: Cooking every meal in Julia Child's cookbook is certainly hard to do, but it's not hard *to want* to do, so who cares? That's why the modern-day portions of *Julie and Julia* fall flat. For that matter, this was another problem with *The Aviator*. Making an expensive movie and deregulating air travel are both hard to do, but they're not hard to want to do, so the movie never took off.

☑ In the end, is the hero the only one who can solve the problem?

Thriller and horror writers love to complain about cell phones. It's now impossible to write a thriller, they say, because rescue is always just a phone call away.

Of course, there are ways around this problem: The battery runs out, there's no signal, the phone gets destroyed, etc., but each one of them has become a cliché in its own right. There's even a YouTube montage of dozens of characters giving these excuses.

But if you find yourself sweating over how to cut off cell phone access, then you've got a bigger problem. If your heroes need only to make a call to get out of trouble, then they're not the only ones who could solve this problem, which means it's not really *their* problem. "Wrong place at the wrong time" is too little to hang your story on. If there's a cop out there who would be better at solving the problem, then you should write a story about that cop.

There needs to be a deeper reason why your heroes are the only ones who can solve this problem. Calling the cops should not be an option, whether or not a cell phone is available.

Of course, most of the traditional reasons why heroes might not call the cops have *also* become clichéd: No one will believe them, they're on a revenge trip, they've been accused of the crime themselves, the cops are crooked, it's the perfect crime, etc. But these have become clichéd for a good reason—they personalize the problem and put your heroes in a position where they and they alone have to solve it, as opposed to contrived cell phone issues, which feel tired and emphasize that the heroes don't have to take care of it *themselves*.

Throughout your story, character should be colliding with plot. The ending is the ultimate collision in which the problem is resolved as both the character and the situation are permanently transformed by their volatile clash.

☑ Does the situation permanently transform the hero, and vice versa?

It's the age-old conundrum for writers: When you're generating a story, do you start with character or plot? Do you create interesting characters and then craft a situation around them, or do you create an interesting situation and then figure out who might be dealing with it? Both methods have their perils.

If you start with great characters, even if they're fascinatingly complex—*especially* if they're fascinatingly complex—then they're going to be resistant to change and unwilling to put themselves in danger. Beware of the "character piece," in which we watch heroes drift from scene to scene, encountering characters who *define* them but don't *challenge* them.

Our challenges tell us who we really are. What we feel and believe is ephemeral. We see ourselves one way and the world sees us another way, and who's to say who is right? We don't know who we really are until we hit a wall. Trying to define yourself or your characters outside of a major challenge is a slippery business.

Up in the Air is a classic example of a good-but-not-great character piece. It's about a rootless efficiency expert who is only happy when he's on an airplane. That's an interesting character, but the situations he encounters (having to compete with a young colleague, falling for a married woman) never seriously challenge that core characterization. The movie is more about *defining* the character than *redefining* him. His character is an unstoppable force that never meets an immovable object, so the story never grabs us.

But it can be equally risky to start with a plot and add your characters later. Let's say you want to start with an alien invasion. Great. But who deals with it? Who's the character? What is the character's relationship to the plot? If you spend a lot of time coming up with a cool situation *before* you pair it with one character's journey, then you could end up in big trouble all over again.

H.G. Wells's novella *The War of the Worlds* features one hell of an interesting situation, and it keeps getting adapted (for radio, for television, for the movies) over and over: Martians attack Earth and shoot death rays at us, but they are ironically defeated by their lack of immunity to Earth viruses. Unfortunately, every adaptation of this story has lacked memorable characters.

In the 2005 movie version, Tom Cruise was an aimless divorced dad trying to redeem himself and protect his kids. Okay, but what does that have to do with aliens getting defeated by a virus? Nothing. The character arc and the plot never intersect. *War of the Worlds* is a big self-sufficient plot that doesn't leave room for any characters.

Great stories have characters and plots that can't thrive without each other. In the book and movie *Silence of the Lambs*, FBI agent Clarice Starling is a great character, but she isn't interesting enough for us to just follow her around at FBI camp. She wouldn't generate enough conflict simply by getting to know herself. If the opportunity to interview serial killer Hannibal Lecter hadn't come along, there would be no story.

By the same token, there would have been no story if another less conflicted agent had been sent to interview Lecter. He only agrees to help solve the case because he finds Clarice so compelling. This *plot* was necessary to spark this *character*, and this *character* was necessary to spark this *plot*.

The key is to let Hegel be your guide: Thesis plus antithesis equals synthesis. Your hero's personality is the *thesis*, and the intimidating opportunity that arrives is the *antithesis* to that. What new synthesis will be created in the wake of this confrontation? When the unstoppable force meets the immovable object, a story is born.

The hero must affect the events, and the events must affect the hero. That's the first test of a great story idea. The hero of *Up in the Air* is a thesis who never meets his antithesis. He is a character who is defined but not redefined by the plot. The alien invasion in *War of the Worlds* simply collapses on its own. It is a plot unaffected by the characters. In *Silence of the Lambs*, however, the plot and the character combust in a volatile reaction.

The Hook

☑ *Does the story satisfy the basic human urges that get people to buy and recommend this genre?*

For the most part, when people recommend a story to their friends, they don't praise the concept, characters, structure, scene work, dialogue, or theme. They recommend it to their friends based on the urges the story satisfied.

Usually, when I get an idea, it gets me excited for a short time, and then I gradually lose interest: I realize that it doesn't make sense, it doesn't mean anything, or the character arc and the plot have nothing to do with each other. Somehow the entire thing fails to coalesce. But then there are other times when everything magically clicks into place. A compelling hero believably finds herself plunged into an exciting plot that builds to a satisfying conclusion! Even better, the entire thing is a powerful metaphor for our modern condition! Victory! But then, something happens: I pitch the idea to a friend, or maybe my management, and get hit with a devastating response: "Well, okay, sure, *but why would anybody want to see it?*"

Oh, right. I forgot about that.

Let's say your co-worker corners you at the watercooler to tell you about a great movie or TV show. What are the odds you'll hear one of these phrases?

"It had a great structure!"

"It really seemed true to life!"

"It had a very satisfying theme!"

"It was a devastating metaphor!"

Not likely. Here's a list of things your co-worker is far more likely to say:

"It was hilarious!" a.k.a. **laughter** (comedies, dramedies)

"It was hot!" a.k.a. **lust** (sex comedies, some thrillers, some horror, some indies)

"It rocked!" a.k.a. **adrenaline rush** (action movies, kids' movies)

"It was gruesome!" a.k.a. **bloodlust** (horror, some thrillers, some disaster movies)

"It kicked ass!" a.k.a. **power fantasy** (superheroes, spies, sports)

"It was so sweet!" a.k.a. **romantic fantasy** (romances, romantic comedies, coming-of-age movies)

"It was devastating!" a.k.a. **pathos** (melodramas, documentaries, indie movies)

"It was gorgeous!" a.k.a. **beauty** (spectacles, some documentaries, animated movies)

"It blew my mind!" a.k.a. **cognitive dissonance** (some art films, some high-concept blockbusters)

Writers must know how to push people's buttons. You have to give them something they *crave*. "But wait," you say, "I don't *want* to push people's buttons. I want to write something smart and a little bit difficult. I want my audience to think about the consequences of real life, not just rock out!" Well, guess what? If you want to write something noble, then you *really* need to push buttons.

David Chase transformed television for the better with *The Sopranos*, proving once and for all that the medium could do dark, morally complex, open-ended, unsettling storytelling. When he was selling his pilot script to a network, several fell in love with it and tried to turn it into a series, but then one by one they each got cold feet. At first, Chase assumed that this was because they were worried about the violence, but then he began to suspect that the *opposite* might be true.

In the end, he realized that he had two problems:

1. Yes, he was asking his audience to empathize with murderers.
2. But, even worse, his pilot script wasn't giving the audience the thrill of actually watching these guys kill anybody!

He certainly wasn't willing to abandon the project because of the first problem, but he was happy to change the second problem. He wrote a new version in which his antiheroes whacked somebody in the first episode, and suddenly everybody loved the pilot even *more*. Only then did the show finally get picked up.

Chase's goal was to subvert the traditional mob narrative (and, along the way, America's self-narrative of our own success), but first he had to assure his audience that, yes, even if this would be an untraditional mob story, it was still going to be a mob story. It was going to conform to the general subject matter of the genre and at least occasionally fulfill the urges that get people to consume those stories. In this case, bloodlust.

☑ Does this story show us at least one image we haven't seen before (that can be used to promote the final product)?

There's nothing that creative types hate more than getting notes from noncreative types, and the most despised of all are the notes that come from, ugh, marketing. How dare *they* be consulted? *Ars gratia artis!* It's *our* job to make a pure, unadulterated masterpiece. It's *their* job to sell it.

But "art for art's sake" has always been an impossible dream. Not only will the publishers or producers eventually have to sell your story to the public, but *you'll* have to sell it to those publishers or producers in the first place. All stories must be inherently marketable. The audience is not going to climb into the ring to wrestle with you; you have to jump over the ropes and pin them down to their seats. So, yes, right from the start, you should ask yourself, *What image is going to appear on the cover or poster?*

When I write about movies, I like to pull iconic still frames to illustrate my points, but occasionally I notice that even though I'm writing about a great movie, there are no unique or iconic images that tell the story of the movie visually. For example, *In a Lonely Place* is one of the greatest movies ever made, but it's always been a hard sell to people who have never heard of it. I searched for stills to illustrate how great the movie was, but all of the imagery is generic. There's nothing *iconic* about it.

Marge's pregnancy didn't have a lot to do with the plot of *Fargo*, but it created very unique imagery that helped sell the quirkiness of the movie before anyone heard the wonderful dialogue.

The cover of the novel *Silence of the Lambs* doesn't show a federal agent interviewing a prisoner, because that's not a unique image. Luckily, novelist Thomas Harris laced imagery of the death's-head hawk moth throughout his story. It had little relationship to the story, but it was a great image, so it dominated the book cover and the eventual movie poster.

So how do you create unique imagery?

- You can create unique "set pieces" or locations we haven't seen before that present unique physical challenges or opportunities.
- You can give characters signature wardrobe choices.
- You can give your characters unique *injuries* like nosy Jake getting his nose cut open in *Chinatown*.
- Most of all, you need to create scenes that *visualize* your conflict rather than just have everybody *talk* about it.

What image will sell your story, no matter how many different media it gets adapted into?

☑ *Is there at least one "Holy Crap!" scene (to create word of mouth)?*

What's the one moment that will make readers perk up and go, "Whoa! I've never seen *that* before. This story actually *went there*! I'm out of my comfort zone now!" This is especially important for these three genres:

- COMEDY: *American Pie* famously revived a dead genre by showing a kid violating a pie in the trailer (a gag so funny they named the movie after it).
- THRILLER: People flocked to see *The Grey* because the trailer implied that Liam Neeson was going to get in a fistfight with a wolf. (Only later did they discover the movie ends with his *preparation* for that fight. The filmmakers did shoot the fight, but it looked too silly. Because of course it did.)

- **ACTION:** Everybody went out and saw *Independence Day* because of the shot where the aliens blew up the White House.

Obviously, it's easy to get cynical about such scenes. When I was writing a broad comedy, I watched twenty recent comedy trailers and jotted down the biggest laugh in each one. A shocking number involved raccoon attacks, or head injuries, or both. But these scenes can actually make your story better.

Your story needs a *reason to exist*. It has to be *the* story that did *that thing* that nobody else would do. "But wait," you say, "I don't want to write an outrageous, over-the-top story!" Okay, let's look at the value such scenes can have for quieter stories.

Sideways is a much gentler movie than the two listed above, but it has not one but two "Holy Crap!" scenes: the one where pretentious wine connoisseur Miles drinks an entire bucket of wine spit at a vineyard, and the one where Miles has to retrieve his friend's wallet from a couple having enthusiastic post-cuckold sex.

Writer-director Alexander Payne excels at little subtle jokes, such as when Miles holds his ear so he can better smell a glass of wine. We find these moments inherently funny, but we aren't sure that we have *permission* to laugh at them because they're so muted.

The value of "Holy Crap!" scenes is that they tell us, "Yes, this is definitely supposed to be a comedy. This is all funny. Laugh." The two "Holy Crap!" scenes in *Sideways* shatter the movie's gentleness (and, one might argue, realism), and the viewer feels liberated. We're shocked out of our happy mellowness to finally enjoy a gut-busting laugh with the rest of the audience, which creates a moment of communal joy and bonding.

And part of that joy is that we now have a scene that we can tell our friends about to get them to see the movie (or read the book). What if these scenes hadn't been there? You'd have to say, "He holds his ear to smell wine!" and they wouldn't get the big deal. Your "Holy Crap!" scene is your calling card and your cultural currency.

☑ Does the story contain a surprise that is not obvious from the beginning?

This is often called the *twist*, but it's a word so abused that writers are tempted to shun it. We all know who's to blame: M. Night Shyamalan, master of the "everything you know is wrong" twist. But when it comes to twists, smaller is usually better. Don't shock your audience; astonish them. Instead of you, the writer, surprising the audience, let your *characters* surprise the audience.

Much worse is the story with no surprises at all. *Young Adult* is a very funny movie. Charlize Theron gives a great performance as a failed children's author slinking back home to pick up where she left off. Writer Diablo Cody and director Jason Reitman both know how to deliver incisive satire, skewering shallow city dwellers and banal exurbanites with equal relish.

There's just one big problem with this movie: If you were to stop the projector halfway in and poll the audience about what's going to happen next, all of them would guess correctly. Once the major characters are introduced, this whole movie rolls downhill. It's painfully obvious what's going to happen every step of the way.

Compare this to *The Color of Money*. This is hardly a twist-driven story, but nevertheless it takes an astonishing turn in the third quarter. If you turned off the projector halfway through, most of the audience would guess that naïve young pool player Tom Cruise was going to eventually reject the corrupting ways of veteran hustler Paul Newman, and find a way to succeed in the world of professional pool playing without compromising his integrity. Instead it's Newman who discovers his conscience and confronts an increasingly sociopathic Cruise. When this plot turn happens, we're astonished but not baffled. In retrospect, the signs were there, but we didn't notice them before. That's a great twist.

The ending of *Young Adult* certainly seemed inevitable but not at all surprising. It felt as if the writer was determined to condemn her own main character, and so she didn't allow the character to surprise her or us. If you set out to "nail" your main character, you'll need to use a hammer, and after you use that hammer, she's going to end up flattened. Let your characters surprise you, and they'll surprise the audience, too.

☑ *Is the story marketable without revealing the surprise?*

It's great to have a big surprise up your sleeve, but beware of a common mistake: The twist is not the concept. The *concept* is the compelling idea that sells the story. The *twist* is what wakes up the story once the original concept starts to run out of steam.

There was a TV show a few years ago called *The 4400*. The creators pitched it to the networks like this: All of these people have been abducted over the years by lights in the sky, and one day they all return at the same time with superpowers. At first, it seems like a standard alien abduction story, but then we get to the big twist: They *weren't* abducted by aliens. They were abducted through time travel by post-apocalyptic humans who have given them these powers to prevent the apocalypse from happening!

Wow, what a pitch! Every network got excited. Then the network execs asked *when* the truth would be revealed. The writers got big grins on their faces and said, "That's the great part: We don't find this out until the end of season five!" Suddenly, all of the joy went out of the room.

The writers hadn't thought this through. By their own admission, it seemed like a generic *X-Files* knockoff until they revealed the twist. They knew that they'd never sell it to the network without revealing the big twist, but they somehow expected the network to be able to sell the generic version to the audience for five years. It gradually sunk in to the writers that their plan made no sense. They hastily came up with a better plan, in which the twist is revealed at the end of the original miniseries.

The makers of *The 4400* belatedly realized that "time travel" wasn't the *twist* but the *concept*, so it had to be set up before the actual series began.

☑ *Is the conflict compelling and ironic both before and after the surprise?*

So the surprise (which astonishes your audience *after* they've shown up) has to be different from the concept (which got them to show up in the *first place*). Now let's turn that on its head: The surprise can't *eliminate* the concept. The concept has to last for the entire story, not just until the surprise happens.

I sometimes come up with what I think is a great concept for a thriller, but then I realize my idea only provides a unique way of *starting* the story, and then all of the uniqueness disappears once the plot gets going.

For instance, an older friend in college told me a wild story from his past. It sounded made up, but I later confirmed it was true: At his previous college, he had been arrested for creating a world-famous computer virus. Like most hackers, he could type faster than any stenographer, so a judge sentenced him to community service working for the government's little-known "Relay" service.

This was a program that allowed deaf people to use a primitive version of "Chat" to communicate online with a relay center. People at the relay center then had to call whomever the deaf person wanted to call and read everything he wrote, then transcribe everything that was said on the other end of the line back to the deaf person. This enabled deaf people to use the phone like anybody else. There were two especially weird things about this service:

- Lonely deaf people would try to chat directly with the relay operators, but the operators were strictly forbidden from responding or conveying anything but what was said on the other end of the line.
- Shockingly, operators were forbidden from interfering with or reporting any crimes committed over the phone using the service, since the government had no right to "listen in" without a warrant, even if the operators were actually facilitating that crime. My friend handled calls to and from drug dealers and wasn't allowed to tell anybody!

My mind instantly reeled: What a great beginning for a thriller! A deaf woman keeps getting threatening calls, and our hero has to relay those threats. She calls the police for help, using the hero's voice, but they don't believe her. She calls her friends, but they hang up. Won't somebody help her? At what point does our relay guy decide that it's up to him?

A great setup, right? Well, here's the problem: As soon as he leaves the relay center to help her, the whole concept disappears. He just becomes one more noir hero protecting a damsel in distress from some crooks. The bizarre relay system no longer has anything to do with the story.

Here are two TV shows from back in the day that have concepts that only start off strong: *Early Edition* is about a guy who gets the next day's paper a day early and then spends every day saving someone who would meet misfortune without his intervention. *Tru Calling* is about a morgue worker who can talk to the dead and find out who killed them, allowing her to avenge them. The problem is, both heroes can *discover* the danger using their superpowers, but they can't *solve* the problem using these powers. After the first commercial break, the concept is gone, and they became routine crime-solver shows.

But no matter how strong your concept, it's just your starting point. Great concepts don't make for great stories; great *characters* do.

4

CREATING COMPELLING CHARACTERS

WHAT IS CHARACTER?

Character is the human element of your story, the aspect that the audience actually *cares* about.

Your characters are also the most *unruly* part of your story to write. Rather than bend them to your will, you need to listen to them and let them do what *they* want. They will make the decisions they want to make, say what they want to say, and create the meaning they want to create. If you generate great characters and throw them into volatile situations, then *they* will generate great stories and take you along for the ride.

In this section, I'm using the term *character* to apply primarily to your main character or hero. Many of the questions in this chapter also apply to other major characters, but I'm focusing on identification, and the audience can only fully identify with *one* character. The chapters on scene work and dialogue will emphasize the interactions between your characters.

MISCONCEPTIONS ABOUT CHARACTER

To begin, let's review some of the misconceptions we covered in the "Thirteen Laws of Writing for an Audience."

- For our purposes, a "hero" is not necessarily male or female, good or evil, or associated with any particular genre. A hero is merely the character the audience most identifies with in any story.
- You can get an audience to care about many different types of hero, whether good or evil, brilliant or foolish, but there are two qualities that every hero must have: The hero must be *active* and *resourceful*.
- Getting an audience to *truly* care about *any* character, even an ostensibly "likable" one, is tremendously hard. It requires an overwhelming act of shared empathy on the writer's part.
- Audiences don't want to *admire* your heroes; they want to *identify* with them. Audiences don't identify with heroes who save cats; they identify with heroes who are *misunderstood*.
- The most successful antiheroes aren't likable but are nevertheless lovable. The creators of these characters work overtime in subtle ways to *force* the audience to empathize.

> **MISCONCEPTION:** Your heroes are real if you say they're real.
>
> **AU CONTRAIRE:** Your heroes are mechanical constructs until you make them come alive.

Pixar had a problem. They had pioneered the idea of computer animation and made some very appealing short films featuring a jumping desk lamp, so they were eager to move into features—but their technology had huge limitations. There was a reason they'd been anthropomorphizing lamps: They just couldn't get the hang of creating hair or warm-looking skin, which meant they couldn't feature human characters.

They parlayed their Oscar-winning short film *Tin Toy* into a first feature called *Toy Story*. While that was in production, they sat down for a now-legendary lunch where they discussed the future of the company. They couldn't make movies about toys forever, but how many movies could they make about heroes without hair or warm skin?

In addition to more *Toy* movies, they brainstormed a list of new ideas, all of which eventually got made:

- Ants: *A Bug's Life*
- Monsters: *Monsters, Inc.* (They didn't know during this lunch that they would master hair in time to make this movie.)
- Fish: *Finding Nemo*
- Cars: *Cars*
- Robots: *WALL-E*

Once they had their list, Pixar realized how challenging it would be to make these films successful: All of these potential heroes would be hard for audiences to identify with, in large part *because* they would lack hair and warm skin. Was there any point in making movies about such unlikely subjects? Yes, but they'd have to make up for the inherent liabilities with additional assets: They would have to create heroes who were extra-lovable, extra-compelling, and extra-*human*.

Pixar realized that if they were going to create five very expensive movies about five different types of hard-to-like creatures, they were going to have to bring back the idea of the Hollywood "story department." Egos had to be replaced by rigorous group critiques. As we discussed earlier, everything was constantly second-guessed by their "Brain Trust," and entire movies were sometimes sent back to the digital drawing board.

The results, as you probably know, were stunning. They created characters so lovable that even people who *disliked* computer animation flocked to theaters. More than any other studio name, "Pixar" became synonymous with quality.

And then a funny thing happened: They ran out of limitations. When they finally developed the technology needed to tell any type of story, the Pixar name began to diminish in the public's eyes. They weren't bending over backward to make us fall in love anymore, because they seemed to assume their new characters would be *inherently* likable.

But no character is inherently human. No matter what you're writing, your characters are just cold constructs until you hook them up to a lightning bolt and jolt them to life. Every character starts off as a bug, a fish, a car, a robot—it only has as much life as you give it.

MISCONCEPTION: Some heroes are winners, and others are losers.

AU CONTRAIRE: Every hero needs to be both a winner and a loser. The audience wants to cheer and fear for every hero throughout every story.

Early on, I would be surprised when I got notes that said, "The hero is too much of a loser at the beginning." I was confused: Why would that be a problem? Shouldn't heroes go from zero to hero? Isn't that common? But true zero-to-hero stories are rare. Even in stories where heroes *seem* totally unprepared for the problem, they usually discover they have useful skills after all.

For example, I remembered *Back to the Future* as a classic zero-to-hero story, until I re-examined it with this in mind: Marty *thinks* of himself as a loser, and we feel empathy for those feelings of vulnerability, but right from the beginning, he's *actually* a badass:

- He has a band!
- He mouths off to the principal!
- He grabs onto the bumpers of cars (even a cop car) as he skateboards to rocket down the street!

But wait—shouldn't these elements keep us from empathizing with Marty's vulnerability? Nope—they have the opposite effect. The badassery *makes* the vulnerability sympathetic. We feel bad about the hero's low self-esteem because we *disagree* with it: Can't you see how cool you are, Marty?

Almost every hero has a surprisingly similar badass-to-vulnerability ratio. The difference between the toughest tough guys and the dweebiest dweebs is about 5 percent. Most great heroes have a lot of badassery *and* a lot of vulnerability, because you need a lot of both to resonate with audiences.

It's tempting to put your heroes under the gun the entire time. This not only maximizes the conflict but also amps up the motivation. This way, your heroes are always outgunned, outnumbered, and reacting instinctively. They don't *want* to do this; they *have* to do this!

Some writers assume the best way to raise the stakes is to pit Bambi versus Godzilla, but a strange thing happens in *Godzilla* movies: People root for Godzilla. Audiences *empathize* with vulnerability, but they *admire* strength.

Anyone who has ever tried to choose a favorite superhero has encountered this paradox. Two factors define superheroes: their levels of power and professionalism. So you want a ton of both, right? Superman has a maximum amount of power *and* professionalism, so he would seem to be the ultimate superhero.

But few comics readers pick Superman as their favorite. He's the ultimate power fantasy. If we could be any hero, he's the one we would all want to be. He's happy, healthy, and very, *very* secure. But on the badass/vulnerability meter, he pings out too far to the left. We cheer for him, but we don't fear for him, which means we don't care about him nearly as much as we should. It's downright unfair to have superpowers *and* super-professionalism.

So who do most comic readers pick as their favorites? The two most popular superheroes, in poll after poll, are Batman and Spider-Man. Batman is a consummate professional, but he has no superpowers. Spider-Man, on the other hand, has powers that landed in his lap, but he's a perpetual amateur at the hero biz.

Either way, they are in over their heads quite often. Batman goes up against powerful supervillains armed with only leather tights and his tool belt. That's brave! That's dangerous! Spider-Man, meanwhile, is taking on armed Mafiosi even though he's just an untrained school kid. Sure, he's got powers they don't have, but he's hardly bulletproof. In both cases, we have reason to cheer *and* fear.

So when it comes to superheroes, powers and professionalism are good, but choosing one or the other is even better. Of course, that leaves a fourth possibility as well: the hero who lacks both, who pegs out to the right on the badass/vulnerability meter. This is exemplified by the would-be superhero Kick-Ass, who is *nobody's* favorite.

Superman is all cheers; Kick-Ass is all fears. Batman and Spider-Man each find a happy medium, each in his own way, which is what the audience wants.

> **MISCONCEPTION:** Heroes should state their philosophy on page 5.
>
> **AU CONTRAIRE:** Stories are more compelling if the heroes start out with the wrong philosophy.

Some storytelling guides recommend that heroes explain their philosophy on page 5, and so many writers dutifully follow along, allowing their heroes to state, right from the beginning, the overall source of personal strength that will carry them through the whole thing—but those stories are over before they begin. When the story begins, heroes shouldn't know what they need to win. That's the point. They have to go on this journey to figure it out.

The original screenplay for *Chinatown* did have a correct statement of philosophy on page 5, but the filmmakers were smart enough to cut it from the finished movie. In the first scene, detective Jake Gittes shows a working-class client named Curly pictures of his wife having an affair, then tells Curly he should probably forget about it. In the finished movie, we then cut to the waiting room of the detective agency as Curly emerges from the office, explaining to Gittes that he can't pay right away. Gittes says he understands and that he was just trying to make a point.

Huh? What point? Did we miss something? Yes, we did. The missing chunk of dialogue from Robert Towne's original screenplay reveals all. This was how that scene in Gittes's office originally played out:

> **Curly:** (*pouring himself a drink*) You know, you're okay, Mr. Gittes. I know it's your job, but you're okay.
>
> **Gittes:** (*settling back, breathing a little easier*) Thanks, Curly. Call me Jake.
>
> **Curly:** You know something, Jake?
>
> **Gittes:** What's that, Curly?

Curly: I think I'll kill her. (*crying*) They don't kill a guy for that.

Gittes: (*examines Curly for a long time, then ...*) Oh they don't?

Curly: Not for your wife. That's the unwritten law.

Gittes: (*pounds on the desk, shouting*) I'll tell you the unwritten law, you dumb son of a bitch, you gotta be rich to kill somebody, anybody, and get away with it. You think you got that kind of dough, you think you got that kind of class?

Curly: (*shrinks back a little*) No ...

Gittes: You bet your ass you don't. You can't even pay *me* off.

Why was this cut? I think it was because the filmmakers belatedly realized that Gittes couldn't say this yet because it's a *correct* statement of philosophy. If Gittes already understands this, then he has no journey of discovery to go on.

The purpose of the story is for Gittes and the audience to learn this. The movie will *show* this to us, so it doesn't need to tell us as well. Like many writers, Towne was giving the game away too soon by giving Gittes a correct statement of philosophy in the first scene. Luckily, the director or the editor was wise enough to snip it out.

But that doesn't mean that characters *shouldn't* have a statement of philosophy right up front. This is your chance to show how *wrong* they are. This is your chance to establish their false expectation that life will work a certain way. That makes it all the more upsetting when it goes wrong.

> **MISCONCEPTION:** The hero's emotional journey should go from A to Z.
>
> **AU CONTRAIRE:** It's often more compelling when a hero goes from Y to Z.

Here's another area where I think many of the most popular storytelling guides steer writers wrong: They insist that audiences always want the hero to go on the longest possible emotional journey, all the way from *A* to *Z*. I disagree, and I think this is where many Hollywood movies get wrecked.

The brilliant graphic novel *V for Vendetta*, set in a dystopian future England, begins when an anti-fascist terrorist saves a miserable young girl from government goons on her first night of prostitution. He then invites her to live in his secret refuge, where he gradually grooms her to be his successor. Even though the girl has already lost everyone she ever loved to the fascist government, she's still horrified by "V" and reluctant to embrace his extreme ways.

The limp movie adaptation has many problems, but one of the biggest is the baffling decision to establish Portman's character as a strong, independent go-getter assistant at a TV station where her biggest problem is an unrequited crush on her boss. We're supposed to believe that this happy-go-lucky girl will soon decide to become an anti-government terrorist leader?

The book takes V's assistant from rock-bottom refugee to terrorist over the course of three hundred dense pages, which makes for an emotionally devastating journey. The movie takes her from rom-com heroine to terrorist in under two hours, which is just silly.

Compare this to a much better Natalie Portman movie, *Black Swan*. This story could have started with Portman as a sweet young ballerina whose life is gradually ruined by her high-stress role and callous director. But the filmmakers and Portman made the daring choice to start off her character pretty far out to sea. Right from the beginning, she's worn down to a state of near madness from years of maintaining an inhuman amount of discipline to get to her current position, and she is already too far gone to save. Winning the coveted lead role in *Swan Lake* is merely the last chink that shatters an already fractured window.

This isn't a journey from *A* to *Z*; it's a journey from *Y* to *Z*, and that's why Portman won the Oscar. Because Portman has less ground to cover, she's able to take time to break our hearts with every minutely observed detail of this final battle. She's not an Everywoman. She's a specific woman, suffering through a crisis that is unique to her own psychology.

You might think that this would make her too unsympathetic, or not worth rooting for, since there's no good outcome to root for, but we actually care more about her because of that. She's already given up so much, but now she fears that she'll have to give up her last shred of dignity to cross the finish line. We respect her accomplishment, empathize with what it has cost her, and feel anguish over this final crisis.

Why waste time dragging her all the way from happiness to the crisis point? Feel free to start with your characters on the edge of a crisis, and trust that your audience is willing to jump right in, up to their necks, as the story begins.

QUESTIONS TO ASK ABOUT CHARACTER

So once you've cleared away all of these misconceptions, how do you create a compelling character? How do you draw the audience in against their better judgment? How do you overcome their jaded cynicism? You have to somehow make them:

- **BELIEVE:** Before they can like or dislike your characters, the audience must overcome the fictional barrier and believe the characters actually exist. How do you overcome the audience's natural resistance and get them to accept your characters as human beings?
- **CARE:** Once the audience has accepted your heroes' existence, can you engage them emotionally? The first part of empathy comes from understanding the vulnerabilities of your heroes. Get strangers to feel for them and fear for them.
- **INVEST:** Caring is only the first half of empathy, because as much as we feel for the heros' flaws, we also need to trust their strengths. This is the area where many beginners fall down on the job. Audiences are naturally inclined to reject heroes until they *earn* their investment. Your heroes need not be do-gooders or Earth savers, but they must be active, resourceful, and differentiated from those around them, even if it means they're extraordinarily rotten.

Believe

☑ Does the hero have a moment of humanity early on?

Your heroes have a lot of work to do, so it's tempting to simply hit the ground running and start dumping problems on their heads until they're ready to stand up and do something about it. But you can't assume that the audience will automatically bond with your heroes just because they're told to identify with them. The audience is actually inclined to distrust and reject your heroes, for all the reasons listed in chapter two.

The audience won't go anywhere with your heroes until they win them over. Logically they know this is fiction and they shouldn't care about a bunch of lies, but you need to overcome their resistance and make them care against their better judgment.

So how do you do that? You need to give your hero at least one *moment of humanity*, which will break through that resistance and bond the audience to the hero. This is the moment the audience forgets that they are watching or reading fiction and starts to believe in the character.

The moment of humanity can take different forms:

SOMETHING FUNNY: This is easiest to do in first-person novels, of course, where the hero can win over the audience on the first page with a snarky point of view. In movies, this just means cracking wise, usually in a perceptive way, as with the heroes of *Casablanca*, *Ocean's Eleven*, *Groundhog Day*, and *Juno*. Humor can also bond the audience to characters who are scared to be funny out loud but have a very funny, perceptive, and self-deprecating voice-over, such as the heroes of *The Apartment*, *Spider-Man*, and *Mean Girls*.

AN OUT-OF-CHARACTER MOMENT, where the audience realizes this character won't just be one-note. This may seem odd: How is it possible to introduce your character with an out-of-character moment? It takes very little time to establish expectations before you start to upset them. Jokes are written according to the "rule of threes": something happens twice, which establishes a pattern, and then the third time something different happens, which upsets the pattern. That's all it takes.

Tony Stark in *Iron Man* proves himself to be a boastful alpha-male billionaire in the first scene as he boldly shows off his new weapon to a group of generals, but then he asks to share a Humvee with some soldiers and becomes self-deprecating and gregarious, making jokes about gang signs in selfies.

COMPASSIONATE: This is tricky, because you want to avoid generically benevolent "save-the-cat" moments, which actually alienate an audience. The best compassionate moments are ones that are *also* out-of-character moments.

Aladdin has a great song about being a fun-loving thief, but after he gets away with his bread, he reluctantly lets starving kids beg it off him. Blake Snyder cites this as a clear-cut "save-the-cat" moment, but it's important to point out that it only works because it's out of character. If he had stolen the bread *for* the kids, we wouldn't like him as much. That would be more sympathetic but less compelling.

Otherwise, compassionate moments should be rooted in the hero's sense of emotional vulnerability. Ben Stiller stands up for Cameron Diaz's mentally disabled brother in *There's Something About Mary* because he feels like a fellow outcast. Katniss volunteers in her sister's place in *The Hunger Games* because she feels she's already hardened herself, and whether or not she survives the Games, she doesn't want her innocent sister to lose her humanity as well.

AN ODDBALL MOMENT, where the character, rather than single-mindedly pursue a goal, indulges in a bit of idiosyncratic behavior that briefly interrupts the momentum of the story in a good way.

- *The French Connection*: We never really get any moments of weakness or humility from Popeye, but we fall in love with him when he suddenly veers off script in an interrogation and starts asking the suspect if he ever picked his feet in Poughkeepsie.

- *Blazing Saddles*: Track-layer Bart is ordered to sing an old slave song as he works, so he smirks and breaks out into an anachronistic rendition of "I Get a Kick out of You." We now love this guy.

COMICALLY VAIN: A variation of the "laugh-with" funny moment is the "laugh-at" moment in which the character is comically vain.

- Han Solo in *Star Wars* is hurt by the fact that Luke and Obi-Wan have never heard of his ship.
- The hero of *Rushmore* daydreams he is a math genius and the hero of the school, only to wake up to a more modest reality.
- Annie in *Bridesmaids* sneaks out of her lover's bed in the morning to do herself up, then climbs back in so it appears that she woke up looking beautiful.

A UNIQUE BUT UNIVERSAL MOMENT that has nothing to do with the story, where the character does something we've all done but have never seen portrayed before.

- My favorite movie, the silent drama *The Crowd*, begins with a dead-simple example: Our hero is nervously preparing for a date in front of the mirror when he notices a spot on his face. He keeps trying to rub it off, to no avail, until he realizes that it's a spot on the mirror.
- *Modern Times* gets us on the side of The Little Tramp by introducing him as he's busy working an assembly line and can't take his hands off for a second—not even to scratch his nose.
- William Goldman, in his book *Adventures in the Screen Trade*, writes about how nobody was bonding with the hero in his movie *Harper*, so he added a brief scene in the beginning where Harper gets up in the morning, starts to make coffee, and realizes that he's out of filters. Harper thinks for a second, then fishes yesterday's filthy filter out of the garbage, brushes it off, and reuses it. Suddenly, the audience is ready to go anywhere with this guy.
- In the case of *The 40-Year-Old Virgin*, it's the very first shot: Andy tries to pee while coping with a painful morning erection. That's

certainly a unique but universal moment I never thought I'd see portrayed onscreen.

No matter which kind you choose, these moments of humanity are essential for building quick identification. You have a very short time to get your audience to say, "I love this person," before they give up and tune out.

☑ Is the hero defined by ongoing actions and attitudes, not by backstory?

Many writers assume a hero will be interesting because of an interesting backstory, but the audience doesn't actually care much about a hero's backstory. Heroes are interesting because of their actions and attitudes as the story progresses, not because of what happened in the past.

Some recommend that you preplan every possible fact about your hero's backstory, all the way back to where her grandfather went to college, but if you actually take the time to list five hundred facts about the past, then you might run into some danger:

- **YOU'LL BORE YOURSELF TO TEARS**, getting sick of your heroes long before they have a chance to come alive on the page.
- **YOU'LL COMMIT YOURSELF TO RANDOMLY SELECTED STORY DETAILS** and feel less willing to change your hero's past on the fly as you write—to add special skills or tangled relationships from the past that can juice up the conflict or provide additional ironies.
- **YOU'LL FEEL COMPELLED TO REVEAL THIS EPIC BACKSTORY**, even though the audience won't care.
- **YOU'LL BE TEMPTED TO USE BACKSTORY AS A SUBSTITUTE FOR FRONT STORY**, differentiating your characters based on where they've been in the past rather than how they act now. This is a huge mistake. You should be far more focused on your hero's present and future.

Every year, there are terrible TV pilots about quirky groups of cops. Each member of the team stops the story dead to reveal a long, complicated backstory, but their current plans and tactics are virtually identical.

Differentiate your characters based on their behavior, language, and attitudes. You want characters who will all react differently to the same situation. Don't differentiate where they *came from*; differentiate where they're *going*.

Don't get me wrong: As long as you're ready to *know more than you show*, it's okay to write out a full bio of each character. Just because your heroes have baggage doesn't mean they should take it out of the overhead bin during the flight.

Most of the time, the audience is content to simply guess the hero's backstory. If your hero became a cop because he came from a long line of Irish cops, or became a preacher because he was always the most pious kid on his block, you don't need to tell us that. We can guess.

The only good reason to reveal a backstory is if it's an *ironic* backstory: Maybe your cop comes from a long line of college professors, or your preacher used to be a gang member. These are backstories worth mentioning.

In *Margin Call*, big-time stockbroker Jeremy Irons quizzes his underling Zachary Quinto about where he came from. We find out that, rather than being a trained stock analyst, Quinto started out as a rocket scientist working at a jet propulsion laboratory, then jumped into finance because the money was so much better. Not only does this give Quinto an ironic backstory, but it reveals the theme of the movie: Our cleverest minds, which once helped us soar to new heights, are now put to use dreaming up crooked schemes that crash our economy and create nothing but wreckage.

Irons's backstory, on the other hand, is never revealed, because we can guess where he came from, and that's fine. Not every character needs to reveal backstory. Most of the time, the audience is happy to fill it in.

☑ *Does the hero have a well-defined public identity?*

Compelling characters are never exactly who they seem to be. The public identity is what your character *seems to be* to the world, and it must contrast with his private identity. The gaps between the two are the character's contradictions. The more contradictions, the more compelling the character.

Now just because you're going to build a rich inner life for your character, one that contrasts nicely with his characterization, doesn't mean the surface characterization can be generic. You can't say, "Sure, this guy *seems* like a million characters you've seen before, but wait until you really get to know him!" Your hero's *surface* characterization must *also* be unique and compelling in its own right.

This is an area where novelists have more leeway than scriptwriters. A novel can start by introducing the hero's interior life, then move on to introduce the hero's public identity. But scripted media, such as plays, television shows, and movies, almost always introduce the external first. Characters' interactions are immediately apparent, but their inner life (without a voice-over) only becomes clear when we see how certain behaviors contradict others.

So how do you create a compelling surface characterization?

The most obvious way is to define heroes in the context of their public role (job, school, function within the family, etc.). You do this by showing unique behavior in this space that quickly defines the character. But it's essential to derive this behavior from your personal experience or research. Your character can't start out by simply doing the sort of thing similar characters do in other stories or your audience will instantly lose interest.

If you're writing about a doctor, and all you've ever seen of doctors is what they do in other TV shows, then it will be impossible to come up with fresh and convincing behaviors to characterize your hero. Every behavior you come up with will either seem overly familiar (they do that on television!) or false (you just made that up!).

Generic is bad. If you want to give your cop character a little personality, don't give him a donut craving. It's believable enough, but it's a cliché. Instead, you should give him something specific. How about a crazy saxophone-playing cop who always has his sax around his neck? That is certainly specific, but it doesn't ring true. The hard part is coming up with something that's unique but also authentic. How do you do this? Research. Go on a ride-along with some cops. Very quickly you'll notice behavior that makes you say, "A-ha! I didn't know that cops did that, but it makes total sense that they would!"

Likewise, if you want to write about doctors, it would be great if you were a doctor yourself, but if you just spend an hour with an actual doctor, or just read one doctor's memoir, you'll note dozens of little behaviors that you can use. *ER* creator Michael Crichton was a doctor, which is how he knew that some doctors dose themselves with saline drips to get ready for work.

Aaron Sorkin, on the other hand, knew nothing about the world of computer programmers when he got the assignment to write *The Social Network*, but he had an amazing resource: Mark Zuckerberg had kept a stream of consciousness misogynistic rant while creating his proto-version of Facebook. That sort of primary document is just as good as being there.

If the audience finds your hero's surface behavior compelling, then you've already got a big leg up. To get them to really care, however, you must soon contrast her characterization with her true character.

☑ Does the surface characterization ironically contrast with a hidden interior self?

All of us see ourselves as having hidden dimensions. Therefore, we identify with heroes who feel misunderstood. Why are superheroes compelling? Because of their secret identities. Batman is an avenger and a playboy. Spider-Man is a wisecracking vigilante and a nervous nerd. Superman, when written well, is a superconfident savior and a humble bumbler. Buffy the Vampire Slayer is a cheerleader and a vampire hunter.

Wolverine doesn't have a secret identity, but he's still a contradiction in that he's a rude, crude killing machine who is secretly sensitive and honorable. His teammate Cyclops, on the other hand, is exactly what he appears to be: He's a sullen do-gooder on the outside and a sullen do-gooder on the inside, too. As a result, he's never been very compelling in the comics or the movies.

Superheroes are the most extreme example, but in every genre, heroes and villains become far more compelling if they embody an inherent contradiction. Dracula is an erotic monster. Equally compelling, Frankenstein is an innocent monster. Jason from the *Friday the 13th* movies, on the other hand, is exactly what he seems.

Character contradictions are important no matter the genre, but in character studies and small stories, they become absolutely essential, because the hero's contradiction is often your only story hook.

Ryan Fleck and Anna Boden made one of the best movies of 2006, *Half Nelson*, starring Ryan Gosling as an idealistic schoolteacher who is secretly a crack addict. Fleck and Boden returned two years later with *Sugar*, an admirable but unmemorable movie about a Dominican baseball player in Middle America. Miguel, their main character, is in an unfortunate situation, stuck in farm teams in farm towns where he doesn't fit in, but he offers no internal contradictions. His whole personality is "lonely Dominican ball player." The movie just doesn't work. You can't write a character study about a character who has no compelling contradictions.

☑ Does the hero have a consistent metaphor family?

So far, I've focused on how to make characters compelling through behavior, but, alas, they eventually have to open their mouths, too.

Predetermining how a character will speak is one of the hardest parts of the job. In fact, it's so hard that it's tempting to simply wait until your characters "talk to you," but this will often result in bland, generic dialogue. You need a separate controlling idea for how each character will speak.

You can simply base your characters on friends and family, but you quickly run into a problem: Your friends and family don't have enough personality. When trouble comes, such characters tend to run and hide instead of acting out like a bigger-than-life character.

One shortcut I like to use is to combine the personality of a friend with the persona of an actor. For instance, as we saw before, Danny McBride created his character in *The Foot Fist Way* by combining the

Tae Kwon Do instructors he knew with Ricky Gervais's persona from *The Office*, and funny dialogue started flowing.

For minor characters, it's better than nothing to simply declare your character will talk like Woody Allen, Vince Vaughn, or Bette Davis. Anyone whose persona you can channel is fair game. The audience *usually* won't notice. But starting with a derivative voice will only get you so far. Ultimately, you need to be able to create a new voice from scratch, and there *are* ways to do so.

Start with a few rules. Does the character talk a lot or a little? Use complete sentences or fragments? Is the character self-aware or oblivious? Lay down these rules, and stick to them. Eventually, an oblivious character can reveal an unsuspected self-awareness, of course, but never be in a hurry to surprise the audience. Let the character act dependably for as long as possible, and only reverse expectations when the audience least expects it.

The biggest mistake is to wait until you have quieter character scenes to reveal all your finely wrought character work. Then, when the plot kicks into high gear, all of that work suddenly vanishes. "There's no time for all that personality stuff now. We've got *important* things to talk about!" Your characters suddenly become indistinguishable, reacting the way anybody would in a crisis.

But personality is not a luxury we shed in times of stress. It's vital to find a governing rule that determines a character's language even in extreme situations—*especially* in extreme situations. This is why your characters each need to have their own *metaphor family*. This can be a go-to source for every swear word they mutter, every compliment they give out, every daydream they indulge in, etc. Sometimes, their metaphor family is based on their job, but it can also be based on their cultural background or psychology.

Let's start with real life. On a normal news day, Dan Rather used the same stentorian language as any other news anchor. But when things got crazy, his language transformed. Those of us who watched his reaction to the 2000 election night crisis are still trying to pick up our jaws off the floor. Dan revealed his unique metaphor family: rural Texas.

> It's too early to say he has the whip hand.

> Don't bet the trailer money yet.

> This race is as tight as the rusted lug nuts on a '55 Ford.

> You talk about a ding-dong, knock-down, get-up race. ...

> The presidential race is still hotter than a Laredo parking lot.

This didn't happen because things slowed down and we got a chance to ask him about his background. This happened because things sped up too fast for him to watch himself. This example shows how writers can reveal character in moments of crisis.

The sitcom *30 Rock* exemplifies the three most common types of metaphor families:

- Jack's metaphor family is based on employment: He speaks corporate-ese (albeit the bizarre and vaguely new-agey language of modern management techniques). That's okay, because he's the only suit on the show.
- The others, however, are all creative types, and they can't all talk alike, so they have non-job-based sources for their metaphor families. Tracy's and Kenneth's reflect each character's home region: the inner city and rural Georgia, respectively. (Even Jack occasionally lapses into his fall-back persona, Boston Catholic.)
- Liz, on the other hand, has a metaphor family drawn from her psychology. She employs the language of adolescence ("I want to go to there," "Blurg!"), a state she's always trying and failing to move beyond.

In addition to these three, there are two infrequent types of metaphor families:

- **IT CAN REVEAL A TOTALLY SURPRISING SIDE OF SOMEONE'S PERSONALITY.** Lily on *How I Met Your Mother* is a sweet Caucasian kindergarten teacher, but when push comes to shove, her metaphor family sometimes becomes hip-hop, which always gets a nice laugh.

- **IT CAN BE BASED ON THE CHARACTER'S AMBITION.** Gareth on the U.K. version of *The Office* is a paper salesman who speaks like a military commander, which tells us everything we need to know.

That last trick can be a lot of fun once you've learned the jargon of several professions, because now you can mix and match. A Starbucks manager can talk like a corporate raider, implying he takes his job too seriously. A general can talk like a quarterback, implying he doesn't take his job seriously enough. An artist can talk like a lawyer. A boss can talk like a therapist. This is a great way to get them to reveal their character unintentionally.

☑ Does the hero have a default personality trait?

Metaphor families are a great way to decide what language a character will use, but it's equally important to establish a default personality trait.

To begin, let's differentiate between three interrelated aspects of a hero's personality:

1. **THEIR EMOTIONAL STATE WILL CHANGE WILDLY FROM SCENE TO SCENE.** As your heroes go on the most momentous journey of their lives, they'll quickly pass from frustration to joy to despair to triumph and everywhere in between.
2. **SEPARATE FROM THEIR EMOTIONAL STATE IS THEIR PHILOSOPHY.** Unlike emotional fluctuations, which happen in almost every scene, characters will engage in one big philosophical change over the course of the story: from selfish to bighearted, from innocent to cynical, from loner to joiner, etc.
3. **NEITHER OF THESE IS THE SAME AS THE CHARACTER'S DEFAULT PERSONALITY TRAIT.** Because characters are in such an extreme state of flux, it's tempting to simply declare that they have no fixed personality for the time being. After all, they're questioning everything, so they're hard to nail down. The danger is that no fixed personality

quickly becomes no personality at all. You need to find a few hard-and-fast rules that always govern how a character talks, even as his emotional state varies and his general attitude shifts.

Our emotions and attitudes may change, but our default personality trait stays the same. If a character's default personality trait is gloomy, then you'll always be able to identify that, even if the character happens to be happy today, because he will say something like, "I'm oddly happy today," or "I'm happy for once."

When you first meet people, it can be hard to tell the difference between their current emotional state and their default personality trait, but it becomes obvious over time. A certain overall aspect of their personality will always shine through, no matter what their mood or their current philosophy might be. Fictional characters should be the same way.

In *Spartacus*, the great Charles Laughton plays a bloated, cynical hedonist named Gracchus, who is more interested in aesthetic pleasures than the moralistic rhetoric of his fellow senators. But he discovers his conscience at the worst possible time—when he realizes it's up to him to take a stand for democracy by martyring himself to protest the rise of tyranny. When we last see him, he picks out a knife to slit his wrists, but then he wrinkles his nose—the knife isn't pretty enough. He chooses a more aesthetically pleasing knife, smiles, and then goes to the bathtub for a luxurious martyrdom.

By sacrificing himself, he's doing something wildly out of character, but he still can't shirk his default personality trait. Paradoxically, that's why the audience accepts his change of heart. Gracchus has undergone a philosophical transformation, but his default trait remains the same. As a result, we still believe in his character, and his sacrifice becomes all the more powerful.

☑ *Does the hero have a default argument tactic?*

Similar to the default personality trait is the default argument tactic. As with the personality, tactics can greatly transform over the course of a story. Frequently, heroes will start off the story naïve and overconfident, using half-ass strategies because they've never been seriously challenged. As the heroes face up to the challenge, they will gain skills, hone weapons, and figure out how to accomplish things.

Nevertheless, each character should have a default argument tactic throughout. Your characters will gain more and more arrows in their quiver over the course of the story, but they will always instinctively reach for this arrow *first*, from beginning to end. In any given encounter, it is only when this tactic fails that they will move on to another.

This is one of the least perceptible aspects of personality. You probably don't think of yourself or your friends as having default argument tactics, but if you think about it now, you might realize that each one does. Start there, instead of with movies or books: Listen to the people in your life and how they instinctively try to win arguments.

We identified metaphor families using *30 Rock* characters, so for default strategies, let's look at that show's former Thursday night companion, the equally brilliant *Community*. Let's say you're withholding a secret from a member of the Greendale Community College study group. How will they try to get it out of you?

- **JEFF:** He tries to trap you with the evidence of your lies in a lawyerly manner.
- **ABED:** He poses faux naïve questions, noticing little details and psychological "tells" in your answers.
- **ANNIE:** She asks genuinely naïve questions, persistently interrogating until she gets the truth.
- **TROY:** He halfheartedly attempts to lay logic traps and ensnare you with your own words.
- **SHIRLEY:** She passive-aggressively guilt-trips you.
- **BRITTA:** She accuses you of hypocrisy, inconsistency, or a general lack of morality.
- **PIERCE:** He doesn't strategize; he just insults. Unsurprisingly, he's the most unlikable character.

These strategies tend to have some overlap with the characters' metaphor families or default personality traits. Jeff, Shirley, and Britta have strategies that relate to their backgrounds (lawyer, evangelical Christian, hippie). Abed's strategy is related to his psychology (Asperger's syndrome). Annie, Troy, and Pierce, on the other hand, use strategies that match up to their default personality traits (sweet, geeky, and arrogant, respectively).

In dramas, the characters will be less broadly sketched but still use distinctive default strategies—silence or verbosity, sexuality or piousness, logic or emotion, etc. A character with a consistent tactic will be far more believable.

☑ Is the hero's primary motivation for tackling this challenge strong, simple, and revealed early on?

In high-jeopardy stories, the size of the motivation must match the size of the problem. The bigger the problem, the bigger the motivation required for the hero to tackle it, and the bigger the risk of *not* tackling it. Ideally, the *reward* for doing it and the *risk* of not doing it will *both* be high.

It's not hard to toss in a few "I have no other options" and "this opportunity is huge" scenes near the beginning of your story. Writers avoid this because they believe these scenes are overused. But everybody uses them for a good reason. Stories—especially big, exciting stories—won't work without them. Without big motivation, we won't buy it when the heroes tackle big problems.

Let's start by looking at an exception that proves the rule: In children's stories, there is often very little jeopardy. The problems are small, so they can be tackled by heroes with small motivations. Fred's, Daphne's, and Velma's motivation on *Scooby-Doo* is entirely capricious: "We heard about a mystery, so we decided to solve it." That's enough for them, *because nobody ever gets hurt*, so they never have reason to reconsider their casual decision.

But in adult stories, things are going to get tough, and the hero will need a *big* reason to stay on the job, or else your audience won't believe that the hero will stick with it. That's why your hero's motivation should have these three qualities:

STRONG. Too little motivation is never good. For a while, it seemed like every comedic film was motivated by two characters making a casual bet: "I bet I can transform a bookworm into a prom queen," "I'll bet you that I can go forty days without sex," "I bet that I can get that guy to dump me in ten dates," or whatever.

The problem with these stories is obvious from the premise: A bet is a weak motivation. Heroes may stick with it through early complications because they're up for a challenge, but if things get emotionally dangerous for them, if they have to change themselves in order to succeed, they won't do it. It was just a bet. So either the story is not going to substantially change the heroes (which is something that always needs to happen), or the heroes will go through hell and really change, all for the sake of a casual bet—and that is totally unbelievable.

SIMPLE. But too much motivation is just as bad. Let's look at some examples from the heyday of overmotivation, the late eighties. In *Lethal Weapon 2*, Mel Gibson has a *huge* amount of motivation to catch criminals:

- First and foremost, there's his civic duty.
- Second, there's his paycheck. It is his job, after all.
- Third, he's suicidal over the death of his wife, so he'll do anything that will put him in the path of a bullet.
- Fourth, he's the one cop who cares about the victims, damn it!
- The bad guys also happen to be the personification of South African apartheid!
- But that's still not enough, because these guys then kill Gibson's *new* girlfriend!
- Then, just to top it all off, one of them is taunting Gibson and suddenly reveals: "Oh, by the way, we also were part of that group that killed your wife all those years ago!"

Now *that's* a lot of motivation!

Tim Burton's 1989 *Batman* movie is another example. Everybody knows Batman's motivation. It's one of the strongest, clearest motivations any character has ever had. A criminal gunned down his parents. He blames all criminals, so now he hunts them down one by one. His personal pain has become society's gain. But in 1989, fighting for society was considered a sucker's bet, so the Joker accidentally reveals that, by an extraordinary coincidence, he was also the guy who killed Batman's parents, all those years ago.

So what's wrong with heroes being supermotivated? The problem is that it makes them less heroic. Saving the city from a criminal is a heroic goal, but now he's just on a revenge mission, and that's not heroic at all. He's overmotivated, so he becomes less interesting.

How on earth do you provide a huge motivation without overmotivating? Here's a warning I got from my mom: "Whenever someone gives you a lot of reasons, none of them is the real reason." Don't increase the *quantity* of motivation; improve the *quality* of motivation.

Piling on additional motivations is bad, but don't be afraid to lift your hero's *primary* motivation all the way to the stratosphere. If your hero gets to page 70 and says, "Ugh, I'm done. This problem isn't worth dealing with anymore," you should definitely listen to that, but you shouldn't have a *new* motivation walk in the door at that late date.

Don't *multiply* the motivation; *simplify* it. Mom was right: Giving too many reasons invalidates them all. It feels desperate and unfocused, and it makes the hero seem weak and vacillating, jerked this way and that by outside events.

REVEALED EARLY ON. If you read a lot of work by aspiring writers, one thing you repeatedly see is stories in which the hero's goal and/or primary motivation are mysterious until the final act. This never works.

Certainly heroes can have an air of mystery. In *The Great Gatsby*, the backstory of the title character is a big mystery and comes out very slowly, but we always know what he *wants*. He wants Daisy. He wants to make it to her dock with the green light.

Aspiring writers know they're supposed to create an air of mystery, so they figure the audience will enjoy solving the mystery of what the main character wants and why. But in fact, the audience *hates* to have to do that. By the time the story gets going, we demand to know enough about the main character's goals and motivations to follow along and engage with the story.

Care

☑ *Does the hero start out with a shortsighted or wrong-headed philosophy (or accept a bad piece of advice early on)?*

In the misconceptions section of this chapter, I countered the common notion that a hero should offer a correct overall statement of philosophy on page 5.

That said, it can be great to have a blatant or an inadvertent statement of philosophy from your hero, but only if it's a *false* statement of philosophy. Then, after most of your story has passed and we're ready for the climax, your hero can have a hallelujah moment and discover a *corrected* philosophy.

Perhaps the most famous false statement of philosophy would be Humphrey Bogart in *Casablanca*: "I stick my neck out for no one." Only later does he reverse himself, declare that his personal problems "don't amount to a hill of beans in this world," and put himself back in harm's way for the war effort.

Another great example: Tommy Lee Jones is a smart actor, and he cleverly stole *The Fugitive* from Harrison Ford when he ad-libbed his own false statement of philosophy. Ford points a gun at him and says, "I didn't kill my wife." Jones looks at him like he's crazy and informs him, "I don't care" (which wasn't in the script). This nicely sets up Jones's big reversal at the end.

Writers talk a lot about ways to "raise the stakes" of the plot, but a false statement of philosophy raises the emotional stakes. It shows the imposing size of the internal barrier the hero must overcome to succeed.

Silence of the Lambs is an example of a character who doesn't have a false statement of philosophy but accepts a false piece of advice. Clarice's boss, Crawford, gives her one cardinal rule for dealing with

Hannibal Lecter: "Don't let him get into your head." In the end, she will realize this is precisely what she needs to do.

☑ Does the hero have a false or shortsighted goal in the first half?

Just as your heroes begin with a false or shortsighted philosophy, they should also pursue a false or shortsighted goal for the first half of your story. This can take many forms:

WRONG SOLUTION TO RIGHT SOLUTION. In 2006, the Lupus Foundation gave the TV show *House* an award for all it had done to spread awareness for the disease. But it was strange because, at the time, Dr. House had never correctly identified a case of lupus. Instead, House's team would *falsely* identify the patient's mysterious ailment as lupus before realizing the patient had a far more exotic disease. Lupus is a little-understood, catch-all diagnosis that can explain all sorts of symptoms that don't normally fit together, so for House's team, it's a tempting but false way to think of the puzzle in front of them. Nevertheless, it gives them tests to run, and these tests unexpectedly lead them to the real diagnosis they hadn't suspected before.

Likewise, on the show *Supernatural*, the demon-hunting brothers always try to exorcise ghosts by finding their graves and salting the bones, even though it's never worked before. It's just their fallback, false goal that gives them something to do until they uncover the real mystery.

Why use the "wrong solution" approach? It gives heroes a reason to get moving so they can learn and grow on the job. While it may seem cooler to have heroes know what to do right away, or at least withhold judgment until they have all the facts, you will often find the audience actually likes them better if you first send them charging off in the wrong direction.

MICRO-GOAL TO MACRO-GOAL. This is a simpler form of false goal. Frodo sets out to merely return the ring to Gandalf in *The Lord of the Rings*. In *Star Wars*, Luke goes from wanting to fix his runaway droid to wanting to blow up the Death Star. John McClane in *Die Hard* spends the first half of the movie just trying to call the cops before he realizes he'll have to take on a terrorist cell single-handedly. These false goals make character motivations far more believable. If the heroes just woke up one day and decided to do a hugely daunting task, it would be hard to swallow. It's far more compelling to watch them get sucked into greatness against their better judgment.

TOTAL REVERSAL OF VALUES. Scrooge in *A Christmas Carol* comes to love Christmas. *Juno* searches for a "cool" parent to entrust her kid to, then realizes in the end that she wants just the opposite. Dave in *Breaking Away* starts off trying to defeat the college kids, then realizes he really wants to join them. Peter Parker in *Spider-Man* wants to use his powers to make his own life better until his callousness gets his uncle killed. Jake Sully in *Avatar* goes from wanting to rejoin the marines to killing them en masse.

These characters grow, and we're glad for it. Although we agreed with their original goal in the beginning, by the end, we've gone on the same journey they have, and we're very happy that they've changed their minds. A total reversal of values is hard to pull off, but when it's done right, it's one of the best ways to get your audience to truly love your hero, since they've shared in the character's astounding transformation.

☑ Does the hero have an open fear or anxiety about his future, as well as a hidden, private fear?

Heroes should have at least one big open fear, preferably a universal one the majority of the audience shares, such as the fear of failure, loneliness, or commitment. Of course, they shouldn't have so much fear they're cowering in the corner. We want the kind of fear that gets them to *actively* forestall a dreaded outcome.

No matter what happens in a scene, it will be far more compelling if we already know your hero hoped or dreaded it would happen. Perhaps your hero is forced to face the one thing he most fears (Indiana Jones in *Raiders of the Lost Ark* gets dropped in a snake-filled tomb). Or maybe what happens to him is a *metaphor* for his fear (Jimmy

Stewart in *Rear Window* is afraid of marrying Grace Kelly, so he becomes obsessed with a worst-case marital situation across the courtyard). Either way, the situation is more compelling to us because we know it's going to tap into the character's emotional anticipation.

Most heroes have a public common fear they express openly from the beginning. But in many stories, they also have a hidden, unique fear that's revealed halfway through. Chief Brody in *Jaws* is openly worried he won't cut it in his new beach-town job. We find out halfway through that he's also secretly afraid of the water. Likewise, Clarice Starling in *Silence of the Lambs* is afraid that she's in over her head at the FBI. Then we find out she's also secretly afraid that her dirt-poor background will show through. In both cases, the key to solving the characters' public fear is to confront their hidden, private fear.

To hook an audience, get them to *anticipate* what might happen next. Of course, your audience will take their emotional cues from your hero, so start the first scene by asking, *What is my hero anticipating?* It could be something good, of course, but it's usually a stronger choice if it's something he dreads. Even if your audience doesn't like your hero yet, they'll find they need to know if the dreaded event happens. That buys you some more time to get the audience on your side.

☑ Is the hero physically and emotionally vulnerable?

I was once in a pitch meeting where they wanted me to rewrite a high-profile project that began with a series of scenes in which a sniper eliminated various clones who were all living separate lives, spread out around the country, unaware of each other's existence. (This was a few years before *Orphan Black*.)

As they pointed out, part of the appeal of the premise was that you could start with the lead actor getting shot and killed, which would shock the audience until they realized this was just one of many clones. I agreed that this presented a neat opportunity.

But then the producer said, "So we start by meeting the first guy, and we're sure he's the hero of the movie because he drives a great car and goes home to his great apartment where he has sex with his hot girlfriend. But then he gets shot in the head! The audience will be so shocked that we've killed off our hero!"

But that's totally wrong, because the audience would not identify with this guy as the hero. The villain, maybe, but not the hero. Heroes are defined by their vulnerabilities as much as their invulnerabilities.

I pitched them a very different fake-out hero: My guy works in a stereo store in the mall. When we meet him, he's down on one knee proposing to a dubious Goth girl co-worker, who laughs out loud and tells him to try again. He thanks her for her honesty and asks for tips on how to do it better—he was just practicing for his real girlfriend, who works in another store in the mall. With the good-natured ribbing of the goth girl, he perfects his pitch. After his shift ends, he rushes over to his girlfriend's place of work only to find that she has already left. He catches up to her in the atrium, but she says she's fed up with his unwillingness to commit and starts to leave, so he decides to propose right there and then. He gets down on one knee and offers her a ring while a crowd gathers, all wondering what she's going to say. Finally, she says yes! The crowd cheers! Then BLAM! His head explodes from a sniper's bullet.

Now that's a shock, because this guy was *really* acting like a hero. Making yourself vulnerable is heroic. Exceeding your capabilities is heroic. Taking a risk is heroic. Schtupping your hot girlfriend is not heroic. Audiences hate it when they're asked to identify with invulnerability. This is why audiences couldn't embrace the second and third *Matrix* movies. By the end of the first one, the hero could already control the fabric of his reality. Who's going to identify with that?

☑ Does the hero have at least one untenable great flaw we empathize with?

It's no secret that all heroes need a great flaw—that's one piece of advice that goes all the way back to Aristotle. Let's look at some of the reasons why:

- **FLAWS ADD CONFLICT:** The hero is his own worst enemy.
- **FLAWS ADD MOTIVATION:** The hero has a big reason to change.

- **FLAWS GENERATE SYMPATHY**: It's easy to feel for a flawed hero.
- **FLAWS FOSTER IDENTIFICATION**: The audience feels flawed and is more likely to identify with flaws than strengths.

Great, so let's add a lot of flaws, right? Well, not so fast. One of the biggest mistakes many stories make is to pile on the pathos with a shovel. In the interest of telling a "brutally realistic" story, they actually present a comically *unrealistic* amount of gloom and doom.

I began to despair the state of American independent cinema after sitting through a grueling one-two punch of *Greenberg* and *Big Fan* in one weekend. The protagonists of these movies are such overexaggerated screwups they literally can't do *anything* right. Even when opportunity is staring them in the face, they are itchy, twitchy, belligerent, and incapable of pursuing their own self-interest. This makes them utterly unconvincing caricatures.

Their behavior is unbelievable, because in real life you can't screw up *all the time* and get through your day. More important, such characters just aren't compelling enough to hold an entire movie. It's impossible to care about a main character who won't meet you halfway.

But the writer of *Big Fan* also wrote a great movie called *The Wrestler*, which accurately captures the tragedy of the *functional* screwup: the stand-up guy who's clever and charming but nevertheless persists in screwing up 5 percent of the time, which is enough to ruin his life. How many decisions do you make in a day? What if every twentieth decision was self-destructive? That's all it would take, isn't it? *The Wrestler* is tragic because Mickey Rourke's character is screwing up a *good thing*. The heroes of *Greenberg* and *Big Fan* aren't tragic at all because they're just screwing up lives that are already hopelessly wretched.

Invest

☑ **Is that great flaw (ironically) the natural flip side of a great strength we admire?**

Writers usually give their heroes too many flaws and not enough strengths. In all the ways adding flaws makes your work easier, adding strengths can make your work harder.

- **STRENGTHS DECREASE CONFLICT:** Fewer things are a challenge to the hero.
- **STRENGTHS DECREASE MOTIVATION:** The hero has less reason to want to change.
- **STRENGTHS DECREASE SYMPATHY:** It's harder to root for an over-dog.
- **STRENGTHS DECREASE IDENTIFICATION:** Deep down, few people think of themselves as strong.

It's tempting to give your hero a lot of flaws and no strengths, but you should resist that urge because flaws only generate pathos in *contrast* to strengths. You need to keep the flaws to a manageable number and ensure each one is the flip side of a great strength because:

- It's realistic.
- It's naturally *ironic*.
- It will make overcoming those flaws something that's not just hard to do but hard *to want* to do. Your hero will be reluctant to overcome that flaw for fear of losing the accompanying strength.
- We'll be less likely to get exasperated by the flaw because we see the good side.
- It will make us worry more about the hero, since the strength is a potential problem.
- We will be more sympathetic to the flaw if we see it as a result of too much of a good thing.

Your heroes' internal struggles are only going to have dramatic tension if they're *reluctant* to overcome the flaw, and we must *empathize* with that reluctance. We need to *see* the potential downside of abandoning that flaw.

Rourke's main flaw in *The Wrestler* is irresponsibility, but this is the flip side of his strength: He loves having a good time and makes sure everyone else in the room has a good time, whether it's the fans at his wrestling matches or the customers at his deli counter. We want him to become more responsible, but we don't want him to stop lighting up the room.

Flaws need to have an upside, which is why some just don't work very well. One of the most overused flaws is alcoholism, but it's not as compelling as some writers think because there's very little upside. It's hard to overcome, but only because it's a chemical addiction. There's never any good reason to be an alcoholic. We'll never identify with a character's desire to keep drinking destructively.

The same is true for other less-than-compelling flaws, such as vanity, bigotry, and ignorance. This is also why mental illness doesn't actually work very well, unless seeing the world in a different way is the character's strength, as with the CIA analyst Claire Danes plays on *Homeland*. Danes is reluctant to overcome her bipolar disorder because she suspects that she does her best thinking when she's manic, and even though we see her suffer, the audience feels the same way. In other words, her flaws come with some strengths on the flip side.

The indefatigable writing guru Carson Reeves came up with a pretty good list of ten common flaws found in heroes. Let's start with his list and then look at how to generate a strength that is inextricably paired with each flaw. As we do so, note that two characters with the same basic flaw can have very different flip-side strengths. You could pair a refusal to grow up, for instance, with being fun loving (*Knocked Up*) or sweetly innocent (*The 40-Year-Old Virgin*) but not both.

FLAW: Puts work in front of family and friends
POSSIBLE FLIP-SIDE STRENGTHS: Hypercompetent, indefatigable, loyal to clients, patients, bosses, partners, etc.

FLAW: Won't let others in
POSSIBLE FLIP-SIDE STRENGTHS: Tough, honest, self-deprecating

FLAW: Doesn't believe in one's self
POSSIBLE FLIP-SIDE STRENGTHS: Humble, openhearted, careful

FLAW: Doesn't stand up for one's self
POSSIBLE FLIP-SIDE STRENGTHS: Nice, sweet, giving, loyal

FLAW: Too selfish
POSSIBLE FLIP-SIDE STRENGTHS: Zealous, hypercompetent, sarcastically witty

FLAW: Won't grow up
POSSIBLE FLIP-SIDE STRENGTHS: Fun loving or (alternately) innocent

FLAW: Uptight, risk averse, anal
POSSIBLE FLIP-SIDE STRENGTHS: Careful, hypercompetent

FLAW: Reckless
POSSIBLE FLIP-SIDE STRENGTHS: Brilliant, independent thinker, aggressive, effective risk-taker

FLAW: Lost faith
POSSIBLE FLIP-SIDE STRENGTHS: Self-aware, rational, sarcastically witty

FLAW: Pessimistic/cynical
POSSIBLE FLIP-SIDE STRENGTHS: Funny, bitingly honest

FLAW: Can't move on
POSSIBLE FLIP-SIDE STRENGTHS: Loyal, sentimental

One of the most entertaining "flaw/strength" scenes of all time appears in Larry Gelbart's wonderful script for *Tootsie*. Michael Dorsey's exasperated agent explains that nobody will hire Michael because he's too intense:

> **Agent:** You played a *tomato* for thirty seconds—they went a half a day over schedule because you wouldn't sit down.
>
> **Michael:** Of course not, it was illogical: If he can't move, how's he gonna sit down? I was a stand-up tomato: a juicy, sexy, *beefsteak*

tomato. Nobody does vegetables like me. I did an evening of vegetables off-Broadway. I did the best tomato, the best cucumber ... I did an endive salad that knocked the critics on their ass!

Casting directors may not want to hire Michael, but we are more than willing to hire him to be our hero. We sympathize with his flaw, even though we hope that he will eventually overcome it. We can work with this guy, because he's well worth rooting for.

☑ Is the hero curious?

Your hero has to *want* to unravel the story. That's all a hero is: the character who has to solve this problem. Your audience wants the entire story to come out, but they can't do it themselves. Instead, they have to trust your hero to get to the bottom of it for them. If the hero doesn't care, what is the audience supposed to do?

But let's say you feel the need to drop some information to the audience that they'll need later, so you have somebody casually mention something important in conversation with the hero, but the hero doesn't notice or care, even though it should be a big clue. This is a *huge* identification killer. If your hero passively receives an incomplete piece of important information and doesn't follow up, then the audience feels betrayed. They say to your hero, "Hey, loser, I'm counting on you to dig up all the information I need to enjoy this story, but you're not asking the follow-up questions I need you to ask! What good are you?"

Now, of course, you can occasionally have your hero "miss" a piece of key information the audience picks up on, but only if the audience feels the hero has a good reason for missing it, like a big distraction. Even better, drop the information and then have the hero and audience both get distracted by something else at the same time, so that they *both* forget about it. Then, later, when it turns out to be important, they'll both be kicking themselves at the same time so that they'll bond even more.

An example of the right way to do it would be when Jake finds the glasses in the pond in *Chinatown*. The audience and Jake both get distracted at the same time and forget all about them. Later, when they turn out to be the key piece of evidence, we don't get mad at Jake for forgetting about them; we get mad at ourselves.

It's an equally big sympathy killer if heroes don't act on the concrete information they do receive. This can be a problem when you try to build tension by ending every scene on an ominous warning of some kind. Oooh—spooky! But then, in the next scene, the heroes have moved on to another part of their day, and they forget all about the warning until it's too late, three scenes later. Heroes may take a while to become proactive, but they should always at least be *reactive*.

When we're watching or reading, we're constantly trying to anticipate what's going to happen next. If we can tell that the hero is not able, or not even trying, to anticipate a consequence that we can anticipate just by looking over her shoulder, we feel powerless. Why are we putting our trust in these schmucks?

Remember on *The X-Files* when they would get a big piece of the alien invasion puzzle at the end of an episode, and we'd all be on the edge of our seats, and then next week they were back in some Podunk solving some dinky little monster mystery, as if they'd never gotten that big clue? Remember how infuriating that was?

A more recent example is the hapless Tom Cruise science fiction epic *Oblivion*. Even though he meets several characters who are more than willing to tell him what's going on, Cruise remains oblivious to the nature of his situation for most of the movie. He just doesn't ask for some reason. The audience collapses in impotent frustration, waiting for him to care about his own story.

☑ Is the hero generally resourceful?

You can't *tell* the audience who the hero is; you need to *show* them. The audience chooses the hero, not the other way around. The audience will choose the character who is trying the hardest to get what he wants.

But just because we've chosen a hero doesn't mean we *trust* that hero. You can do everything else right but still lose us if you don't give us what we crave: a moment where your hero does something clever that makes us say, "Okay, this hero is resourceful enough to care about!"

Jason Bourne in *The Bourne Identity* is an example of a character who doesn't really get a "moment of humanity," simply because he has just woken up with amnesia and, as a result, has no real personality when the movie begins. So why do we bond with him? Because of the one aspect of his mind that he held onto: his extreme resourcefulness.

This goes way beyond being good in a fight. The moment where we really fall in love with him is when he's trying to escape from an embassy and rips a fire evacuation plan off the wall so he'll have a map of the place. We love to see something like that.

But you might protest: "Not every hero has to be Jason Bourne! Maybe my hero *isn't* clever. Maybe he's not even a hero. Maybe he's just a fool. Can't I tell a story about a fool?" The answer is yes, of course you can. But he has to be a *resourceful* fool.

How does that work? As my brother likes to point out, "It's hard to make things foolproof because fools can be so clever." If you think about this, it's absolutely true. Nothing in this world is foolproof because resourceful fools always figure out *some* way to screw it up. If you're going to write about a fool, *that's* the kind of fool you want to write about.

As filmmakers go, you don't get more admirably artsy than the Dardenne brothers of Belgium, who make beautifully observed but grueling portraits of pitiful figures who somehow manage to spiral even further down. Why are these movies so compelling, despite their painful subject matter? It's because of the brothers' ability to create great heroes. Of course, no one thinks of their characters as heroic, and certainly not clever, but in their own way, they are.

Bruno in *The Child* is an aimless junkie who discovers that his ex-girlfriend has just had his baby, so he immediately sells the child on the black market to get money for drugs. Later, he is truly shocked to see how upset she is, and he tries to get the baby back.

At one point in this process, Bruno is forced to wait in a back alley before the person inside will speak with him. There's just one problem: Bruno can never wait around for *anything*. He can't sit still for a second—that's his entire problem. But he doesn't whine about this problem. Instead he finds clever ways to solve it.

When he is told he must wait five minutes, we instantly sense that this is like a prison sentence to him. We share Bruno's anxiety as he looks around desperately for something to do. Then he spots it: a mud puddle by a white wall. He goes over, soaks his boots in mud, then leaps up against the wall repeatedly, putting black boot prints all over the wall. This happily occupies him until they come to get him. Problem solved. Fools can be so clever.

☑ Does the hero have general rules for living that he clings to (either stated or implied)?

So far, we've focused on how *you* would define your characters, but you also need to know how they would define *themselves*.

You need to ask yourself, *What are the rules they live by?* Every character has these, though most don't state them out loud the way John Wayne does in *The Shootist*: "I won't be wronged, I won't be insulted, and I won't be laid a hand on. I don't do these things to other people, and I require the same from them." In *Margin Call*, Jeremy Irons has a far more cynical philosophy: "Be first, be smarter, or cheat."

Stick to what the people would actually say if asked. Nothing like "I can't stand germs," or "I don't like kids," or "I'll never get off the couch." Those may be the real rules that actually define a character, but the purpose of this exercise is to get to know their self-image.

Once you've got your rules, you can start playing with them. Which rules are they forced to break over the course of the story? Which ones *should* they break but are too proud to do so? Which rules are they just deluding themselves about, since they've never *really* followed them?

The advantage of listing these rules is that doing so forces you to listen to your characters and allow them to define themselves. It's easy for characters to become just a bundle of flaws: a false goal, a false statement of philosophy, a limited perspective, and a long host of ironic failings. *But they don't know that.* They're just living their lives, doing their own things in their own time, so you need to know what those things are, as *they* see it.

☑ Is the hero surrounded by people who sorely lack her most valuable quality?

Many of the misconceptions mentioned earlier in this chapter can be summed up with the false notion that a hero is a character who would be heroic in any situation. The truth is, most heroes only become "heroic" as a result of a unique situation and might seem downright monstrous in any other.

This is another problem with cat saving: It's generic, not specific. A hero who is likable in one situation might be entirely unlikable if placed in a different story. Every crisis situation has something lacking, a vacuum that's just begging for a certain personality type to come in and fill it. Sometimes the situation calls out for a hero who will speak truth to power, but other times, it just needs someone to come in and start a keg party. The writer must find the right vacuum for every hero and the right hero for every vacuum.

In the book, movie, and TV show *M*A*S*H*, we're happy to have a martini-swilling, ultracynical hero like Hawkeye Pierce dropped into an uptight military base, where he can puncture all the gasbags and bring a breath of fresh air. In contrast, nobody is rooting for the Grinch to bring *his* cynicism to Whoville. Hawkeye is a hero because he's just the right interloper to fill the vacuum he finds himself in. The Grinch is a villain because he's the wrong interloper at the wrong time.

Heroes can't be generically heroic. Writers are always trying to search for a universally applicable key to heroism. After all, when we seek ways to make our heroes more likable, we secretly hope we're also gaining life skills for ourselves. Perhaps once we've discovered what makes Jimmy Stewart so likable, we can become just as appealing in our own lives!

But the truth isn't as encouraging. It turns out the secret to creating a hero is often to simply make everybody around the hero look awful. As Rodney Dangerfield says in *Back to School*: "You want to look thin? Hang around fat people!" That's *not* a solution writers will want to transfer to their real lives.

This seems, on first blush, like a very cynical and manipulative way to write. You're tricking your audience into liking your heroes simply by placing them into an extreme world. You're not playing fair. You're stacking the deck!

But this actually makes good sense. In fiction, as in life, nobody gets any credit for doing what everybody else is doing. Most stories aren't about morals, which are universal; they're about ethics, and ethics are entirely relative. In the same way that actions are only heroic if they're hard to do, personality traits are only admirable if you have to go against the grain to act that way.

☑ And is the hero willing to let them know that, subtly or directly?

But it's not enough to stand out from the crowd simply as a counter-example. Most heroes should feel compelled to point out the flaws of those around them, either loudly or quietly (or sometimes just in muttered asides).

It's funny that what we consider sympathetic in a hero is very different from what we find sympathetic in real life. We want our friends to be sensible, but we have very little patience for sensibility in fiction. We want our heroes to be *willful*. This doesn't mean that every hero needs to be brashly defiant. There are a lot of ways for heroes to stand up for themselves.

- Sometimes, yes, heroes will engage in angry confrontation.
- Other times, they subtly mock or impeach what the other character is saying.
- Sometimes they'll just quietly and brazenly ignore all opposition, which is a more direct type of defiance.
- Weaker characters may acquiesce but mutter sarcastic asides as they do it.
- In some cases, heroes fail to stand up for themselves, but they at least get their own say in first-person narration or voice-over. If

characters won't hold their own in person, they at least let *us* know about their defiance.

But if you don't want your heroes to be compliant, how do you straighten them out? After all, they have big flaws. Don't they need to accept a lot of good advice? No, they need to reject a lot of *bad* advice. In a great scene from the classic drama *Hill Street Blues*, the chief desperately seeks out his AA sponsor, hoping to be convinced not to relapse. He finds the sponsor at a restaurant, where the sponsor unexpectedly mocks the program and our hero's problems. Then the waitress brings out that drink the sponsor ordered. Our hero has seen what a relapse looks like, and that's what he really needed. Rejecting bad advice is far more powerful for him than accepting good advice.

Our urge to see heroes defy authority can go to ludicrous extremes. The producers of *24* joked that whenever a script came in short, they had one stock scene they could use repeatedly because the audience would love it every time. Before President Palmer took whatever action he had decided to take, they'd have one of his aides run up to him and say, "Mr. President, wait! We just got some new poll numbers about this issue, and everybody disagrees with what you're about to do!" Palmer would consider this gravely for about five seconds, then issue a stentorian statement: "I don't care if they impeach me—it's the right thing to do." With that, he would boldly stride off into the situation room while his aide's mouth hung agape.

Is this how we want a president to act in real life? Absolutely not. In real life, when presidents double down on their current agenda, even after the polls are screaming for them to reverse course, the American people become dispirited and depressed, and we blame their intransigence on corruption. But in our fiction, it's a different story.

Compare this to later seasons of *24* in which President Palmer's more pliable, poll-following brother inherited the Oval Office. He was perfectly nice, but the audience *hated* that guy. We all dream of saying no to our boss, and we want our fictional heroes to live that dream, even if the hero's boss happens to be the American people.

☑ **Is the hero already doing something active when the story begins?**

The audience must know that this hero is the sort of person who actively pursues things. Heroes are often *literally* active in the first scene: jogging, swimming, bicycling, playing tennis, etc. Assure your audience as quickly as possible that the character is going to be active, both literally and figuratively.

Sometimes the hero will begin by doing something cool or admirable, but it can also work well to have a character pursuing something active that makes him look bad. Amiable goof Lloyd Dobler in *Say Anything* wants to be a kickboxing champion until he unexpectedly gets a date with the girl of his dreams and changes all of his goals. Even though his kickboxing spiel sounds very loserish, it's actually far more appealing than if he simply said, "Eh, I don't know what I want to do yet." We like him because he wants something, even if we think what he wants is dumb.

You might assume the audience will more easily root for a smart hero who can see all the angles and who would therefore rather do nothing than act rashly, but they actually *hate* heroes like that. Nobody wants to watch somebody do nothing. The audience wants to be reassured right away that heroes aren't passive sticks-in-the-mud. Many weak heroes never take the initiative. Nothing is ever their idea, good or bad.

In a lot of stories, and especially in comedies, you have heroes who are plunged into over-the-top situations where everybody wants them to do something wild and stupid. Stupid isn't sympathetic, right? So you show how smart your hero is by having him tell everybody else that they should be sensible, right? Nope.

For instance, Ted Mosby is the titular hero of *How I Met Your Mother*, but he's by far the least likable character because he's a scold, and audiences get irritated with scolds. We like heroes who dive in enthusiastically and then make plans on the fly.

Defiance is *usually* good, but one problem with Ted is that he says no to his friends' schemes even though he has nothing more interesting to propose. He doesn't want to play laser tag with Barney, but he wants to sit around his apartment? Playing laser tag certainly is a dumb way for grown men to spend an evening, but it's better than nothing, so we're always going to be on Barney's side. The writers failed to give Ted his *own* alternate set of enthusiasms.

☑ Does the hero have (or claim) decision-making authority?

Every year there are a lot of TV pilots about rookie cops, medical students, and young crusaders just out of law school, but these shows almost always flop. Why? It's because these characters are very hard to write. In the end, a hero needs decision-making power, which is one thing rookies don't have.

This is somewhat counterintuitive. Everybody loves an underdog, right? And if the heroes are just learning the ropes, the audience is right there with them, learning everything by their side, so that's a great way into the story, isn't it? Yes, following low-power heroes through their day is a great way into a new show, but then you run into trouble.

A classic example is *The West Wing*. When Aaron Sorkin conceived and pitched the show, he imagined it would feature only the president's staff, but we would never see the president himself. So he wrote the pilot, in which the staff vigorously debates about how to advise the president on a difficult decision, and that worked well enough for most of the episode. But then Sorkin got to the end of the story. He suddenly realized it would be enormously *unsatisfying* to end the pilot (and each of the next hundred episodes) with his heroes sending their advice up the chain of command and then powerlessly waiting for the outcome. So, suddenly, in the very last scene, the president walks into the room after all and lays down the law. This show needed a decider.

Before long, it became a show that centered on the president as the main character—exactly the opposite of what Sorkin originally wanted.

And indeed every show tends to trend in this direction—away from the flunkies and toward the bosses. The *30 Rock* pilot is about put-upon comedy producers Liz and Pete, with NBC boss Jack as a mere antagonist. Before long, Jack is Liz's co-equal co-star, and Pete is rarely seen. Stories are about the consequences of decisions, so it's much easier to write stories about people who actually have decision-making power.

There's a reason why most kid heroes are orphans. They need the ability to commit fully to whatever they decide to do without anybody preventing them from rising too high or falling too far. They need to be on the hook for the consequences of their actions.

If you're writing about rookies, you need to ask yourself why the audience should trust them to be the heroes instead of their boss. Is there a value to their newness that makes them more interesting heroes? You need to make the audience trust them even while you're establishing that they don't trust themselves yet.

Maybe the smartest pilot of all is for *CSI*, in which the audience follows a rookie as she (and viewers) learn all about the squad. At the end of her first day, she takes her newfound knowledge and goes out to her first crime scene, where she is promptly shot and killed. She is a great point-of-view character, but now we need to put ourselves in the hands of the power players.

☑ Does the hero use pre-established special skills to solve problems?

Why are some stories memorable but others fade in your mind a day later? Why do some heroes win your heart while others make little impression?

David Mamet's thriller *The Spanish Prisoner* is the very definition of "fun but forgettable." Campbell Scott has invented a process that will revolutionize his industry. Steve Martin is a con man who tricks Scott into stealing his own formula and handing it over, and then frames him for murder. Once Scott realizes he's been tricked, he does a lot of poking around, investigating, running through alleyways, etc.

Scott is the classic Everyman hero. He shows no special skills in the first act, and he doesn't need them to get through the rest of the movie. In the end, he just needs to reach within himself and become a little smarter, a little savvier, and a little more courageous to get out of the trap. Basically, he muddles his way out. Because the movie has a good cast, a twisty plot, and Mamet's crackling dialogue, we may not notice right away how uncompelling Scott's character is, but the movie has no weight to it.

Compare this to Harrison Ford in *The Fugitive*. Like Scott, Ford is framed for murder. He's arrested and has to escape with Tommy Lee Jones hot on his heels. How does Ford get out of it? He doesn't transform into a generic hero. Instead, he finds a way to use his pre-established skills to solve the problem. Since he was a doctor, he spends the entire movie in and out of hospitals, using the resources of those settings at every turn.

Audiences prefer their heroes to get out of trouble in the second act using talents they already displayed in the first act. Even heroes who *seem* to be starting from scratch are actually *adapters*. They find ways to use skills from a completely different job to surmount their current problem.

What about that supposed zero-to-hero story *Back to the Future*? On the surface, it seems like a story about a neophyte who's hopelessly floundering when faced with the biggest challenge of his life. Marty has not trained to be a time traveler, nor has he studied up on the fifties. He seems totally unprepared for and baffled by this situation.

But, like most heroes, Marty *does* have a hidden reserve of special skills, and those are what he relies on to get out of trouble, time and time again. In this case, most of his skills, like skateboarding and playing rock guitar, shouldn't apply to 1955, because they don't exist yet, but he figures out how to use them anyway. He actually *invents* skateboards and rock and roll just so he can use them to save himself. *That's* how dependent heroes should be on their pre-established special skills.

Let's look at a complex adventure story with three competing heroes: *Pirates of the Caribbean*. Of the three heroes, only one is in his element: Johnny Depp is using his long-honed pirate skills. But the other two, though totally out of their element, still rely on pre-established special skills. Orlando Bloom is a blacksmith by trade, and he finds all sorts of ways to use those skills, from his experience with forging swords to his knowledge of how to pry open a cell door using a makeshift lever. Keira Knightley has never prepared for *any* trade, but she makes use of her copious *reading* about pirates and knows, for example, that they can't turn down a demand of parley. Depp is already an expert, but Bloom and Knightley adapt using their preexisting knowledge.

Relying on past knowledge gets you past the "wouldn't the bad guys have thought of that?" problem. There's a good reason our hero can outsmart the villains: He knows something they didn't know he knew (but *we* know he knew it, because we saw it in the opening scenes). Otherwise, in a movie like *The Spanish Prisoner*, where the hero doesn't reveal any special skills, you can really only credit his success to the villain's incompetence. It turns out that "every man" could have defeated this villain.

It is, however, crucial that a special skill be established in an organic way. When it's set up in a clunky way, and then it comes back later, the audience groans.

- One laughable example is the girl who gets past the dinosaurs using her parallel-bars gymnastic skills in *The Lost World: Jurassic Park*.
- Even dumber is the spy-thriller *Salt*, in which Angelina Jolie uses her husband's random spider-venom advice to create a special venom bullet.

So can you ever write a successful story about a hero with no skills whatsoever? Yes, you can, but only if things get truly harrowing for the poor unskilled hero. Horror stories sometimes have unskilled heroes, as do some stories that aren't horror but *feel* like horror for the protagonist: Poor Linda Hamilton never finds a use for any of her waitress skills when fighting an evil robot from the future in *The Terminator*, but that's okay because she's just trying to survive. Ultimately, she gets saved by someone else.

Audrey Hepburn's newly blind housewife in *Wait Until Dark* seems like a truly unskilled heroine. When she comes under siege by thugs who want to retrieve a heroin-filled doll that ended up in her apartment, she feels that she lacks even the basic tools of the average person. Not only does she not have any assets, but she has a huge liability. But, eventually, she decides to smash all the light bulbs and use her superior ability to navigate without light to her advantage. She turns her liability into her only asset.

You can't become a hero by doing what anyone would do. You have to do that thing that *you* do.

I could go on much longer about character, but, ultimately, even if you have a wonderfully compelling hero, you still don't have a story. These hypothetically perfect characters have to get up, get going, and test themselves.

SHAPING A RESONANT STRUCTURE

WHAT IS STRUCTURE?

Structure is the hidden grunt work of your story. It's your job to carefully and skillfully construct the emotional roller coaster your hero and audience will ride together, without your audience ever noticing what you're doing.

Your audience doesn't want to be aware of an "inciting incident," "act breaks," or a "shift to proactivity" but will demand that the progress of your story rings true, is increasingly satisfying, and resonates with their understanding of human nature at every turn.

To achieve this, you have to shape your structure subtly and precisely. You need to understand which steps and missteps naturally occur while solving a large problem, and what effect each step will have on your audience. You need to know how to carefully skip or rearrange certain steps to meet the needs of your story. One of the biggest advantages of mastering structure is that it gives you the ability to skillfully play with it!

MISCONCEPTIONS ABOUT STRUCTURE

MISCONCEPTION: Whether they like it or not, story structure is a straightjacket all writers must wear.

AU CONTRAIRE: Most of the steps associated with the most common story structure can be identified in most great stories, but few stories hit every step, and there are many great stories with totally unique structures. The story structure we'll be defining applies primarily to stories about *solving a large problem*.

What sort of writers should study story structure? I think it's useful for all writers, but some will use it more often than others. Without a doubt, beat-by-beat structures like the one we'll be exploring are most often associated with screenwriting. Movies tend to be far more homogenous in their structure than any other type of writing because:

- All movies are expected to be about the same length. (Nobody really knows why moviegoers demand a strict conformity in length, whereas novel readers and even theatergoers will happily accept different lengths.)
- Movies cost a lot more money to make, so they need to make more money, which means they need to have a much more universal appeal.
- As a result, almost every movie is about solving a large problem, because it's the foundation that creates the greatest audience identification. In this limited amount of time, it's much easier for audiences to invest in one hero and one problem.

But this structure isn't just for movies. In recent years, other types of media—including novels, plays, and comics—have grown increasingly similar to movies, meaning they are now more focused on solving a large problem.

Nevertheless, there are still a lot of great stories in every media that *aren't* about solving a large problem and therefore won't conform to classical story structure. Let's acknowledge some of these up front.

- A long novel like *David Copperfield* is not just about one of its hero's problems but every aspect of his life. It begins with the first line, "I am born," and then progresses through several problems, treating many of them with equal weight.
- Likewise, a slice-of-life play such as *Our Town* is not focused on any one problem in the town of Grover's Corners. It's a cross section of the town as a whole.
- Even in the supposedly homogenous world of American movies, there are great classics such as *Nashville, Slacker,* and *Pulp Fic-*

tion that are not about solving one problem. As a result, each of these movies has its own revolutionary (and enthralling) structure.

- For that matter, there are even some American movies that *are* about solving a large problem but nevertheless successfully employ extremely unusual structures, such as *Memento* or *Eternal Sunshine of the Spotless Mind*. It should be noted, however, that these are very peculiar cases, because in both movies the hero is experiencing memory problems, and the structure has been chopped up to reflect the change in perception. Every rule can be broken if you *know* you're breaking it and have a strong reason to do so.

Beware of any attempt to impose the same order on *everything* and deny *any* exceptions. It's counterproductive to search for a structure that applies to absolutely every story, because no such structure exists, and we can all be thankful for that.

If you base your story on something besides solving a large problem, you'll be required to chart an atypical structure. And, of course, even if you are writing about solving a large problem, you can attempt something wild. (But don't forget that even wild things tend to settle down. Richard Linklater had a wonderfully audacious debut with *Slacker*, but he soon proved he could also produce excellent mainstream fare such as *School of Rock*.)

Despite many wonderful exceptions, most stories *are* about solving a large problem and don't use strikingly disjointed points of view. So this chapter is going to focus on those stories and attempt to discover why the best ones tend to share a strikingly similar underlying structure, whether or not the writers have ever read any advice books.

So, yes, there is such a thing as a common story structure, and it does apply to most stories. But now that I have defended the orthodoxy in general, I'd like to second-guess most of its particulars. I find the version of this structure that's become gospel has in fact misidentified the steps found in the most common type of stories. Let's look at some of the major misconceptions that have built up over the years.

MISCONCEPTION: Heroes should be happy and content with their lives before an "inciting incident," and then they should spend the rest of the story attempting to restore the status quo.

AU CONTRAIRE: If your story is true to human nature, then your hero will be *discontent* when your story begins, and then, after that discontentment is made acute by a social humiliation, your hero will pursue an intimidating opportunity to solve that problem.

One problem I have with most structure guides is how *vague* they are. They're presented as magic one-size-fits-all prescriptions for success rather than lists of common trends in successful stories, so they feel the need to phrase everything as generically as possible. As a result, *everything* the guide says is true for *every* story. There's just one problem: A rule that's true for every story provides no actual guidance.

As a result, we get generic terms like "inciting incident" that are essentially meaningless. The problem is, it's impossible to create a story without something that could be called an inciting incident. The purpose of rules should be to *separate* strong choices from weak ones, so you can explain why some stories work and others don't (or at least why some stories have broader appeal than others).

A classic example often used to demonstrate an inciting incident is *Jaws*. Everybody in the town is happy, and then a shark attacks. In the end, they kill the shark so they can all be happy again. But in most stories, things aren't that tidy.

Here are some problems with the idea of an inciting incident:

- **"RETURN TO NORMALITY" IS A WEAK MOTIVATION.** If you define the inciting incident entirely negatively ("something bad happens"), then the hero rarely has enough motivation to get through the story. Heroes should be trying to *improve* their lives, not just return to zero.

- **IT DE-EMPHASIZES THE IMPORTANCE OF CHANGE.** Stories will not be very interesting if they are merely about a return to the status quo. Audiences prefer stories about *transformation*.

- **IT ISN'T PERSONAL ENOUGH.** If the inciting incident is defined externally, then the heroes are merely *reacting* to outside events instead of *choosing to act* based on their volatile personal psychology.
- **IT IMPLIES THAT THE CHALLENGE ARRIVES TIED UP IN ONE BIG PACKAGE INSTEAD OF DEVELOPING INCREMENTALLY.** One reason many stories bog down in the middle is that the heroes jump in with both eyes open way too early. Something bad happens and the heroes understand the nature of the problem right away, but then they wait until the end to defeat it. So what's the purpose of the middle?

Instead of experiencing one big inciting incident, well-written stories tend to show a much more volatile and, yes, *ironic* relationship between heroes and the situations they encounter.

In most stories, the inciting incident actually consists of three distinct events:

1. A longstanding social problem
2. An intimidating opportunity
3. An unforeseen conflict that arises from pursuing that opportunity

For example, the setup for most romances is as follows:

1. **LONGSTANDING SOCIAL PROBLEM:** The hero's loneliness (or dissatisfaction with a current relationship) intensifies.
2. **INTIMIDATING OPPORTUNITY:** A new love interest appears who is unavailable or out of the hero's league.
3. **UNFORESEEN CONFLICT:** Someone is opposed to the match (sometimes another lover, parent, or the actual love interest, who isn't interested).

Here's the setup for most crime thrillers:

1. **LONGSTANDING SOCIAL PROBLEM:** The hero becomes more desperate for money.
2. **INTIMIDATING OPPORTUNITY:** The hero gets roped into committing a crime.
3. **UNFORESEEN CONFLICT:** The cops close in and/or the hero finds out it's a setup.

This three-fold inciting incident is stronger for these reasons:

- **HEROES HAVE MUCH STRONGER MOTIVATION.** The journey is one they've needed to take for a long time, and their goal is to change their lives for the better, not just return to zero.
- **IT'S ABOUT CHANGE.** The hero is trying to break out of a rut, not just return to the status quo.
- **HEROES ARE MORE ACTIVE.** He is proactively choosing to seize an opportunity that's materialized rather than to merely react to a problem (which is something anyone would do).
- **THE STORY PLAYS OUT MORE GRADUALLY AS THE HERO REALIZES THE UNFORESEEN TRUE NATURE OF THE CONFLICT.** This only works if the hero seizes what seems like a positive (albeit intimidating) opportunity in the beginning, *without realizing* how much conflict it will cause.

Now that we've established these three steps, let's go back to *Jaws*, the book/movie that supposedly exemplifies the inciting incident paradigm. Is it really as simple as it seems? The attack that begins the story certainly could be described as something bad happening, and for most of the islanders, it is indeed an unwelcome intrusion into their complacent status quo—*but not for our hero*. Our hero, Chief Brody, is unhappy with the status quo. He feels unwelcome and disrespected in his new job. He needs an opportunity to establish his authority. The shark attack is atrocious, but it's just the opportunity he needs. That's why he's the hero.

In the end, in order for Brody to attain his fondest wish (reestablishing the authority and self-respect he lost when he left the city), he must confront his greatest fear (going out on the ocean). Both the wish and fear predate the arrival of the shark. The story is driven by his volatile psychology, not merely by the arrival of an external event.

MISCONCEPTION: Audiences love it when a plan comes together.

AU CONTRAIRE: Audiences get bored if the hero doesn't have to improvise.

As a general rule, if someone hands your heroes a map and plan at the beginning of the story, he should realize at some point that the map is wrong and the plan is inadequate. From that point on, he must improvise.

On the old *Mission: Impossible* TV show, a team of brilliant spies would pull off elaborate con jobs for Uncle Sam. Every week, just before the first commercial, the entire plan would seem to fall apart before it ever got off the ground. But when we came back after the commercial, it would turn out that (surprise!) getting caught was all part of the plan: The group member that got caught *wanted* to get put into the jail cell to complete the con.

The problem was that the writers sometimes got lazy and tried to use the same trick for all three commercial breaks: Nothing ever *really* goes wrong, and every plot turn from start to finish turns out to be part of the heroes' original master plan. The network execs at CBS got fed up with this and wisely dictated a new rule for the show: At the midpoint, every week, the original plan had to *genuinely* fall apart, and the team had to improvise from that point onward. The show became a lot more fun to watch.

The result is what I call the *Mission: Impossible* rule: By halfway through, your heroes should always be making it up on the fly.

> **MISCONCEPTION:** The audience wants to see your great structure.
>
> **AU CONTRAIRE:** Your audience will subconsciously expect you to hit the beats of the most common structure, but they don't want to see you do it.

Your audience subconsciously craves structure, but on a conscious level they hate any story that seems formulaic. This is why your structure must always remain completely invisible to your audience.

A hilarious example of what *not* to do is provided by the monster movie *Van Helsing*. One of the movie's producers presumably read a book that said every hero has to engage in self-realization in the third quarter. So after a full hour of back-to-back action scenes, Hugh

Jackman and Kate Beckinsale suddenly decide to take a thoughtful walk around the grounds of a castle, where they have this delightful nineteenth-century conversation:

> **Kate:** Why do you do it, this job of yours? What do you hope to get out of it?
>
> **Hugh:** I don't know ... Maybe some self-realization.

Sorry, guys, you're not supposed to tell us that the hero wants self-realization; you're supposed to show it. We're not supposed to *hear* it; we're supposed to *feel* it.

A wisely deleted scene from the movie of *Silence of the Lambs* illustrates this point: After Hannibal Lecter escapes, the angry director of the FBI calls Clarice and her boss, Crawford, into his office, where he summarily fires Crawford and kicks Clarice out of the academy. As they leave, Clarice says to Crawford that she's now sure the killer must be in Ohio, and she's going to go there and find him, save the day, and get them their jobs back. (A similar story beat happened in the book, but in a less overheated way.)

These scenes were still in the movie for the early test screenings, but veteran writer William Goldman (*Butch Cassidy and the Sundance Kid, The Princess Bride, Misery*) attended one of those screenings and implored Jonathan Demme to cut them. Demme realized this was good advice. Once the scenes were gone, nobody missed them.

Yes, it was vitally important to shift into proactivity and create a finale in which Clarice is the only one who can solve the problem, but she shouldn't have to announce it. The audience should *feel* this shift, not see it. In the final movie, she's never kicked out of the academy and Crawford is never fired. That escalation is simply unnecessary in the slimmed-down, propulsive narrative.

If you've done your job right, the audience will get frustrated and think to themselves, "Dammit, the Feds are totally screwing this up! It's all up to Clarice now!" But if you actually force Clarice to say *out loud*, "My bosses are screwing this up! It's all up to me!" then your audience will get annoyed and feel manipulated.

> **MISCONCEPTION:** The important turning points in a story oc-
> cur at the first-quarter and third-quarter marks, resulting in a
> short first act, a long second act, and a short third act.
>
> **AU CONTRAIRE:** It's fine to use this three-act terminology, but
> don't be misled into thinking those two turning points are the
> most important ones in your story.

It used to be that only theatrical plays had "acts" (five acts were the most common in Shakespeare's time, and two acts are the most common today), but then the late Syd Field changed everything. His 1979 screenwriting guide was so influential it became almost universal for producers, screenwriters, and even critics to think of all movies as having three acts, with dividing points at the thirty- and ninety-minute marks. This terminology has even begun to seep into other media as well, as even novelists talk about their "third-act problems."

It's far too late to turn back this tide, and even I use this terminology at certain places in this book, but the omnipresence of this idea has had a somewhat baleful influence on the art of writing. The problem is that this way of thinking creates a vast, undifferentiated second act that turns into a long, hard slog. If the first-act break happens when the hero commits, and the second-act break happens when the hero finally turns proactive, it turns the second act into an interminable series of minor obstacles as the hero marks time before going into action.

There are a lot of steps that get lost in this terminology, but the most important is the big crash that usually happens at the midpoint. Not only does this change everything in terms of the external situation, but it slams the hero into a radically new outlook. The first half of a story can often be summarized as "the easy way," and the second half as "the hard way."

This ties back to the need for unexpected antagonism. The three-act structure implies that the hero spends the entire story headed toward the big finale, which is always in sight, but this isn't true to human nature. When we start to solve a large problem, we don't perceive the size of the problem—and that's good, because if we did, we would never begin. In most stories, heroes shouldn't have any idea how long or how much work it will take to solve this problem. They should fully intend to wrap everything up in almost every scene and be overconfident about imminent success until the big crash wrecks those delusions.

Only at this point do the heroes realize this *external* problem can only be tackled by confronting an *internal* flaw, which means this will be a much more harrowing process than they could have predicted.

> **MISCONCEPTION:** If you love this structure formula, you should memorize it.
>
> **AU CONTRAIRE:** Once you've had some time to think about it, you should look at your own life and see if this jibes with your experience of problem solving.

Structure is the "inside baseball" of the writing world. If you think about it too much, you can drive yourself and those around you crazy. Your best bet is to read guides like this, puzzle over them, wrestle with them for a while, and then reject them utterly and try to forget all about them. Only then will you discover you've internalized these ideas, and you're now creating stories that naturally hang together.

Look around you and see if you don't see this structure replicated in your life, and then look at your stories and figure out if maybe your characters might be more believable and compelling if they found themselves following these same steps.

QUESTIONS TO ASK ABOUT STRUCTURE

In this section, we'll break structure into these four parts:

- **FIRST QUARTER:** In this section, we'll quickly do away with the overly vague concept of the "inciting incident" and replace it with three specific parts: the long-standing personal problem, the intimidating opportunity, and the unexpected conflict. Together these form what I call "the challenge."
- **SECOND QUARTER:** I refer to this section as "the easy way," in which the hero tries to tackle the challenge without any self-examination, sure of an early success, until everything wrecks in a big crash.

- **THIRD QUARTER:** It's only after the big crash that our hero finally tries "the hard way" and engages in self-examination—until a further setback plunges our hero into a spiritual crisis.
- **FOURTH QUARTER:** The hero comes out of the spiritual crisis with a corrected philosophy and proactively pursues a corrected goal, which culminates in "the climax."

As you review the questions, you'll notice I'm limiting myself to movies for this section. Movies are much more structure-bound than any other type of storytelling, so they make the best examples, but this structure also underlies many great novels, plays, TV episodes, and comics, though they're less likely to hit every step or do so in the same order.

First Quarter: The Challenge

☑ *When the story begins, is the hero becoming increasingly irritated about her longstanding social problem (while still in denial about an internal flaw)?*

In real life, we tend to let a mess of troubles mount before we finally choose to act. In fact, we only take on the massive work of solving a large problem once we have been discontent for some time. So rather than start with a happy status quo that gets ruined by the inciting incident, most stories begin the opposite way: The hero starts out with a long-standing social problem, and the inciting incident (even if it's something horrible) presents itself as an *opportunity* to solve that problem, as we'll see in the next two steps.

The long-standing social problem is usually either something the hero is already aware of when the story begins or something that suddenly becomes acute because of a social humiliation in the first scene. Because this is something the hero acknowledges early on, it must be stated in the way the hero would state it. This is because most of us define our problems externally, not internally, until we're forced to become self-critical.

In the outline version of your story, the problem should usually be phrased nonjudgmentally, as the hero would phrase it herself: The hero is "broke" or "disrespected," or "overworked," etc. These are the sorts of personal problems that people will admit to even if they haven't engaged in serious self-reflection.

- In *Kramer vs. Kramer*, it's tempting to say Dustin Hoffman's problem is that his wife has abandoned him and their son, but that's not a *long-standing* problem that predates the story, so it doesn't fit into this category. Alternately, one might be tempted to say his problem is that he's not a good father, but that's not something he's aware of yet (it's his flaw, not his problem). If we limit ourselves to *long-standing* issues he's *already* aware of, we see his real problem: He's distracted. His work takes him away from his family, and he can't decide which is more important. As horrible as it is, the disappearance of his wife will give him just the opportunity he needs to address this problem.
- In *Swingers*, Jon Favreau's problem is that his ex-girlfriend won't call him back. Even though the audience can see right away that he should just move on, we can also see that, for the time being, *he's* defining his problem in an entirely external way, putting all of the onus on his ex. In this case, we, like his friends, have a lot of *empathy* for his pain but little *sympathy* for his suffering, because we see he could suffer less simply by changing his attitude.

The great flaw, on the other hand, is something internal that most heroes remain stubbornly unaware of for most of the story, and it should always be phrased negatively: The hero is "sanctimonious" or "disloyal," etc. In other words, it should be a true flaw.

When someone asks us about our flaws, we prefer to say, "I'm too nice" or "too much of a perfectionist," etc., because those aren't true flaws and we don't really want to change. A hero must have a true flaw that requires change.

When I was evaluating the classic screwball comedy *Easy Living*, I was tempted to say that the heroine's flaw was that she was "too nice," but I realized I had to look deeper to identify an actual flaw. Sure enough, I found one: She may think of herself as "too nice," but her real flaw is that she's too naïve and deferential. When you put it that way, it's obvious that it's bad. Everybody wants to be nice, but nobody wants to be naïve and deferential.

The flaw must be something that needs to change for the hero to become a better person. Otherwise, you'll go too easy on your characters.

☑ Does this problem become undeniable due to a social humiliation at the beginning of the story?

In real life, we may be aware we have a problem and feel troubled about it, but we are unlikely to confront it until that problem has been exposed to the world in a humiliating way. The hero may have been only dimly aware of the problem beforehand, but the social humiliation makes the problem *acute*. Now that it has been made visible and exposed to the world, it can no longer be ignored.

Humiliation scenes are tricky. They should illuminate a real personal problem, but to create more sympathy, the size of the humiliation should *exceed* the size of the problem. The best humiliation scenes are ones that are *somewhat* unjust but not entirely. Your heroes should deserve a comeuppance but get a much bigger humiliation than they deserve.

The first *Iron Man* movie shows how to do it right. We have a cocky and callous arms dealer who clearly deserves to be taken down a peg, but then he becomes a prisoner of sadistic Afghan warlords. Even though it's something he's brought upon himself, it's even worse than he deserves, so we have no trouble sympathizing with his plight. Compare this to the lame sequel *Iron Man 2*, where a U.S. senator is upset that our cocky millionaire has his own personal weapon of mass destruction. We're supposed to boo the senator, but why would we? The senator may be a jerk, but he's totally correct. This is the tricky line you have to walk: The humiliation must be somewhat deserved but disproportionate.

- In *The Awful Truth*, the couple have been cheating on each other for some time, but it's only when both parties are exposed while they have a house full of guests that they decide it's time to divorce.
- In *The Apartment*, Jack Lemmon's private humiliation spills out onto the street, where he gets hassled by the cops for spending the night in the park.
- In *Witness*, Harrison Ford hides a young Amish murder witness and his beautiful mother (Kelly McGillis) at his sister's apartment. The next day, after McGillis gets annoyed at Ford's boorishness, she cheerfully conveys to him what his sister *really* thinks of him, laying out a litany of his personal flaws. Coming from a witness, this embarrasses him both personally and professionally.
- In *Donnie Brasco*, both the feds and the Mafia brusquely tell Donnie his mustache violates their regulations, drawing the first of many ironic parallels between the two institutions. After he dutifully shaves it off, his wife says the mustache was the only thing she *liked* about his new identity. Clearly, he's being pulled in every possible direction.

☑ Does the hero discover an intimidating opportunity to fix the problem?

Simply restoring the status quo is never a strong motivation. In real life, as a general rule, our crises are not just temporary accidents that must be undone but crucial opportunities to fix long-standing problems. It may be a myth that the Chinese use the same character for crisis and opportunity, but that myth persists because it rings true.

To build sympathy, the opportunity should be obviously intimidating. This shouldn't be a no-brainer decision, but to avoid losing empathy, the full size of the potential conflict should not be immediately apparent, as we'll see in the next three steps.

- Many intimidating opportunities, such as the shark in *Jaws* and the runaway train in *Unstoppable*, are disasters for everyone ex-

cept the heroes, each of whom needs a chance to prove his continued usefulness. A classic *positive* intimidating opportunity can be found in *Superbad*: While the characters get to go to a real party and become heroes to their crushes by providing the beer, it's illegal and they've never tried it before. It's clearly intimidating, but they don't yet know *how* bad it'll be because they don't imagine they'll get mugged.

- Some intimidating opportunities exist only in the hero's mixed-up mind. In both positive and tragic ways, Kevin Spacey's volatile chemistry gets unexpectedly set off by the sight of his daughter's cheerleader friend in *American Beauty*.
- Others are only intimidating because of the hero's flaw, as with Andy's terror in *The 40-Year-Old Virgin* when his co-workers offer to help him get laid.

☑ Does the hero hesitate until the stakes are raised?

This is what distinguishes a big life-changing problem from a small no-brainer problem. Hesitation proves the opportunity is intimidating, indicating it carries both high risk and high reward.

While it's tempting to skip hesitation to speed up the first quarter and make the hero seem more forceful, it's equally important to cheer *and* fear for a hero. A healthy wariness reminds us to worry about the dangers and trust that the hero is not foolhardy.

Hesitation scenes often establish the role of the hero's friends, who either counsel caution or recklessness. The good friends in *Salvador* and *Juno* are dubious, but the more reckless friends in *Risky Business* and *Mean Girls* say to go for it. Or, as they say in the dubbed-for-TV version of *Risky Business*: "Sometimes you gotta say, 'What the hey!'"

These scenes can also ease the audience into suspension of disbelief by giving the hero a moment to stop and say, "Hey, this is crazy! This can't be happening, can it?" as seen in movies such as *Back to the Future* and *The Terminator*.

☑ **Does the hero commit to pursuing the opportunity by the end of the first quarter?**

As Woody Allen says, "Eighty percent of success is showing up."

It's easy to overemphasize the commitment scene. It's okay for heroes to be knee-deep before they realize they're committed. Bruce Willis spends the entire first half of *Die Hard* just trying to call the cops, not realizing that as soon as he stole those detonators, he had pretty much committed himself to taking down the bad guys alone.

Sometimes it's possible to skip over the actual commitment scene, jump-cutting right from hesitation to a conflict that arises after committing. In *Some Like It Hot*, the guys are still having a heated debate about whether they should dress up as women when we suddenly cut to the two of them wobbling down the train platform in heels.

Second Quarter: The Easy Way

☑ **Does the hero's pursuit of the opportunity quickly lead to an unforeseen conflict with another person?**

As any artist considering a follow-up project will tell you, it's much easier to commit to a big undertaking if you *don't* know what you're getting into. Just because you know an opportunity is intimidating doesn't mean you comprehend how much trouble pursuing that opportunity will cause.

It's best if your heroes are not fully aware of the scope of the problem before they commit. Audiences prefer heroes with a limited perspective, who quickly get in over their head. Given how bad things are going to get, it's hard to sympathize with anyone who would *intentionally* put himself at risk.

This is a dangerous moment where the story can lose its momentum. You've finally arranged all the pieces on the playing board, so it's tempting to take it easy for a few pages, but you need to wallop the hero right away to keep the reader from putting down your manuscript.

- The couple in *The Awful Truth* has just one problem with their divorce: Who gets the dog?

- The hero of *Speed* has accepted the danger of leaping on the bomb-rigged bus, but he doesn't know that a passenger will freak out and accidentally shoot the driver, instantly making the entire task a lot tougher.
- In *Goldfinger, The French Connection,* and *Silence of the Lambs,* the hero realizes the villain is a lot smarter than anybody thought.
- Almost always, the unexpected conflict should come from an actual person, as opposed to an animal, the weather, a physical obstruction, or a faceless bureaucracy. Sheriff Brody in *Jaws* isn't just opposed by the shark or "the townspeople." He's specifically opposed by the *mayor,* who refuses to protect his own town.

☑ Does the hero try the easy way throughout the second quarter?

Even when we've accepted that we have to solve a large problem, and even after we've run into unexpected conflict, we are absolutely hardwired to try the easy way first and stick to it until it ends in disaster. The easy way can take many different forms, but what they all have in common is an insistence on treating the problem as an external obstacle rather than an internal dilemma.

Audiences quickly get bored with a story in which the hero has five tasks to complete and then dutifully knocks them out one by one until arriving at the end of the story. The hero should be trying and expecting to solve the entire problem in almost every scene. The second and third quarters will usually consist of two different attempts to solve the same problem, not two halves of one attempt.

- Some heroes spend this section juggling different lies, assuming that the targets of their lies will never compare notes, such as in *Some Like It Hot, Tootsie,* and *How to Train Your Dragon.*
- Some heroes spend this time escaping from the danger, without realizing that they'll eventually have to face it head-on, such as in *Witness* and *Die Hard.*
- Some use this time to unsuccessfully seek allies, such as in *High Noon.*

- Others devote this time to elaborate schemes, such as in *Double Indemnity, The Producers*, and *Body Heat*.

☑ Does the hero have some fun and get excited about the possibility of success?

We are more likely to tackle a huge challenge if we think we might have *some* fun doing it. Of course, we only have fun when we're doing it the easy way, and we're not going to make real progress until we stop having fun and get down to real work.

In this area, there's a huge difference between horror and almost every other genre. Some call this step "fun and games," and that's true for every genre *except* horror, where our heroes have no fun at all in this section. Nevertheless, the audience has fun, because they experience the creeping dread that sends a tingle up their spines. In most genres, they totally identify with the hero's ups and downs, but in horror, they identify only partially with the heroes, because they also want to see the heroes punished for their sins. As a result, they are able to enjoy both the characters' triumphs and suffering.

As Blake Snyder points out in *Save the Cat*, this section tends to provide the big moments that make it onto the book cover or the movie poster. It's where the hero does the thing the audience has come to see him do, and has fun doing it, right before the disaster hits and things get serious.

- Picture the posters: The parents and their baby sunbathe together in *Raising Arizona*; the lovers have steamy sex in *Body Heat*.
- Think of the trailer: The Millennium Falcon jumps into light speed in *Star Wars*; the therapist and the prince practice rapid nonsense sounds in *The King's Speech*.
- It's not *just* in horror movies, such as *The Shining* and *Alien*, that we're having more fun than the heroes are; it's also true of some especially tense thrillers. The big trailer moment in *The Fugitive* happens when he leaps into the waterfall to save his life. Presumably, that's a lot more fun to watch than it is to do.

☑ **Does the easy way lead to a big crash around the midpoint, resulting in the loss of a safe space and/or sheltering relationship?**

In real life, we will stick with the easy way, stay in our safe space, cling to sheltering relationships, and refuse to examine our motives for as long as possible. It takes a huge, hubris-fueled failure, in which we lose that safe space, to force us to try the hard way and consider the possibility that we're our own worst enemies.

Don't go easy on your hero. Bigger is usually better. The further they fall, the more inspiring their rise back up will be. And beware of the false crash. Remember the *Mission: Impossible* rule: At the second-act break (the midpoint) the team's plan has to *genuinely* fall apart, and the team has to improvise. At this point, your hero should throw away the map.

- Often the loss of safe space is literal: Rick's bar is trashed by the Nazis in *Casablanca*, Bruce's house is burned down in *Batman Begins*, and Tony's house is blown up in *Iron Man 3*.
- Sometimes it's figurative: Sheriff Brody gets slapped in *Jaws*, and Michael gets slapped in *Tootsie*.
- Some stories prefer to pile on multiple big crashes. *Bridesmaids* has several huge disasters in a row as the heroine loses her job, her apartment, her potential boyfriend, her lover, her car, her role in the wedding, and her best friend in rapid succession.
- Likewise, *Raiders of the Lost Ark* has two crashes. First, Marion seems to die in the bazaar chase, and then, a few scenes later, Indy gets some good news and some bad news: Marion's still alive, but he's lost the ark and been sealed into a tomb of snakes with her.

A few things to keep in mind: In tragedies like *American Beauty*, we sometimes get the opposite: the midpoint peak, followed by the point when the hero starts heading for a fall. Even nontragedies like *How to Train Your Dragon* can sometimes do something similar. Hiccup gets everything he's ever wanted at the midpoint, and it doesn't fall apart until the third quarter, when his lies finally come crashing down.

Third Quarter: The Hard Way

☑ *Does the hero try the hard way from this point on?*

As with cleaning your house, things have to get worse before they can get better. Trying the hard way should not be instantly rewarding and shouldn't yet lead to any better results than the easy way. The advantage of trying the hard way is that it forces us to lose our illusions and leads us to a spiritual crisis, and that crisis becomes the secret of our success.

It can be tempting to regard the entire third quarter as a string of betrayals, reversals, and assaults, but it's important to remember that this is all happening now for a good reason: The hero is finally tackling the problem head on.

- After pretending to be poor in the first half of *Sullivan's Travels*, our hero really loses everything.
- Max in *Rushmore* learns to struggle through public school.
- The prince in *The King's Speech* finally agrees to talk about the troubled childhood that caused his stutter.
- The heroes of *Fatal Attraction* and *Silence of the Lambs* both admit they lied their way through the first half of the story and try to reestablish trust.
- The heroes of *Some Like It Hot*, *Tootsie*, and *The Talented Mr. Ripley*, on the other hand, continue to lie throughout the third quarter but have to deal with the steadily increasing consequences of those lies.

☑ *Does the hero find out who his real friends and enemies are?*

Only in a crisis do we discover whom we can really count on and who has been sabotaging our efforts all along.

Warning: The easiest way to drop a huge reversal on your hero is to reveal that his "success" is actually part of the villain's plan, as seen in movies like *Total Recall* or *Flightplan*, but this is never a good idea. It inevitably creates huge plot holes and makes the hero seem way too stupid and predictable. Instead, reversals should come about because of the hero's blind spots and hubris.

- A lot of heroes get betrayed at this point. Richard realizes that his best friend ordered his death in *The Fugitive*. Tony gets his heart ripped out by Stane in *Iron Man*, only to realize what Pepper really means to him.
- Sometimes it can be positive: Bart befriends Mongo and Lili Von Schtupp in *Blazing Saddles*. Max finally realizes that Helen is a natural ally in *Rushmore*.

☑ Do the stakes, pace, and motivation all escalate at this point?

At a certain point, when dealing with a large problem, things slip out of our control and we are overtaken by events. This feels horrible, but it's ultimately necessary for us to have the motivation and urgency we need to solve the problem.

Again, it's tempting to *over*motivate the hero in this section. Beware of the tendency to prop up a flagging story by tacking on additional motivation, such as revealing that the villain *also* killed the hero's family years ago. If you want to strengthen your hero's motivation, then simplify it instead of multiplying it.

- This is frequently where the "double-chase" begins: The hero is both hunter and hunted now. The heroes of *Some Like It Hot* and *Blue Velvet* discover that the bad guys now know who and where they are, and they're coming for them.
- This is where the ticking clock sometimes comes in, as in both *Alien* and *Aliens*.
- Or where a family member is threatened: The baby is kidnapped in *Raising Arizona*, and Mary Jane is kidnapped in *Spider-Man*.
- This is sometimes where events happen that force a decision, such as David's marriage proposal in *An Education*.

☑ *Does the hero learn from mistakes in a painful way?*

It would be nice if we all had enough perspective to spot our mistakes from far away and deal with them coolly, but in reality, we almost never admit our big mistakes until bad consequences have resulted.

This is frequently where mentors and love interests get killed, where illusions get stripped away, and where lies are exposed.

- Mentors are killed off in *Star Wars* and *The Untouchables*.
- Partners get killed off in *Speed* and thousands of other cop movies.
- In most comedies, the hero's lies are exposed at this point, at the worst possible moment.

☑ *Does a further setback lead to a spiritual crisis?*

The easy way tends to end in a disaster and loss of safe space, but trying again the hard way is no guarantee of success. In fact, it often leads to another failure. The difference, this time, is that our eyes are wide open, and suddenly we can see *why* we failed. Now we need to come face-to-face with the factor within ourselves that's causing these failures.

Most heroes discover they need to change their personalities at this point, but others realize they need to be true to themselves and *stop* trying to change. This is usually the point at which the hero replaces a false goal with a true goal, and a false philosophy with a corrected philosophy.

- The couple realizes divorce just isn't fun anymore in *The Awful Truth*.
- The parents decide they'll probably split up in *Raising Arizona*.
- After admitting he's not Italian, Dave in *Breaking Away* visits his father's quarry and admits he's not really a stonecutter, either.
- Andy in *The 40-Year-Old Virgin* freaks out about selling off his action figures.
- The heroes of *Blue Velvet* and *Donnie Brasco* realize how far they've fallen when they each hit a woman.
- The spiritual crisis is quite literal in *Witness* when the cop and his Amish crush finally kiss.

Fourth Quarter: The Climax

☑ *Does the hero adopt a corrected philosophy at this point?*

And then, one day, the light of truth begins to dawn. The magic words pop into the hero's head and guide her out of the darkness. It can be advice she desperately needs to hear, or simply her own pithy summary of every hard lesson she's learned.

- Rick in *Casablanca* realizes, "The problems of three little people don't amount to a hill of beans in this crazy world."
- The heroine of *The Babadook* says to her husband's ghost, "You're trespassing in my house."
- Ripley in *Alien* stops taking the company's side and says to her remaining crew members, "We'll blow it the fuck out into space. We have to stick together."
- As with the false statement of philosophy, sometimes the corrected philosophy is stated by someone else and accepted by the hero: "Be a mensch," in *The Apartment*, and "Use the force," in *Star Wars*.

☑ *After the crisis, does the hero finally commit to pursuing a corrected goal, which still seems far away?*

Any recovering addict will tell you that once you stop sabotaging yourself, you still have a long, long way to go to get your life back on track. All you've done by committing to a corrected goal is get back to zero with a better plan.

Remember: Everybody hates a lucky man. The solution shouldn't land in the hero's lap, and it shouldn't be within easy grasp. Even at this late point in the story, once the hero has a corrected philosophy, there should still be a long way to go and a short time to get there.

- The heroine of *An Education* realizes that she must now try to get into Oxford without a high school degree.
- Jason Bourne decides he must take the fight back to the CIA all alone.

- Phil in *Groundhog Day* realizes that he must help as many towns-people as possible, honing his schedule over hundreds of repeated days.
- Danny realizes that he must somehow stop his father himself in *The Shining*.

☑ **By the time the final quarter of the story begins (if not long before), has your hero switched to being proactive instead of reactive?**

Eventually you realize you can't solve your problems without getting in the driver's seat.

While this is the *latest* possible moment for the hero to turn proactive, I should emphasize that it's also fine for the hero to become proactive, starting way back when the hero commits or at any point in between.

- Mike in *Swingers* finally goes out and meets a new girl.
- Cady in *Mean Girls* begins to make amends and joins the mathletes.
- Clarice in *Silence of the Lambs* decides that the answer must be back in Ohio.
- Tired of sneaking around, Steve McQueen steals a motorcycle and peels out in *The Great Escape*.

This is usually considered the one unbreakable rule of fiction, but there are rare exceptions: The hero of *Witness* never becomes proactive, and the hero of *Raiders of the Lost Ark* suddenly becomes totally passive. (He decides to follow that old bumper sticker's advice: "Let Go and Let God.") The first cut of *The Terminator* included a proactive turn, but it was cut out in the editing room to speed up the movie. (Originally, they were on their way to blow up Skynet's future manufacturing plant when the robot caught up with them, but that decision was cut out of the final version, so that storyline became the basis for *Terminator 2*.) Because the movie is so exciting, the audience doesn't care that the heroes never become proactive.

In very rare cases, it can be heroic *not* to go on the offensive: The dad in *Kramer vs. Kramer could* redouble his efforts when he loses his custody case, but he decides it would be too hard on his son. When his wife relents and surrenders custody anyway, it feels like he earned it by *not* fighting. Likewise, in *Sideways*, Miles simply waits for Mya to call him at this point, but because he has a history of hostile drunk dialing, it seems heroic for him to summon up the patience to wait for her call.

☑ **Despite these proactive steps, is the time line unexpectedly moved up, forcing the hero to improvise for the finale?**

We always begin a huge project with a proposed end in sight, but we rarely finish unless there's an externally imposed deadline to kick us in the ass. And, *surprise!*, that's when we do our best work. Self-motivation peters out, but, to paraphrase Samuel Johnson, impending doom sharpens the mind.

This deadline is necessary to resolve a sympathy paradox. The audience wants the hero to be smart and proactive at this point, but it's still inherently unsympathetic for a hero to fight the final battle "at a time of our choosing." To resolve this paradox, the hero should be proactively *preparing* for a final confrontation, but then those plans should be ruined when the antagonist unexpectedly moves up the time line.

- Most famously, George Lucas realized in the *Star Wars* editing room that the ending wasn't exciting enough if the characters simply used the stolen plans to attack the Death Star on their own schedule, so he recut and redubbed the scene in postproduction to make the Death Star unexpectedly attack first.
- Joel in *Risky Business* finds out his parents are coming home early.
- The heroes of *Rear Window* and *Blue Velvet* find that the objects of their voyeurism are coming over to pay them a visit.
- Clarice in *Silence of the Lambs* finds herself accidentally dropping in on Buffalo Bill without backup.
- The title character in *Goldfinger* literally moves up the ticking clock on his nuclear bomb!

This step gets skipped more often than some of the others, and that's fine. It's good to knock the hero off balance one last time, but sometimes the story already has enough momentum, or you have a setting like the jury room in *12 Angry Men* where, by design, there's no ticking clock.

In some rare cases, it's more powerful to do the opposite of this step. In movies like *Bringing Up Baby* and *The Apartment*, the chaos ends early and the hero finally gets what he originally wanted (the bone and the promotion, respectively), but does he still want it? Only when he's no longer being dragged along by events can he really decide.

☑ Do all strands of the story and most of the characters come together for the climactic confrontation?

In real life, most projects (whether relationships, confrontations, or criminal enterprises) *eventually* culminate in success or failure, but this is usually a gradual process. Fiction heightens and compresses these moments, creating something far more definitive and impactful than real-life climaxes, which, let's face it, are often underwhelming.

Most heroes win, some heroes lose, some lose by winning (the hero of *Downhill Racer* realizes how meaningless victory is), and some win by losing (*Spider-Man* sacrifices love for higher responsibilities), but in each case, the story climaxes and the hero has a catharsis.

- The hero defeats the villain in most thrillers and action movies.
- Boy gets girl (and vice versa) in most romances (and also, for that matter, in most action movies).
- The discontented heroes of *Sullivan's Travels* and *Rushmore*, in addition to getting the girl, mature and find more inner peace.

One reason many first-time writers insist on writing unhappy endings is that it's a lot easier to write a story in which the hero fails. After all, you don't need to master the structure of problem solving if your hero doesn't solve the problem, right? But whether your heroes win or lose, they *must* see their problems through to their climax. An unhappy ending cannot arrive at an earlier point in this structure and bring the story to a premature end. Such endings are only *tragic* when the hero loses at the *last possible moment*. (Rick gets the girl and *then* has to give her away in *Casablanca*; Michael loses the last bit of his soul *after* defeating his enemies when he closes that door in *The Godfather*; Jack loses his life *after* saving the girl in *Titanic*.)

While audiences usually hate stories that don't climax, you can use that tool to force them to think. *Mutiny on the Bounty* denies its antagonists a final showdown, forcing the audience to decide who's right. *Limbo* pulls a similar trick when it ends right before the climax. In the case of *Monty Python and the Holy Grail* and *Blazing Saddles*, the lack of proper finales is an "F you" to convention. Finally, *Killer of Sheep*, *Funny Ha Ha*, and *Old Joy* all end on quiet moments that provide little catharsis. All three are excellent, but it's telling that each of these micro-budget movies was self-financed by the filmmakers. You may be able to *tell* a story without a climax, but you can't *sell* it to a buyer. That doesn't mean such stories aren't worth telling.

☑ Does the hero's inner struggle climax shortly after (or possibly at the same time as) her outer struggle?

Catharsis only comes about because of crisis. We put off personal change until the last possible moment, at the crux of the crisis or afterward.

The inner conflict should not end too early. Once when a producer was quickly summing up the problems he had with my script, we got to the third act and he said, "It's very exciting, but after a certain point it all runs downhill." I asked him to explain, but he couldn't, since he considered the point self-evident. I thought he was crazy. Was he saying I didn't have enough conflict? There's no way: It was an over-the-top, one-man-against-an-army-of-crazies finale. How does that roll downhill?

I think that now, years later, I've finally figured out what he was saying. My hero hadn't run out of exterior conflict; my hero had run out of dilemma. He still had a lot of bad guys to be defeated, but he no longer had internal tension caused by those actions.

Once I figured this out, it was an easy fix: I had to send my good guy into the final confrontation still seeking the temptation the bad guy had offered. I had to push the good guy's final rejection of that temptation as late as possible, right at the heart of the climax. The hero's dilemma should be exacerbated by the conflict, and vice versa, until the last moment, when the resolution of the dilemma and the resolution of the conflict should happen at about the same time.

- In any movie where it might be all in the hero's head, the inner struggle and outer struggle automatically end at the same time, such as in *The Babadook* and *Groundhog Day*.
- The hero of *How to Train Your Dragon* reconciles with his father during the heat of battle.
- *Die Hard* is very tidy: Willis wins his wife back by shooting the bad guy dead.

Note: Sometimes the inner struggle happens early in sports movies. In both *Breaking Away* and *The Fighter*, the emotional breakthroughs happen before the hero competes at the end. The real story is over, and the final triumph is essentially a victory lap.

☑ **Is there an epilogue/aftermath/denouement in which the challenge is finally resolved (or succumbed to), and we see how much the hero has changed?**

Real life is mostly epilogue. The ramifications of our crises linger for years, and we're never sure if it turned out right. In fiction, we want tidier concluding moments, although not too tidy.

- In exciting stories like *Speed*, this is often the moment when the hero and heroine take a breather and confirm that they really do care about each other, which often results in a first kiss.
- The surviving heroes of *The Great Escape* get dragged back to prison, content in the knowledge that they've caused a huge distraction.

- Many comedies, like *Date Night*, wrap up the dilemma (the marriage problems, in this instance) in a quiet scene just after the climax, which is fine.
- In movies like *Rear Window*, we see that the underlying dilemma (the different interests of Kelly and Stewart) has not been resolved at all, though the climax brought about a temporary truce. This can work, too.

We've covered concept, character, and structure, but so far we've only looked at the big picture. For the next two chapters, let's zoom in on the nitty-gritty details that actually get you from page to page.

6

STAGING STRATEGIC SCENE WORK
....

WHAT IS SCENE WORK?

Scene work is the blood, sweat, and tears of writing. At any given point in your story, the audience will be far more interested in the conflict within the current scene than in the *overall* conflict. If you allow yourself to create weak scenes in service of the larger story, you will sabotage your work. You cannot let your characters simply seek each other out, exchange vital plot points, and then go about their business. Each scene must be a self-sufficient microcosm of your total work: filled with personality, conflict, mini-triumphs, mini-defeats, and, yes, irony. (I told you that would show up a lot!)

MISCONCEPTIONS ABOUT SCENE WORK

MISCONCEPTION: The most powerful conflict occurs when characters directly dispute each other.

AU CONTRAIRE: Direct disputation is the least interesting type of conflict. Indirect conflicts are far more compelling.

You can perfect your concept, characters, and structure only to discover that everything is still falling flat. You can't just have scene after scene of low-conflict information exchanges, no matter how interesting that information may be. Every scene must be compelling in its own right.

Here are three key elements that make every scene stronger:

1. There must be *conflict* between the scene partners.

2. As a result, at least one of them should end up *doing something he or she didn't intend to do* when the scene began.
3. At least one of them should use indirect *tricks and traps*, not just direct confrontation.

Mix and match those elements and you get the five levels of scene work, ranked from weakest to strongest:

1. **THE LISTEN-AND-ACCEPT SCENE:** Two characters listen to each other and accept each other's information. One may be surprised or upset by what the other person has to say but doesn't reject it as untrue. There's no conflict, nobody does anything unintended, and nobody is clever.

2. **THE LISTEN-AND-DISPUTE SCENE:** Two characters tell each other things, but one or both reject the other's statement, so they argue and then leave. There's conflict, but still nobody does anything unintended, and nobody is clever.

3. **THE EXTRACT-INFORMATION-OR-ACTION-DIRECTLY SCENE:** Two characters disagree, directly confront each other, and, in the process, one talks the other into giving something up. There's conflict, and one person does something unintended, but nobody is clever.

4. **THE EXTRACT-INFORMATION-OR-ACTION-THROUGH-TRICKS-AND-TRAPS SCENE:** This is the same as above, but instead of using direct confrontation, one person tricks or traps the other into *unwittingly* giving something up. There's conflict, one person does something unintended, and one person is clever.

5. **THE BOTH-TRY-TO-TRICK-AND-TRAP-EACH-OTHER-AND-ONE-OR-BOTH-SUCCEED SCENE:** This is the most lively type of scene. There's conflict, at least one character does something unintended, and both are clever.

Once you start holding yourself to this standard, all of your scenes will come to life (but writing will become a lot harder!). It's okay to have a few ones, twos, or threes, but as often as possible, it's preferable to have more fours and fives.

MISCONCEPTION: Your plot will give your characters a lot to talk about.

AU CONTRAIRE: Figuring out the plot is not your characters' job.

Most of your plot should be conveyed by imagery. Sometimes we will see more of the plot than the characters do, sometimes we will see exactly what they see, and sometimes we will see less than they do, but in all three cases, the plot should primarily be seen, not discussed.

Let's talk about a particularly famous plot hole. In Alfred Hitchcock's *Vertigo,* detective Jimmy Stewart is following around a seemingly possessed housewife played by Kim Novak. Along the way, many spooky things *seem* to happen, but in the last half-hour of the movie, we find out this was all an elaborate con job, and there was never any actual supernatural element.

And for the most part, that works. Once we know what was really going on, we see everything in a new light and it all makes sense, except for one scene: At one point, Stewart follows Novak into a hotel, where he's told that she's gone upstairs, but when he goes up, he discovers she's vanished into thin air. What happened? The explanation we get at the end doesn't cover that.

It's not hard to imagine an explanation for Novak's disappearance: Perhaps she paid off the hotel front desk clerk to lie to Stewart. Or maybe she rigged up a way to escape from the hotel room without being seen. We can guess, but we'll never know for sure.

Of course, Hitchcock could have given us the answer: Why not tidy up the story by having Stewart ask Novak (an hour of screen time later) how she pulled that off? Because the audience would *hate* that. Plotting is the job of the writer, not the characters. We don't want to hear characters clarify the intricacies of the plot.

This is why it's so hard to write thrillers. You don't want to reveal the twist too soon, so you play your cards close to the vest. Then, after the twist goes down, it's very tempting to toss in a lot of "backfill" where the characters belatedly explain why everything happened the way it did.

Don't do this. Once the plot twists, it should be instantly obvious how everything now fits together. If anything is still unclear, just leave it. Producers and editors sometimes ask writers to "hang an explainer on it," which is almost always a terrible idea. Your characters, and your audience, should be way too caught up in what's happening next.

If the plot doesn't quite make sense, that's your problem, not theirs. Whatever you do, don't have your characters stop and discuss the plot until it all makes sense. Keep the characters moving forward. *Vertigo* was recently voted the best movie ever made. Nobody cares that one small part of it makes no sense.

MISCONCEPTION: Lovers love to talk about love.

AU CONTRAIRE: They need something else to talk about, so the love interest can't just be the love interest.

Dating scenes, or any scene where the hero is there for no reason other than flirting, can be tough. It's hard, because the intentions are too obvious, which gives you too little subtext to work with. But if there's some *other* context for the meeting, and you add flirting on *top* of that, then there's going to be a lot more energy in the scene. You need some other goal for the romantic inclinations to push and pull against.

Ideally, heroes should be required to run into their love interests, even if they definitely don't want to see them, so you can have a lot more variety in your love scenes. If heroes just go home to their sweethearts at the end of the day and tell them what's going on (like the leads in so many cop movies do, such as *Bullitt*), then those scenes are going to be limp.

It's great if the love interest has vital information that the hero needs, or can otherwise be a potential obstacle, as well as an attractor. *Hill Street Blues* has a perfect setup: It features a relationship (and eventual marriage) between a police chief and a public defender, professions that constantly put them at odds. When they argue about the case at work, it can also be a metaphor for their love life. When they talk about their love life at home, it can be a metaphor for the case. Every scene has instant subtext.

But Ross and Rachel on *Friends* were a much harder couple to write well. Part of the tension in their relationship is that they don't care about each other's jobs (paleontology and fashion, respectively), but that's the sort of tension that kills stories rather than launches them. Ultimately, it gives them nothing to talk about except their relationship in scenes that lack subtext. In the end, the only way to wring interest out of the relationship is to repeatedly watch them break up and get back together.

Take heed: There's a reason everybody gets worried when they hear the phrase "Let's talk about our relationship."

> **MISCONCEPTION:** The best way to keep your story lean is to whisk your characters through scenes as quickly as possible so they can keep pushing the story forward.
>
> **AU CONTRAIRE:** Yes, stories should be as lean as possible, often cutting out the beginning or end (or even the middle, as we'll see later), but the portion of the scene that we *do* see must also contain odd little nonplot elements that create verisimilitude, even though the resulting friction will slow down the story.

When I got started, I would write a thirty-beat outline in which my heroes would dart from place to place, getting overwhelmed by and then overcoming their personal problems. I figured that, as long as each of my thirty beats was accomplished in four pages or less, I would come out with a screenplay that was under the 120-page limit.

No problem, right? Wrong. As I wrote, my scenes would balloon in size, and they would have unforeseen consequences that required me to add more scenes. I was chronically underestimating how many pages it would take to get through each beat.

Remember high school physics? In order to make the theoretical problems easier to solve, they would always say, "Assume that all surfaces are frictionless." Of course, in real life, there's no such thing as a frictionless surface, so your calculations would be way off, but those classes were just supposed to teach us the abstract concepts, not how to get anything done.

The problem with story outlines is that they assume your *characters* are frictionless. In an outline, your hero glides into a room, collides with another character, and then the force of that collision sends the hero ricocheting off into the next scene. And you can *try* to write the first draft that way, too, but it'll be pretty bad, and you'll just need to rewrite it later.

The more authenticity, verisimilitude, and *texture* your fictional world has, the more friction your characters will experience when they encounter it. Your characters may walk into the scene with a straightforward confrontation in mind, but to reach that goal, they'll first have to overcome some tactical mini-challenges and navigate some swirling emotional crosscurrents.

Here are some typical causes of friction you may have failed to account for in your outline:

- What the character in the room is doing (and may want to continue doing) when the other character walks in
- The physical challenges of the room's layout
- Additional characters in the room who aren't part of the main confrontation but may butt in
- The decorum of the room, where a confrontation may be unwelcome
- Unresolved emotions carried over from your hero's previous scene
- Unresolved emotions carried over from the last scene these two characters had together
- One or more characters who refuse to do what you want them to do
- An encounter that turns out to be far more emotional than you thought it would be because of unexpectedly volatile reactions within each character

If you ignore all of these factors and write each scene as if it's happening in a vacuum, you'll get to where you're going much faster than if you don't, but the scenes will suck. The more sophisticated a piece of writing, the more friction it creates and the less plot it needs.

Each episode of *Mad Men* has only a thin wisp of a plot, just enough to start these richly textured, electrically charged characters sparking off against each other. The acclaimed episode "The Suitcase" had a ridiculously simple plot description: Don and Peggy work to come up with a slogan for a luggage company. That sounds like a dead-simple goal, but on this show, the characters encounter so much emotional friction along the way that they wind up being torn apart.

On many of CBS's crime procedurals, by contrast, the characters have very little personality, which creates a frictionless surface, allowing dozens of plot points to glide by effortlessly—and meaninglessly.

Obviously one way to keep your story lean is to strip away extraneous material: Start every scene late, end it early, and avoid meandering digressions. But in order to be lean, it needs to be dense. You need to pack every moment of every scene with as much metaphorical meaning as possible.

Let's look at one little throwaway scene from *Breaking Away* that's extremely dense with meaning. First, some background on the story: Our hero, Dave, is a directionless kid growing up just outside the college town of Bloomington, Indiana. As part of a subconscious urge to prove he can be just as cosmopolitan as the college kids, he begins to emulate the Italian bicycle racers he reads about in his cycling magazines. That's his *false* goal. By the end of the movie, he will realize the Italian bicyclists are actually a bunch of jerks and the college kids aren't so bad. In the end, he will enroll at IU himself. That's his unsuspected *true* goal.

Now, let's look at one little scene that metaphorically encapsulates both his false goal and his true goal: Dave gets a magazine saying the Italian bicycle team, sponsored by Cinzano vermouth, is coming to race in Bloomington. He goes out to practice so he'll be ready. He bicycles to the highway, where he pulls up behind a tractor trailer, which happens to be hauling Cinzano, which only spurs him on all the more. Dave keeps up with the truck even as fast as 50 mph. The shooting and editing switch from bucolic to tense, showing that it's now a real race. But just as Dave is about to pass the trucker, a state trooper pulls the trucker over and gives him a speeding ticket. With a big smile on his face, Dave whips past the miserable trucker. As he does so, he barely notices a sign that says he's now entering the city limits of Bloomington.

Every aspect of this scene is packed with ironic meaning. First, it drives home Dave's false goal: He doesn't tell anyone in this scene that he wants to become Italian, but he doesn't have to. He's dressed himself as an Italian racer, and he's cheering himself on using little bits of self-taught Italian. The scene is even scored to an Italian symphony. And, of course, the race against the Cinzano truck foreshadows Dave's upcoming race against Team Cinzano.

But the scene *also* foreshadows Dave's hidden *true* goal. In his mind, he's in Italy, and he doesn't even notice that he is actually racing toward the university the entire time, which is his true destination. He also doesn't notice that, by projecting his fantasy onto this trucker, he is actually screwing the trucker over, causing him to get a ticket. This foreshadows the subplot in which Dave courts a college girl (the "enemy") by pretending to be an Italian, not realizing how much it will hurt her feelings when his deception is revealed.

Cramming so much meaning into a little throwaway scene takes a huge weight off the *actual* dialogue scenes. The more you can *show* to your audience in nonverbal ways, the less you'll need to *tell* them through dialogue, and that leaves you with more space to let your story breathe.

QUESTIONS TO ASK ABOUT SCENE WORK

Scene work breaks down into three areas:

- **SETUP:** Does this scene begin with the essential elements it needs?
- **CONFLICT:** Is this a compelling collision of competing agendas?
- **OUTCOME:** Does this scene change the story going forward?

Setup

☑ *Were tense and/or hopeful (and usually false) expectations for this interaction established beforehand?*

Writers of standalone stories (most novelists, screenwriters, and playwrights) have a wonderful tool that writers of serialized stories (TV writers, comic book writers, series novelists) sometimes lack: They can write *backward*. If you're writing a self-contained work and you find you've run into trouble with a scene, character, or plot, you don't need to plow forward and write your way out of it. Instead, you can plow *backward* and bury the seed of the solution far enough in the past that it'll be ready to sprout just when you need it. As with most other problems in life, the best time to fix a scene problem is before it starts.

CAN YOU ESTABLISH THAT THE CHARACTERS HAVE PAINFULLY UNREALISTIC EXPECTATIONS ABOUT WHAT'S GOING TO HAPPEN? A reversal is so much more upsetting if we know the character (and the audience) was fully expecting (and possibly *depending*) on a totally different outcome. Maybe you can add a brief scene beforehand where the hero rehearses how well he thinks it's going to go. *(500) Days of Summer* has a great scene where the character's hopeful expectations are shown on a split screen with the harsh reality.

Once you start looking for these, you will notice them everywhere: mini-scenes before each real scene where the character takes a moment to rehearse or boasts about what's about to happen or gets nervous. These scenes key up the real scene, making the outcome far more powerful because now we know what it means to the heroes, how it contradicts (or gratifies) their expectations, and what they had riding on it.

Tolstoy is a master at this. He has huge casts of characters and constantly jumps from head to head, having readers identify with different characters in each scene, but he makes sure they only identify with one character at a time. The identification is often intense because he gives that one character a little moment of prep time. Once readers know how anxiously invested the character is in one outcome, they're ready to hope for the best and fear for the worst.

CAN YOU PRELOAD THE ACTIONS WITH MEANING? If the hero said, many scenes back, "I always know she's not leaving for good because she never takes her cat with her," then when she *does* take the cat, we instantly guess how serious it is *at the same time our hero does*. That's when the audience feels the *most* bonded with your hero: when they understand the hero's expectations so well that they can share those feelings *as they happen*.

There's a great scene in *Singles* where Bridget Fonda sneezes and her humbled ex-boyfriend Matt Dillon automatically mumbles, "Bless you." That's it, but it's a wonderful love scene, because we had heard her tell a friend many scenes before about how heartbreaking it was that he never said that. Rather than put them in that elevator and force them to spew reams of dialogue about how he's changed and how she's maybe ready to believe him, we get a wonderful two-word scene that convinces us they should get back together, because the writer was clever enough to lay the groundwork beforehand.

Audiences love this. They love learning the secret language of characters. They love knowing that, for her, "Bless you" means "I love you." They love it especially when they forget all about it, then see it suddenly pay off much later. Only if they know the characters' expectations beforehand can they experience the same emotional reactions *at the same time* as the characters. This is *true* emotional identification.

☑ Does the scene eliminate small talk and repeated beats by cutting out the beginning (or possibly even the middle)?

When you're chopping down your first draft, one classic trick is to simply cut out the first two lines of every scene so that the audience has to hit the ground running each time. The first two lines serve to "set the scene," but you don't really want to do that: The audience *likes* to play catch-up and figure out on the fly which scene they've leaped into.

But why stop there? You can also cut out the *middle* of scenes. In *Easy Living*, we see Jean Arthur and Edward Arnold start to argue about compound interest in the back of a car, then we cut to an exterior shot of the car crossing town, then jump forward to them getting out of the car once the argument has reached a crescendo. In a later scene, she walks into work wearing her new mink, which raises eyebrows, so then we jump inside the boss's office as she's already halfway through trying to explain how she got it. In each case, writer Preston Sturges uses a cut from outside to inside to hide the excision.

Earlier I quoted a scene from *Chinatown* where the director belatedly cut out a line that was overly prescient about the philosophy of the movie. Nobody misses this cut because the conversation moves out of the office, which allowed the film editors to cut outside a little early and hide the fact that part of the conversation is missing.

But you can also cut chunks out of the middle of scenes even *without* cutting away from the space you're in. If you've got multiple conversations going on in the same space, you can hide time jumps whenever you cut back and forth between them. *The 40-Year-Old Virgin* cuts between four guys who are speed dating and manages to compress an hour down to five minutes, without resorting to jump cuts.

☑ Is this an intimidating setting that keeps characters active?

Kitchens are better than bedrooms. Tennis courts are better than coffeehouses. Semaphore is better than the Internet. Do your characters a favor: Put objects in their hands!

Independent films love to set scenes in coffee shops. Coffee shops are easy to scout, cheap to shoot in, and they lend themselves to long-winded discussions. They're also terrible locations for any scene. If you love your characters, let them play basketball, dig a ditch, or try out a pastry class. They need something to do with their hands. Giving characters stuff to do accomplishes so much:

- First of all, it gives each character a secondary goal beyond "I need to have a conversation." This physical goal can become an obstacle to having this conversation or a reason to get out of there or an excuse to linger where they're not wanted, all of which will amplify conflict.

- It also gives you a way to accidentally express hidden emotions. You can simply have the characters *say* that they have mixed feelings, but it's a much better solution to have your characters say one thing and then betray a different emotion through their actions. The more objects you put in their hands, the easier it is to do that.
- The characters can use body language instead of dialogue. Bodies don't have much language when you're sitting in a coffee shop. You can only play with the sugar cubes for so long.

The tennis scenes in the razor-sharp family drama *The Squid and the Whale* did a great job with this. At the beginning, everybody is supposedly one big happy family, but we can tell how they really feel when they aggressively play tennis during seemingly innocuous conversations. As a result, we need fewer scenes of "Honey, I'm unhappy."

For the same reason, kitchens are better than bedrooms. There's only one thing to grab onto in a bedroom, and you can't even do that in a PG-13 story. In the kitchen, characters always have things in their hands: That's a lot of body language. Bonus: These are frequently *dangerous* objects. If characters are upset with themselves, they can accidentally cut themselves, so that internal emotion suddenly becomes external. If they're upset with someone else, they can accidentally set that person on fire.

In a coffee shop, of course, you can throw a cup of coffee in someone's face, but that takes a lot of rage. The character has to have a huge emotion and totally own up to it. It has to be on the surface. In a kitchen, you can allow suppressed emotions to express themselves violently in *unintentional* ways. That allows nonviolent people to *accidentally* show violent emotions.

You should not only choose locations that keep your characters on their feet but search for locations that *emotionally* heighten scenes as well. Every scene will become much more interesting if you can set it in a place that your heroes either *long* or *loathe* to go rather than in a neutral place they have no feelings about. Either way, you'll make it tougher on them.

If your heroine has to say something to her now-married crush, and he ushers her into another room to have the conversation, have it be his bedroom and not his living room. Every time she takes a step closer or farther from that bed, she'll feel it.

The bank-heist movie *The Town* had a lot of limp scene work. Ben Affleck plays a bank robber who realizes that one of the tellers may know too much, so he decides to talk her out of calling the cops by romancing her. Luckily, he already knows all about her, so he's able to drop in on her in all sorts of neutral locations: He strikes up a conversation at her Laundromat, then they meet at a Dunkin' Donuts, then they visit a community garden, etc.

But what if he *didn't know* where she did her laundry, or even her name? What if the *only* thing he knew about her was that she worked at that bank? In that case, his only option would be to go back *to the bank* to hit on her. Even though he was wearing a mask during his previous visit, that's still a very uncomfortable location for him. It will constantly remind him and the audience of the essential danger of this relationship, both literally and symbolically.

Instead, those Dunkin' Donuts scenes are low-stakes, low-conflict moments, so Affleck (as writer/director) had to balance them out with a lot of additional scenes where the other gang members keep visiting to remind him about how dangerous this relationship is. These repetitive scenes would not have been necessary if we'd been more acutely aware of that danger in the courtship scenes themselves.

This is your world. If you create a setting with subtextual meaning, then that's one less thing you need to cram into the text. You take the burden off the dialogue. Don't make your characters keep *saying* what they're worried about; put what they're worried about in the room, between them and their goal, and force them to physically go over, under, or through it to get what they want.

Don't get embarrassed. The audience is far more accepting of melodramatic locations than of melodramatic dialogue. If you give your characters a *lot* to react to, then they get to underreact. If you make them churn up all the drama through dialogue, then they have to overreact. Make it easy for them by choosing a location that is as extreme as you can get away with.

Look at the Indiana Jones movies: Don't just lower your archaeologist into an ancient crypt. Make it an ancient crypt filled with snakes (after you've preloaded the scene by making it clear that he really hates snakes). Don't just toss him into a Nazi rally. Put him face-to-face with Hitler! Now you've got a memorable scene.

☑ Is one of the scene partners not planning to have this conversation (and quite possibly have something better to do)?

You're writing a scene. A man learns some shocking news. He goes home to tell his wife. He walks into his apartment, where she's been waiting for him to come home. She asks what's wrong. He tells her everything.

What does she say in response? Well, we don't care *what* she says because the scene is already dead. Why was she just waiting for him to come home? She had nothing better to do?

In how many ways does this sabotage the scene?

- She has nothing to do but talk, because she has nothing in her hands and no business to complete.
- She has no goal of her own to accomplish rather than have this conversation.
- The scene is drained of conflict because she *wants* to have this conversation and in fact *needs* to have it, since she has nothing better to do.

No matter how loving she is, what if she doesn't want to get into this discussion *and* she needs to complete something else important? That's two more sources of conflict right off the bat.

But, more important, you've hobbled your own thought process. If you had taken the time to figure out what she would actually be doing all day, then you would have had to create a much richer, fuller character, because you would have thought about what these people do for work and play. In other words, you would have thought about what they *value*. And that would inform *every* conversation.

Look at *Star Wars: Attack of the Clones*. In this airless, weightless, computer-rendered world, every actor stands around in front of green screens and blandly converses about who gets to control the universe. If you listen to two seconds of dialogue, you know the movie is bad, but you don't even have to listen that long. Just look at any still frame that features their homes and offices. Where is all their *stuff*? How do these people live without *stuff*?

As far as I understood it, Natalie Portman's character is queen of a planet *and* a senator in the galactic legislature. Those are two big jobs! Where is her desk? Where are her papers? Is there no paper at all in this universe? Okay, so do they use computers instead? No? Do they write everything on their hands? Can she at least have a pen? No? There's not a single usable prop on any set.

This lack of stuff makes the visuals look hopelessly unconvincing, it makes the performances painful to watch, and, more important, it makes the highfalutin ideas they're discussing sound vapid and pointless. Why should we listen to you people? You obviously don't *do* anything.

These people have very important jobs, or so we're told, but they do nothing, and they have nothing, so they *are* nothing. And out in the audience, nobody cares. Don't make the same mistake. Never let anybody enter a room and find somebody waiting around to have a conversation.

☑ Is there at least one nonplot element complicating the scene?

Stories must be lean, and we've already established you have a lot of work to do in a small amount of space. And yet, you'll end up with a totally unappealing story if your characters only say what needs to be said to move the plot forward. The best way to combat this is to make sure that in every scene you have some element that has nothing to do with the larger story, something that doesn't serve your purpose, something that just makes the scene feel real.

Add a counterpoint. By that I mean an oddly funny note in a serious scene or a serious note intruding into a comedy scene. On TV, *Mad Men* always does this beautifully. At the movies, the Coen brothers have made a career out of this type of scene: In their noir-homage *The Man Who Wasn't There*, there's a scene where Frances McDormand, imprisoned for murder, tries to confess her infidelity to her husband, but she can't stop complaining about the blubbering inmate next to her.

Make sure at least one character talks about something that has nothing to do with the plot. This can be an oddball distraction that adds to the hero's frustration whenever he tries to move the conversation back to more serious topics.

- In Alfred Hitchcock's final masterpiece *Frenzy*, the police inspector prefers to solve his cases by discussing them with his wife over dinner, but she's now taking an exotic cooking class, which makes that task a lot more daunting.
- In *Unforgiven*, Gene Hackman's villainous sheriff keeps insisting on talking about house building whenever anybody wants to talk about more serious matters. He even wants to talk about it as he's dying.

Or the distraction can be a red herring that threatens to derail the conversation. My all-time favorite dialogue scene is not from a screenplay, stage play, or TV script, but from a novel. No one wrote better dialogue than the late Ed McBain, who wrote fifty-five novels about the detectives of the 87th precinct. My favorite scene was from way back in the second novel, 1956's *The Pusher*. The detectives are trying to track down a big drug dealer, and so they arrest a small fry to get information. They ask him his last name: "Hemingway." They ask him his first name: "Ernest." They get mad and threaten to beat him, but he doesn't understand why. They say they highly doubt that's his real name. He insists he has no idea what they're talking about. They gradually realize this guy has gone through life without ever hearing about the author of the same name, which makes it very clear how utterly bleak his upbringing was. The dealer, meanwhile, is stunned to realize that his father, whom he'd never met, gave him the name of some famous manly man before he disappeared—and that it was a message about how to act that he'd failed to receive until now.

All of this is just a distraction from the business of the scene—getting the guy to give up his supplier—but what a distraction! I can't remember whodunit at the end of the novel, but this heartbreaking little scene has always stayed with me.

☑ Does the scene establish its own mini-ticking clock (if only through subconscious anticipation)?

We all know that the overall plot needs a ticking clock to ramp up motivation, but you can also add time limit countdowns to almost every scene. Now that I've started doing it, I find that it's surprisingly easy. At the beginning of every scene, toss in a line like one of these:

> "I have to go, so I can only talk for a second."

> "Let me ask you something before she comes back in the room."

> "Let's do this quick before anybody notices we're gone."

If one spouse wants to discuss something at the breakfast table, the other spouse should be running late for work. If they're in bed at night, one of them should have taken a sleeping pill that's about to kick in. The one with the problem now has a limited time to get an answer.

This technique has additional benefits: Writers should always try to build events toward a climax, even though that's *not* how life naturally works. In real life, when people kiss, or say, "I love you," for the first time, or get in a fight, they tend to talk about it afterward, right? But that's a problem for stories, because talking about it afterward is inherently anticlimactic. To make your story more dramatic than real life, you need to create a way to cut off that scene *before* they have a chance to talk about it. If you have a pre-established excuse to cut the scene short, you can go out with a bang by yanking one character away right after the big breakthrough.

If your scenes keep getting cut short by outside events, then your characters won't get to resolve their issues too early. If a character says,

"I love you" right before someone shows up to arrest her love interest (or freeze him in carbonite, in the case of *The Empire Strikes Back*), that creates a natural cliff-hanger, and you can let that emotional dilemma dangle for a while.

This is also a good way to get unemotional characters to say emotional things. When the pressure's on, our defenses drop. (Although, in that case, Han Solo managed to hang onto his *sang froid* and not reply with his own "I love you," even though his *sang* was about to be literally *froid*ed.)

One advantage of mini-ticking clocks is that you don't need to focus as much on the major ticking clock, and this can also take the heat off your villain. The more you allow minor, incidental pressures to provide the conflict, the less you need to write overheated rhetoric about the major conflict. Instead of forcing the characters to endlessly fret about one big conflict, remember that the pressure they're under can complicate their lives in a dozen *smaller* ways, keeping them on edge even when they're not under attack from the main bad guy. The best way to keep your readers reading is to make sure they're always anticipating something that's about to happen, both in the story as a whole and within each scene.

Michael Powell's creepy horror masterpiece *Peeping Tom* has the ultimate example of the ticking clock for a scene. Our "hero" is a troubled young man who invites actresses to his apartment for screen tests, then kills them with a blade attached to one leg of his tripod, filming their hideous expressions as they die. But a compassionate young woman in his building, unaware of his madness, has started reaching out to him. In one scene, while he's in the middle of developing the film of his last victim's death, the young woman stops by. The conversation makes him happy, but if he talks to her for too long, the developer fluid will ruin the film of his previous kill. Powell literally intercuts the ticking timer in the darkroom with their flirtatious conversation until our hero is ultimately forced to decide between the two.

But not all ticking clocks are so literal. Sometimes it can be something minor that only has a *subconscious* effect on the reader or viewer. If you don't have an excuse to yank one character away at the end, there are all sorts of subtle ways to create a minor climax within a scene:

- Begin a kitchen scene with the toaster lever being forced down. The audience will subconsciously sense the scene will end with the toast popping up.
- In a comedic scene, have a character unable to think of a word at the beginning, which is driving her crazy. Just when the audience has forgotten about that, the scene ends with her exclamation of the word.
- If two characters are loudly arguing, add a meek person who keeps trying to get the attention of one of the two arguers, then comes up with a clever solution to get what he needs.
- Add a dog that's trying to get one of the characters to feed him for the length of the entire scene, and then have him come up with a clever solution to get the food at the end. Good examples would be Asta in the *Thin Man* movies or Momo on *Avatar: The Last Airbender*.
- Have a character hastily cover up the evidence of some mistake she's made at the beginning of the scene. Then have it pop up again and get revealed at the end of the scene, causing much embarrassment.

There's no better example of this than the Nazi monkey from *Raiders of the Lost Ark*, who ultimately dies from eating his own poisoned dates. What could have been a dull exposition scene comes to life, only to end tragically for one poor monkey. Who is a Nazi.

Conflict

☑ Does each scene both advance the plot and reveal character through emotional reactions?

As we established in chapter two, the audience doesn't care about the plot. They only care about the hero and her *reaction* to what's happening. This is true of the overall story and of each scene.

Beginners write scenes in which big plot points happen, but readers (or viewers) aren't in any one character's shoes when they happen.

The audience is just supposed to float above it all and say, "Oh my god, what a big story development!" But audiences don't actually care about the plot; they only care about the characters. They don't care about the outside action; they only care about the hero's volatile *re*action.

Let's say that in your first scene a crowd of co-workers watches a nuclear bomb go off outside the window. You expect your audience to say, "Oh, that's terrible! A nuclear bomb! Just think of all those people who must have been killed!" But your audience has no good reason to feel that way. They don't know anybody outside that window. That world isn't real yet because you haven't made it real. If you haven't *created* any people outside that window, then there *aren't* any people outside that window, and your audience knows it.

But if you make your audience identify with one member of that crowd, and the audience knows she's trying to get out of there early today to pick up her daughter from school, and maybe she was talking to her daughter on the phone when the signal cut out, then the audience will be *devastated*.

Plot for plot's sake is meaningless. Stop trying to upset the expectations of the audience with shocking events—the audience isn't emotionally involved in *events*. Instead, get the audience to love the *characters*, and then show how events *upset the characters' expectations* to upset the audience.

☑ Does the audience have (or develop) a rooting interest in this scene (which may sometimes shift)?

Obviously, in most scenes you write, your hero will be in the scene *and* will also be the hero *of* the scene—the person we admire and want to see triumph in this interaction. But that's not always the case.

What about scenes that don't feature any of the story's heroes? There still needs to be conflict within that scene, and the audience should be able to pick a favorite to root for in that conflict. There's a fun little scene in *Die Hard* where we cut away to the local news coverage: The anchorman mistakenly refers to Stockholm syndrome as "Helsinki syndrome," and his co-anchor rolls her eyes. Even this small scene has its own hero and villain: We side with the anchor who spots her colleague's mistake.

Even if the scene merely consists of two villains, then that scene also needs its own "hero" whom we want to see "triumph" in this interaction. We should admire one villain's reaction to this situation (even if it's only to admire the competence of his villainy), and we should disdain the other.

And in some scenes, even if the overall hero of the story is present, the audience is actually rooting for someone else. For instance, sometimes we're rooting for someone else to set the hero straight. When Buffy and Willow disagree on *Buffy the Vampire Slayer*, the audience almost always sides with Willow. Buffy is better in a fight, which makes her the capital-*H* "Hero" of the show, but Willow is wiser, which makes her the "hero of the scene" in most of her interactions with Buffy.

When you let different characters establish dominance in each scene, you build up potential energy. If your hero and villain keep running circles around inferior scene partners in separate scenes, then the audience will get more and more excited about their eventual confrontation. The audience will start saying, "Wow, these two each dominate every scene they're in! What happens when they're finally in a scene *together*?" Which one will be humbled for the first time?

Sometimes you can allow your audience to have *ambiguous* identification in a scene. In some scenes, we will be rooting for some heroes *not* to get what they want. For one reason or another, we know they are pursuing a false goal, and what they're attempting to do will only make their problem worse. In these scenes, we root for the heroes to realize that what they want is not what they really need. One thing to be aware of: It's very hard to watch characters do anything and *not* root for them to succeed, even if they're taking an action we disagree with. This can be dangerous: French filmmaker Francois Truffaut claimed it was impossible to make an anti-war film, because anytime you show someone doing something difficult, the audience starts to root for them to succeed—even if they don't approve.

A perfect example is the swamp scene in *Psycho*. We've spent the first half of the movie rooting for Janet Leigh, but when she's killed by serial killer Norman, our identification switches to him very quickly.

At what point do we suddenly realize we've come to sympathize with Norman? With much difficulty, he's killed our heroine, put her body in the trunk of her own car, and then dumped that car in the swamp. We're horrified, but we can't help but get wrapped up in his grim determination. Then, suddenly, the plan hits a hitch—the car bobs back up instead of sinking. And what do we think? We *should* think, "Hurray, our heroine's killer will be caught!" but we don't. Instead we say, "Oh no, our new hero, Norman, might get caught!"

It turns out that what's really required to generate sympathy is to closely watch someone who is (a) making decisions, (b) doing something difficult, and (c) overcoming setbacks.

Hitchcock is forcing us to root for what Norman wants (to get away with it) and what he needs (to get professional help) at the same time, even though they conflict. But it's okay for each audience member to have two competing rooting interests. The problem is when the audience has *no* rooting interest in a scene: "Why are they showing me this? This isn't moving the story forward. I can't figure out what's supposed to happen here or how to feel about it."

Instead, you must either trigger straightforward feelings in your audience (stand up and cheer!) or trigger two ambiguous feelings (I want the hero to succeed *and* fail, and I can't decide which I want to see more). What you can't do is fail to trigger *any* feelings.

As soon as a scene begins, let your audience know that one of several things might happen. Then get them to root for one or the other, or maybe, if you're really good, for more than one irreconcilable option. Once they're rooting for a certain outcome, the way you end the scene will either make them feel good, bad, or something more complex, but you must make them feel *something*.

☑ Are two agendas genuinely clashing (rather than merely two personalities)?

The Cary Grant and Rosalind Russell newsroom comedy *His Girl Friday* (loosely adapted by Ben Hecht and Charles MacArthur from their play *The Front Page*) has justifiably famous dialogue, so much so that it's now become the template for every fictional male-female relationship: "We bicker all the time with rapid-fire, razor-sharp wit, but we really just want to jump each other's bones!" Unfortunately, too many writers do it wrong because they fail to understand why that movie works.

The heroes of that movie don't just have conflicting *personalities*; they have conflicting *agendas*. Grant wants to win Russell back, both as his wife and his best reporter, while she wants to get free and move on with her life. They disagree about the past (what ruined their marriage), the present (the best way to cover the current news event), and the future (whether they should get back together). That's *genuine* conflict.

The problem is, so many modern stories, in a failed attempt to imitate *His Girl Friday*, show a man and woman *instantly* launching into combative, flirtatious banter the very first time they meet.

Let's return to an article I cited before: Tad Friend's tragicomic *New Yorker* profile of floundering *John Carter* writer/director Andrew Stanton. Friend describes yet another attempt at an intervention: Stanton is meeting with his composer, Michael Giacchino, who is desperately trying to identify an emotional throughline in Stanton's sprawling mess of a movie. Giacchino shows Stanton a problematic scene: American prospector Taylor Kitsch has been transported to Mars, where huge green aliens have enslaved him. Suddenly two warring groups of *another* alien race show up to have an airship battle right above their heads. This is the first time John has ever seen anything remotely humanoid on this planet. Minutes later, he sees one of those humanoid aliens fall out of one of the ships, and he leaps up to catch her in mid-fall. (Stanton calls this the "Superman catch.") They land and automatically team up, pulling out swords and killing a lot of other aliens together, flirting with each other the entire time.

Friend describes the composer's attempt to explain the problem to the director:

> They watched Taylor Kitsch soar up to save Lynn Collins as she fell from her airship—the Superman catch—and the newly met couple then carves up an enemy platoon.
>
> "Do you have a take where Lynn isn't smiling when she says, 'Let me know when it gets dangerous?'" Giacchino asked. "She just met the guy. Why would she be smiling playfully?"
>
> "Mm-hmm," Stanton said. He folded his hands behind his head. "It was a bump in the movie for me."
>
> "Interesting."
>
> Afterward, Stanton told me, "I was mentally kicking my own ass, because I don't think I have a take where she didn't smile—and I don't want my learning curve to be the reason a scene doesn't work."

Stanton still didn't realize the entire scene (indeed, the entire movie) is unsalvageable because he directed it on autopilot. He had his hero and heroine flirting and bickering because he'd been told that's what heroes and heroines do. He didn't think he actually had to provide a reason *why*.

The movie version of *Daredevil* is even more ridiculous. In the comics, Daredevil and Elektra are college sweethearts who cross paths many years later only to discover they're now on opposite sides of the law. The movie cuts out all the history but still has them sparring like old lovers from the moment they meet. They meet in a café, flirt like crazy, then walk outside and start playfully beating each other up in a playground. It's hard to say which is worse, his decision to beat up a random woman who turned down his advances or her desire to beat up *a blind man*! Once again, the writers were on autopilot.

Yes, every scene needs conflict, but that should be because the characters have conflicting goals. Until their goals conflict, they should get along just fine. Both of the aforementioned creators were in too much of a hurry to generate empty conflict.

☑ *Does the scene have both a surface and a suppressed conflict?*

The topic of conversation does not always determine the true substance of a scene, and it should never contain *all* of the conflict in a scene. Every good scene needs a surface conflict and a suppressed conflict, either one of which can be the primary conflict.

There are ways that one character might confront another one *indirectly*.

- In pursuit of a goal, the character chooses to mask a hidden agenda behind an innocuous topic.
- The character is genuinely attempting to have an innocuous conversation but unintentionally pursues a subconscious agenda.

Either way, the other agenda will be revealed not through the text but through the subtext, so you must ask …

☑ *Is the suppressed conflict (which may or may not come to the surface) implied through subtext (and/or called out by the other character)?*

You can write without using any subtext—just have everybody honestly state their emotions and charge directly at each other full force—but it will ring false. It's vital to imitate real life, and real people are rarely direct. That's why writers learn the art of subtext.

Subtext is an odd thing: It's both the most naturalistic way to write and the most artificial, since the writer must put a lot of work into layering multiple levels of meaning within each scene, setting up and paying off complex x-equals-y algorithms. And yet the results, if done right, will seem totally organic.

Here are some of the many types of subtext and an example or two of each:

- **TALKING ABOUT THE PRESENT INSTEAD OF THE PAST:** On *Modern Family*, Mitchell frequently criticizes his dad's mistreatment of his new stepson, Manny, instead of complaining about his own mistreatment as a child.

- **TALKING ABOUT THE PAST INSTEAD OF THE PRESENT:** In *It's a Wonderful Life,* Donna Reed keeps trying to talk to Jimmy Stewart about the time they sang "Dance by the Light of the Moon" because she wants to indirectly let him know that she still likes him.
- **TALKING ABOUT OR EXCHANGING AN OBJECT INSTEAD OF AN EMOTION:** In *The Apartment,* keys represent souls: Jack Lemmon loans out his apartment key to get an executive washroom key, but when he finally gets the key he wants, he realizes what it's cost him and hands it back.
- **COMPLAINING ABOUT SOMETHING TRIVIAL INSTEAD OF SOMETHING MAJOR:** In the first episode of *The Sopranos,* Tony worries about the ducks flying away rather than his guilt over his mother.
- **COMPLAINING ABOUT SOMETHING YOU HAVE NO CONTROL OVER TO AVOID COMPLAINING ABOUT SOMETHING YOU DO HAVE CONTROL OVER:** Andie MacDowell frets about a garbage barge instead of her marriage in *Sex, Lies, and Videotape.* Woody Allen rants about the Warren Report instead of his marriage in *Annie Hall.*
- **TALKING ABOUT AN OBSTACLE INSTEAD OF A CONFLICT:** The hero of the play *A Thousand Clowns* always claims that he can't look for a job until he completes various small tasks.
- **ATTRIBUTING ONE'S DESIRES TO A THIRD PARTY:** In *Husbands and Wives,* married Mia Farrow is attracted to Liam Neeson, but rather than admit it, she suggests her friend date him.
- **CRITICIZING A THIRD PARTY INSTEAD OF THE PERSON YOU'RE TALKING TO:** In *Breaking Away,* Dennis Christopher talks about how the Italians cheat as a way of indirectly confronting his father about his dishonesty.
- **TALKING ABOUT A WORK DISPUTE INSTEAD OF A HOME DISPUTE, OR A HOME DISPUTE INSTEAD OF A WORK DISPUTE:** On *Cheers,* Sam and Diane initially break up because they keep arguing about whether to have a fortune-telling machine in the bar rather than arguing about their future.
- **FEIGNING AN OPPOSITE EMOTION:** In *Pride and Prejudice,* the couple feigns aloofness instead of fascination. In the classic film noir

Gilda, the couple feigns hate instead of lust. In *The Awful Truth*, the couple feigns annoyance instead of attraction. In *Match Point*, a young groom feigns devotion instead of contempt.

- **TALKING IN BROAD GENERALITIES TO AVOID TALKING IN SPECIFICS:** Harry in *When Harry Met Sally* keeps debating about the general rule that a man and a woman can't be friends instead of telling Sally he's in love with her.

- **TALKING ABOUT SELF BUT REALLY TALKING ABOUT SOMEONE ELSE:** Kevin Smith's character in *Chasing Amy* tells a story about himself in order to get Ben Affleck to admit that he's in love with the title character.

- **TALKING ABOUT SOMEONE ELSE BUT REALLY TALKING ABOUT SELF:** On *Game of Thrones*, Peter Dinklage's character says to his sister, "It must be hard for you to be the disappointing child."

- **A CHARACTER CHOOSES TO MAKE A HUGE LIFE CHANGE RATHER THAN RISK A RELATIVELY MINOR CONFRONTATION:** This last example is sort of the reverse, so I suppose you could call this supertext. One son becomes Italian rather than confront his father in *Breaking Away*, another son stops speaking rather than confront *his* father in *Little Miss Sunshine*, and a third son changes his first name rather than confront *his* father in *Breaking Bad*.

Subtext doesn't have to happen in dialogue. Characters can also use behaviors to sublimate their desires, as in the following examples: eating in place of having sex in *Tom Jones*, attempting to kill each other instead of having sex in the 2005 version of *Mr. and Mrs. Smith*, and chopping wood instead of busting heads in *Return of the Secaucus 7*.

In each of these cases, it would have been so much easier for the writer to simply have the characters walk right up and confront each other about what's really bothering them. Such scenes are tempting because they're big, bold, packed with attitude, and full of conflict. But they're flat because they lack multiple layers.

People avoid direct conflict. It's usually in the best interest of both parties to keep the real conflict suppressed and stay focused on the surface conflict. It spares both parties pain, allows each to keep personal goals hidden, and gives an excuse to ignore the other's ploy to force them to do something they don't want to do.

☑ Are the characters cagey or in denial about their own feelings?

Another problem with direct confrontation is that it turns every scene into a "big scene." Your story gets buried in *sturm und drang*, with everybody yelling too much. The trick is to learn to write "small scenes" that pack in even more conflict than you might find in a big scene.

Let's look at a randomly selected example in *Breaking Bad*, from the second season episode "Down." Mild-mannered meth dealer Walter White has recently been kidnapped by a rival, and when he finally returns to his family, he gives an unconvincing lie about where he's been. No one wants to confront him directly, but roiling suspicions are tightening the tension in every scene.

This is a seemingly inconsequential scene, but it contains four confrontations, each of which could have been its own "big scene":

1. Walt Jr. tells his dad he now wants a new name and separate identity.
2. Walt and his wife argue about supporting the name change.
3. Walt's wife confronts him with her hurt feelings about his disappearances and lies.
4. Walt's meth partner, Jesse, reaches out to him for help, but Walt refuses him.

Instead of presenting these confrontations as separate scenes, the show layers all four on top of each other in one fluid, small scene: A friend comes to pick up Walt Jr. in the morning and accidentally calls him by his new name. Walt asks his son about this, and the son meekly confirms the new name on his way out the door. Walt, shocked, heads to the bathroom to ask his wife if she knew about this. She says she did, and explains it by saying, "He wants his own identity," and "Your disappearance really hurt him." Walt realizes that she's talking about herself, not their son, and so he's about to say something, but just then the phone rings. Jesse, his drug-dealing partner, is calling about yet another crisis. Walt lies to his wife about who is on the phone and tells Jesse to buzz off. But by the time Walt is off the phone, his wife is already angrily leaving the house.

All of these confrontations can happen at the same time because they're more subtle:

1. The first confrontation is replaced by symbolism: The name change says it all, relieving the need for an "I want my own identity" confrontation. The friend's slip of the tongue allows the information to come out indirectly without forcing Walt Jr. to confront his dad at all.
2. Walt's larger confrontation with his wife about his lies hides as subtext within the smaller confrontation about their son's name change.
3. Walt doesn't need to tell his wife, "There are things I can't tell you," because Jesse calls and she sees that he's still lying.
4. Walt doesn't need to tell Jesse, "You're messing up my life," because we see that happen.

Four potentially melodramatic confrontations all happen at once, but the way it plays out, *none* of them *feels* melodramatic. Indirect confrontations are less upsetting to the characters than direct confrontations, which means that you get to have more of them.

☑ *Do characters use verbal tricks and traps to get what they want, not just direct confrontation?*

Until the nineteenth century, most armies would just march right at each other, but Napoleon perfected the "flanking maneuver," in which one army would sweep around and attack the other from the side. This became many nineteenth-century generals' preferred method of attack, even though it quickly turned comical. In the American Civil War, both sides were obsessed with Napoleon and determined to outflank each other most of time, so the result was thousands of armed men endlessly circling each other in the woods, only fighting when one army accidentally backed into the other.

Here's what this has to do with scene construction: Once you know what your characters want and what obstacles are in their way, it's time to figure out what strategy they'll use to get it. In every scene, one or more of the scene partners are pursuing an objective and encountering an obstacle. If that obstacle is another character, then the solution will probably involve seduction, friendship, or belligerence (and sometimes all three). Each of these three methods requires strategy.

Of course, your characters can walk right up to one another, state their case plainly, reasonably discuss every possible objection, come to a resolution, and then move on. But they won't seem like human beings. We won't even admit what we want to ourselves, much less to each other. As a result, we hide our true objectives in every possible way. Real-life conversations, even with people we love—*especially* with people we love—are full of little verbal tricks and traps.

In any negotiation, the one who lays out his position first usually loses because it allows his opponent to reposition accordingly and outflank him. This is true whether you want a kiss, a confession, or a treaty. Clever people play their cards close to the vest and lead their verbal sparring partners on until they can trap them with their own words.

Don't assume that only unsympathetic or devious characters do this. All people who are clever and persuasive know they must pepper their conversation with tricks and traps.

Take, for example, the famous knife scene from *12 Angry Men*. As a lone holdout juror in a murder trial, Henry Fonda pretty much plays the ultimate embodiment of human decency. He's one of the most humble and noble heroes in the history of storytelling. *But he does it all with tricks and traps!*

Fonda's character, Juror 8, sits there throughout the first half of the story hiding a big secret that's burning a hole in his pocket: He has gone out the night before and found a knife identical to the one that was supposedly used in the murder. But he doesn't walk into the jury room and present his exculpatory evidence right away. No, he waits and lays traps for his eleven opponents.

He insists they speak first, laying out their cases for conviction, knowing that ultimately they will have no choice but to brag about the supposed uniqueness of the murder weapon. He's hoping they'll literally throw the knife in his face so he can dramatically produce his identical knife and do the same. Ultimately, his patience pays off.

Juror 8 is not some righteous blunderer who stumbles upon the truth. He's a steely but wily crusader who verbally traps and defeats his opponents one by one. That's what makes him *heroic*. All compelling characters, whether heroes or villains, best serve their own cause by laying verbal traps and outflanking their opponents at every turn. Those who get fed up with maneuvering and simply plow straight ahead (as if they were at Pickett's Charge) lose their battles and our sympathy.

☑ Does the scene utilize "re-blocking," including the literal push and pull between scene partners?

In the world of television and movies, some producers say scripts can't have any scenes over two pages. That's a little extreme, but it's true you can't have more than two pages of conversation without any written directions breaking up the dialogue. If the scene goes longer (or even if it doesn't), you must seek opportunities to "re-block" it, as they say in the theater.

Force the characters to their feet, and give them a lot of stuff to do. Break off two people from the group for a brief, private conversation, and then reintegrate them. Even if your characters are at a large dinner table, you can create mini-scenes for any pair so that the other characters seem to fade away.

Characters need a goal in each scene, and the other characters need to be the obstacles in their way, literally and figuratively. You already know human interactions have "push and pull," so why not physicalize that? Let them actually shove or yank on each other. For physical interactions, I generally stick to a "one-touch" rule: Two characters should touch each other once, and only once, in each scene.

- Flirtation scenes contain a significant touch on the shoulder, arm, or wrist, which is met either with a recoil, a shirk, or a meaningful look.
- Romantic scenes often build up to a single kiss (whether it's accepted or not) or begin with a single kiss and then unravel from there.
- Manipulation scenes often build to the moment when the manipulator puts a pseudofriendly arm around the scene partner's shoulder or gives him a forceful pat on the back or a firm grasp of the arm, applying some literal pressure.
- Antagonism scenes often build to a single poke, slap, shove, or punch.

This is payoff for both the literal and figurative chasing that has occurred throughout the scene. Whether you're writing a dramatic work or simply prose on the page, you can dictate how far apart the characters are at all times and then use that distance to convey meaning. When they touch, it's the clincher in every sense of the word: One character has literally reached the other. Can they seal the deal?

☑ Are objects given or taken, representing larger values?

Just as relationships involve "push and pull," they also involve "give and take," so why not make that literal as well?

In chapter eight, I'll stress the importance of investing objects with meaning and giving characters "totem objects." Once you invest objects with meaning, every time they're handled or exchanged, a tremendous amount of meaning will move with them.

A dating scene should not be about whether he can call her sometime but about whether she'll take his card. Words are just words. If you say someone can call you, it doesn't mean much, but the physical act of accepting or rejecting a card is powerful.

- He doesn't have to be as intentional. He can give her the card under a false pretext, with the understanding that she'll get his true meaning (as in *Bridesmaids*, where the cop writes a mechanic's number on the back of his card). This is part of the very realistic dance single people do to downplay their intentions (and it's why I was hopelessly inept at being single).

- The look she gives the card will tell us far more than the look she gives the person doing the asking. People are guarded in their looks toward each other, but they reveal their true emotions when they look at objects, secure in the knowledge that the object isn't looking back. What they don't know, of course, is that the writer is there to register those looks that reveal their true feelings.
- In the end, she doesn't have to say yes or no; she just has to accept the card, preferably without saying anything, because actions are always more powerful than words.
- The exchange of a card is physical. Something has changed hands. There is concrete evidence that this scene happened. Part of him has been accepted onto her person now. It's intimate, in its own way.
- This card can carry meaning into future scenes. If she's considering calling him, she can look at the card and then put it away. If she decides she's done with him, she can throw it away. If she changes her mind again, she can fish it out of the trash.

All of these invisible internal decisions have now been made visible, without saying a thing. By relieving characters of the need to say things they wouldn't say out loud, objects eliminate dialogue and allow your story to move at a faster clip.

Sometimes the exchange of the object provides the turning point in the scene: Take the diner scene in *Groundhog Day* in which Phil tries to convince Rita of his powers. It's only when he gives her a slip of paper predicting exactly what Larry the cameraman is going to say that she's finally convinced. He slides the paper to her facedown, she accepts it, listens to Larry, and then turns it over and sees that Phil is uncannily correct. Now it's not just talk anymore; there's physical evidence in her hand, so she is convinced and the scene is over.

Sometimes the exchange of an object merely provides subtext. In *The Shining*, while Jack is hallucinating that he's attending a ball, a waiter spills a drink on him and invites him back to the restroom to clean off his jacket with a washcloth. Jack recognizes the man and accuses him of being the previous caretaker who chopped up his family. As he does so, he gets fed up and takes the man's washcloth away to try to clean his own jacket. The waiter just smirks and says, "You're the caretaker here. You've always been the caretaker here." Jack throws the washcloth down, but it's too late. He's taken on the other man's clean-up role, so now he's the one who will try to chop up his own family.

Outcome

☑ *As a result of this scene, does at least one of the scene partners end up doing something she didn't intend to do when the scene began?*

As I said before, nobody wants to see a "listen and accept" scene where one character passively receives information. But by the same token, a "listen and dispute" scene, where two characters merely argue about some piece of information, is little better. One or more characters in a scene should try to convince or force another to do something he doesn't want to do:

- divulge a secret (though the divulger may not know it's a secret)
- give up an object
- change an important decision
- shift affection
- grant some sort of permission

A scene should have a concrete outcome. The hero's agenda should either succeed or fail in such a way that things get worse rather than stay the same. Things should never return to the status quo at the end of a scene.

Of course, just because the agenda succeeds doesn't mean that things have to go as planned ...

☑ Does the outcome of the scene ironically reverse and/or fulfill the original intention?

As we've now established, irony is the heart of meaning, and it should suffuse every aspect of your story. This means you need to keep upsetting your heroes' expectations, but it doesn't mean your heroes need to keep failing.

Audiences love to see characters succeed or fail in *ironic* ways. That's what keeps stories interesting. If a girl says to the glum boy she likes, "I'm going to take you to the carnival and cheer you up," then the audience is not going to want to see either a *straightforward success* (he loves the roller coaster and thanks her for a fun time) or a *straightforward failure* (he hates the rides and says, "Thanks for nothing.").

The audience would much rather see one of the following:

- **AN IRONIC FAILURE:** He loves the rides and starts to cheer up, but from the top of the Ferris wheel he spots his ex kissing a new guy behind the ring toss, and he becomes more depressed than ever.
- **AN IRONIC SUCCESS:** He hates the rides and tries to sneak away, but as he does so, he sees a carnie kicking a mangy dog out of the camp, so he rescues the grateful dog, who proceeds to make him totally happy.

In *Romeo and Juliet*, Romeo doesn't go to the party to meet someone new. He goes to win back Rosaline's affections. He finds the love he craves, but he does so ironically. He forgets his former infatuation and finds someone new.

This is another thing to be aware of when it's time to turn your outline into a finished project. The broad strokes of the scene may be "He goes to the party, meets Juliet, and falls in love," but when you're painting in the details, you should make it more interesting. Try to have every plot point, positive or negative, be an ironic reversal of what the audience *and* the character expected. Your audience will love you for it.

Scenes that lack irony can do real harm to a story. Look at any scene involving a misunderstanding. *Captain America* was a lot of fun, but the weakest plot turn in that movie showed the danger of relying on an *unironic* misunderstanding.

At mid-movie, everything is hunky-dory with Cap and his love interest. They're both supernice and only interested in each other, so there's no room for any real drama in their relationship. But the writers nevertheless felt the need to put a bump in the road, so they fell back on an old standby. Out of nowhere, a vixenish secretary grabs Cap for an unwanted passionate kiss just as he's leaving the war office. Before he can push her away, his crush walks in, sees them together, and then runs away. Ugh.

This false conflict could be resolved with a simple explanation, but, as usual, the misunderstanding snowballs out of control. Why do this? Why not generate an *actual* difference of opinion between the two so a genuine dilemma can help fuel the drama instead of a meaningless mix-up?

The Apartment, on the other hand, shows the value of an *ironic* misunderstanding. Baxter's neighbor spends the entire movie convinced that Baxter, and not his bosses, is bringing all those women back to his apartment. This adds a thick layer of irony to their discussions.

Baxter accepts the criticism because he wants to be gentlemanly and to conceal his bosses' affairs, but as a result, he looks like a massive heel. The audience bristles with indignation to hear our hero falsely accused, but we also know Baxter's actions *are* wrong and he does deserve criticism, even if it's misdirected.

This irony is compounded when Baxter's boss, Sheldrake, jilts his mistress and she attempts suicide in Baxter's apartment. When the doctor comes over to help, Baxter covers for Sheldrake and claims that *he* jilted her. As the doctor's criticisms get more severe, Baxter must totally adopt the persona of his boss, quoting Sheldrake's dismissals of her as if they were his own.

This attempt to identify with his boss has the opposite effect on Baxter: It forces him to finally realize just how despicable Sheldrake is. Baxter has to become what he fears, which shows him what he really wants to be. It also results in the advice he most needs to hear, even if he hears it for the wrong reason: "Be a mensch."

Imagine a different version of this scene: Baxter truthfully explains the situation, and the doctor sympathetically suggests that Baxter should stand up to his terrible boss. That would be far less powerful.

The misunderstanding in *Captain America* is not ironic and tests the audience's patience. The many misunderstandings in *The Apartment* are wickedly ironic, juicing every scene with additional layers of meaning.

☑ Are previously asked questions answered and new questions posed?

Which questions will be answered and which new questions will be asked? Often the first question you're answering is the one posed, explicitly or implicitly, by the last shot of the previous scene. But if you want to move the plot forward, you'll reach back and answer other outstanding questions as well, and then ask some new ones.

The most obvious way to do this is to have the character ask an unanswered question out loud ("How could he be murdered in a locked room?"), but questions can also be posed implicitly (*Whose point of view is this?*). Cutting to a new character always implies a question (*Who is this person? Are they important?*). Showing a mysterious action works, too (*What's this character trying to do?*).

In a movie like the 2001 version of *Ocean's Eleven*, sometimes we know what the heroes are doing and the question we ask is, "Will it work?" Other times we don't, and our question becomes, "What are they up to?" Usually, the next scene answers these questions, but sometimes we don't get an answer until the end, when we can finally see the full picture.

Of course, if you put too many enigmatic scenes in a row, you'll lose your audience. Look no further than the terrible sequel, *Ocean's Twelve*. The audience quickly realizes they'll never be able to follow what's going on, so they stop trying and sit there bored for two hours, waiting for the filmmakers to reveal how smart they are.

But if you have too many scenes that just set up questions and knock 'em down, then the story will seem plodding and episodic, and it won't build a larger narrative. So you have to mix quick payoffs with longer mysteries.

☑ Does the scene cut out early on a question?

I already mentioned the possibility of chopping out the first two lines of scenes and chopping out some of the middle as well. While you're at it, why not chop out the last two lines of every scene? These lines wrap up the events and set the stage for the next progression, but you don't want that, either. Instead, just yank the audience out of this scene and into the next at the earliest possible moment.

Whenever you can, end on a question and have the circumstances of the next scene instantly answer that question. Don't have the characters discuss what they're going to do next; just have one ask, "What can we do now?" and cut to a shot that answers the question. "You're losing in the polls. What do you intend to do about it?" Cut to the candidate knocking on doors in a sketchy neighborhood.

This is a great way to trim unnecessary dialogue. You don't need to show the hero answer the question and then consider his next move. Just let the transition answer the question. The same trick even works for crosscutting between different characters. "What else could go wrong?" Cut to the villain's office.

Perhaps the question at the end of the scene is answered by the circumstances of the next scene. Perhaps it goes unanswered for now and becomes a mysterious undercurrent. Either way, we are propelled out of the scene before we have a chance to "put a button" on what's happened.

Every scene should have its own beginning, middle, and end, but that ending should usually be a cliff-hanger. You don't want to waste valuable time watching your characters pause to process what's happened, much less what it might mean, because your story will suddenly go slack.

☑ *Is the audience left with a growing hope and/or fear of what might happen next?*

Usually the question that ends the scene is a practical one that's instantly answered by the circumstances of the next. But you should keep your audience looking *further* ahead, breathlessly wondering how the events they've just witnessed will affect the rest of the story.

If your scene has pushed both the outer and inner journey forward, then the audience will be left with more and/or different hopes and fears. By now, their initial hopes for what the hero might accomplish in this scene have been gratified or dashed, resulting in a surge of hope or a deepening dread (and sometimes both). For example:

- I'm excited by the romantic potential of the person the hero just met.
- I'm scared by this villain scene and increasingly tense about what will happen when the villain collides with the hero.
- I'm becoming confident that the hero's plan will work.
- I can see what the heroes can't see, and I'm dreading the consequences of their limited perspective.
- I'm rooting for what the hero is doing, but I'm also dreading the inevitable consequences of this action.

A scene can be very well written, but if it comes to its own self-sufficient ending and tries to create its own meaning rather than propel the audience toward future events, then it can still hurt the overall story.

Most writers spend too much time looking at the big picture and not enough time down in the mines doing the nitty-gritty of scene work. If you can master this skill, you'll be way ahead of the game.

DRAFTING ELECTRIC DIALOGUE

WHAT IS DIALOGUE?

Dialogue brings your story to life. In our heads, we are all great heroes, filled with deep thoughts and profound insights, but when we actually open our mouths, we discover those insights are never as impressive as we thought. Only our spoken words, pitted against worthy opponents, reveal who we really are and what we really represent. They force us to go *on the record*, determining whether we're as persuasive or clever as we imagine ourselves to be.

Dialogue is how we reveal what we want, both intentionally and unintentionally, and it's our best tool for achieving our goals, *if* we can find a way to out-talk our opponents. That pitched contest is at the heart of all dramatic storytelling.

MISCONCEPTIONS ABOUT DIALOGUE

MISCONCEPTION: Well-written fictional characters should speak just like real people.

AU CONTRAIRE: Fictional dialogue should mirror the language and syntax of real people with startling accuracy, but characters should be more *concise* and have more *personality* than real people.

Many writers get this backward. When they try to write realistic dialogue, they simply write the same old phony and clichéd syntax except with a lot of extra hemming and hawing and trailing off. In other words, they make it less concise. This is wrong on both counts. Audiences have very little patience for stammering, no matter how realistic it is, and they also have no patience at all for unrealistic sentence structures.

Yet your dialogue must *seem* realistic. In fact, it should seem *startlingly* realistic. The way to do this is not to imitate the inarticulate meandering of real talk but to imitate the unique sentence structure this type of character would use.

And *please* don't attempt to capture the dialect of real speech. If you find yourself tempted to spell out a character's pronunciation to indicate he comes from a certain culture or region, stop. Instead, try to indicate that subculture or region through culturally specific sentence structure. For example, instead of having a British cabbie say "'At's right!" have him say, "Too right." It's a writer's job to capture unique syntax, *not* pronunciation.

> **MISCONCEPTION:** You can learn to write dialogue by watching great plays, movies, and television.
>
> **AU CONTRAIRE:** All fictional dialogue is abstracted from real life, and any imitation of that dialogue will be an abstraction of an abstraction. Writers must constantly listen to *real* language and then learn to boil it down to its purest essence.

Chicago journalists Charles MacArthur and Ben Hecht broke into playwriting with a newspaper-themed play called *The Front Page*. MacArthur then went to Hollywood to tackle the challenge of writing dialogue for movies, which had just added sound. He soon sent a telegraph back to his old writing partner: "Come quick, millions are to be grabbed out here, and your only competition is idiots. Don't let this get around." (Sometimes this quote is attributed to Hecht and sometimes to Herman Mankiewicz, but you get the idea.)

Of course, the other would-be screenwriters of the time weren't *really* idiots; they just didn't have the superior skills that journalists like MacArthur and Hecht had spent a lifetime mastering.

Journalists learn to write on the job, where the hectic environment and cheap wages ensure they can screw up every once in a while without getting fired. They send that work out the door every day no matter what and move on to the next story, which gives them a lot of practice and a good work ethic. But there are two more things journalists do that make them great dialogue writers:

- They transcribe hundreds of hours of actual dialogue, spoken by all types of people, about life-or-death situations. When it comes time to write fiction, they don't have to imagine what a poor man might say on his way to the gallows. They just have to check their notes.
- But the most important skill of all is learned *after* they transcribe all that dialogue, because they have to take the actual conversation and *cut it down*.

Hecht's collaborator on the great spy movie *Notorious*, Alfred Hitchcock, summed up this skill: "Drama is life with the dull bits cut out." That's a somewhat fanciful description of fiction, but it's *literally* true of journalism. A newspaper story is everything that happened *except* the dull bits.

Writing with verisimilitude is tremendously hard, and once you craft a conversation that captures the feel of real life, it's tempting to pat yourself on the back and call it a day. But your job is only half finished: You need to cut down the scene to just the good stuff.

This doesn't mean cutting down a scene to *just* its essential information. You should leave in the essential information and the moments that have a lot of character. Even entertainment journalists master this skill. This was driven home for me when I read an *Entertainment Weekly* preview issue with short sidebar interviews with various movie stars. When you read something like this, it doesn't occur to you that each profile is chopped down from a larger interview.

Presumably, each uncut interview began with "Hi, how are you?" which got a bland response, so that question-and-response simply got cut. In the print version, only one of the interviews includes that question and answer:

EW: Hi, how are you?

Will Smith: Man, I am so good, it's almost a damn shame (laughs).

In that one case, they leave the question and answer in because it's packed with *personality*. Even if you'd never seen a Will Smith movie, you'd fall in love with the guy right there. Journalists become great fiction writers because they know how to hit us with a surgical strike of personality and snip out the rest.

There are many ways fiction writers can imitate journalists. Anybody is allowed to go to court and transcribe proceedings, and you can also do ride-alongs with cops and detectives. It won't take long to log a lot of real-life details nobody's ever seen on TV.

But if you only want to transcribe a lot of real dialogue, there's a way to do that without ever leaving your couch. If you have digital cable, you may never have checked out channels 101 through 200. They tend to be oddball sister networks to those in the lower one hundred. And they burn through a ton of content, so they're kind of a gold mine for transcription.

Reality shows on the lower channels tend to be overly scripted. Don't try to copy the dialogue from a show like *Celebrity Rehab*, because it was probably written by a scriptwriter. But up in nosebleed channels, they can't afford to script their reality shows. They actually point a camera and let people talk.

Writing about war? The Military Channel has shows where they cut together actual combat footage in which all of the soldiers are wearing head-cams with microphones. It used to be that you had to put yourself in danger as a war correspondent to hear this sort of stuff—and you couldn't rewind to make sure you got everything.

Writing a cop drama? Well, The Biography Channel has a quality show called *The Interrogators* that consists of fly-on-wall footage of police interrogations. I've learned a lot about dialogue from transcribing episodes of that show.

Even on the more popular channels, there are shows less scripted than others. If you're writing about young people, stay away from shows like *Jersey Shore*, but check out *True Life*, which seems to show genuine, unprocessed teen talk.

So, good news: These days anybody can figure out how to write dialogue as well as a journalist without ever leaving the couch. You just need to be willing to transcribe reality television.

> **MISCONCEPTION:** Ironic dialogue is sarcastic dialogue.
>
> **AU CONTRAIRE:** There are many types of ironic dialogue. Some, such as sarcasm, are intentional, and others are unintentional.

Sarcastic dialogue uses intentionally disingenuous phrasing to highlight the hypocrisy of a situation. We've all known lots of sarcastic people, so this type of dialogue is certainly true to life. It can be a strong element of a character's voice, but it's important to remember that this sort of *intentional* irony is not going to create the same sort of meaning as *unintentional* irony.

The audience prefers to see what the characters can't: We want to be one small step removed from the story, seeing some things they miss. By contrast, we want the characters themselves to be in it, not outside of it. Sarcastic characters should only *think* they see the full irony of their situation, but we see that they don't really get it. George Bailey in *It's a Wonderful Life* is a great sarcastic character, but he's unaware of the larger ironies of his life until Clarence the angel points them out.

Then there are times when characters **blatantly discuss irony**. This should almost always be avoided. Irony should be the air your characters breathe, but they shouldn't be aware of it. Whenever characters talk about how ironic something is, the audience groans.

Here's a particularly atrocious example of blatantly discussed irony: Bette Davis followed up her big comeback, *All About Eve*, with a very similar role, but this time the results were disastrous. In *The Star*, she plays a washed-up ex-starlet who tries to settle for a down-to-earth longshoreman played by Sterling Hayden. Eventually, the grubbiness of her new life causes her to snap, and she smashes a store display to steal a bottle of expensive perfume. The result is one of the worst scenes ever written: When Hayden comes home, Davis confesses her impetuous crime and hands the unused perfume bottle over to him.

He sternly lectures her, but when she breaks down crying, he has no choice but to comfort her. He finally opens the bottle and says she might as well try some on, but they're surprised to discover they can't smell anything. The display bottle was just a prop. This causes Hayden to wisely opine, "You thought you had a bottle of the world's most expensive perfume, but it was just colored water. [Dramatic Pause] That's just like your life."

No, no it isn't. When irony is openly discussed, it withers on the vine. If your audience hears it, they won't feel it.

There are other types of unintentional ironic dialogue more useful to writers. The first is **an ironic contrast between what the character says (or does) and what the audience knows.** (This is sometimes referred to as "dramatic irony," but given how many types of irony we're throwing around, I find that term imprecise.)

This type of irony might occur because we know something that *no* character in the story does. The first episode of the fifth season of *24* has a very funny line from the first lady, who is trying to reassure her husband: "We just have to make it through today and we'll be fine." By that point, *24* fans knew a lot of crises could fit into one day.

Or, it can be even more ironic if we share knowledge with *one* scene partner but not the others. Look at the first three seasons of *Lost*. In each episode, we *see* a character's painful memories flood over him through a series of flashbacks, which are ironically juxtaposed against a painful dilemma that same character now has to face on the island. But *only we* know how these emotions affect his ultimate decisions, because he never shares his conflicted feelings with fellow islanders. Hurley never sits down with Jack and says, "You know, what happened today reminded me of something that happened several years ago, and now I think I have a better understanding of what this all means. If you'll hear me out …"

We see how his past experiences influence his current actions, and the episode is more meaningful for *us* because these actions ironically contrast with the current events. But Hurley isn't necessarily able to process the meaning of that irony, and if he does, he keeps it to himself.

The second type of unintentionally ironic dialogue is any **ironic contrast between word and deed**. If you want to reveal emotional baggage, then find an active and ironic way to do so instead of having your characters reveal their own baggage to others. Characters should rarely speak perceptively about their own feelings, especially to people they don't trust. In real life, we don't understand our own feelings, and even when we *think* we understand them, we will almost always lie about them if asked.

> "Do you like that boy?"
> "No!"

> "Are you still in love with your ex-wife?"
> "No!"

> "Do you feel appreciated by your grown children?"
> "Of course I do. What a silly question!"

Yes, you want to reveal your characters' complex emotions, but the one thing you're not allowed to do is have them explain those complex emotions to their friends (or, for that matter, their enemies!). Your characters shouldn't do that because we don't do that in real life.

So how do we reveal our feelings? When our mouths lie about our feelings, our body language and actions betray us. Make your characters reveal emotion through *behavior*. It's unlikely that a character would baldly state, "I want to stay a kid forever." Instead, have the character ask, "Why won't you treat me like a grown-up?" while wearing Spider-Man pajamas, or cutting the crusts off a sandwich, or sticking gum under the table.

Unity of word and action is not ironic. If word and action match, then you, as author, aren't showing any powers of observation. The audience need not even pay attention to the visuals you're creating, because the character is simply telling us what's going on. If the audience is told to believe what your characters say, then there's no way to *interact* with your story.

Your audience wants to play sleuth. They want to make their own observations about your characters instead of being forced to listen to and accept the characters' observations about themselves. Stories thrive on tension, both external and internal, including the tension between what people say and what they mean.

> **MISCONCEPTION:** When writing comedic dialogue, you should ask yourself, "What's the funniest thing this character could say?"
>
> **AU CONTRAIRE:** You should ask, "What's the funniest thing this character *would* say?"

One of the reasons writing comedy is so hard is that you need to serve two sometimes opposing goals: You want everything to be as funny as possible, but you also want everybody to stay in character. You quickly realize you can't always use the funniest possible line or action. Instead you should limit yourself to the funniest line or action *this character* would say or do *in this situation*.

On *How I Met Your Mother*, if the writers came up with a funny Barney joke but he wasn't in the scene, they had to resist the temptation to give that line to Ted, who wouldn't naturally say it. (The worst possible solution is to give a Barney line to Ted and then have Ted say something like, "Sorry, Barney's not here and somebody had to say it!" Ugh. Do not do this.)

Bridesmaids has a wonderful ensemble of actresses, and the script features strong character arcs for four of the six ladies in the bridal party. As for the other two, Ellie Kemper and Wendi McLendon-Covey, they have a lot of funny lines but don't really get storylines of their own. The proof that moviemakers aren't sure what to do with them is in the airplane scene. They have a funny conversation about their very different marriages, but the writers didn't seem to know how to end it, so they have the two women suddenly kiss.

It gets a big laugh, but it really doesn't come from character, and it doesn't get paid off later. In an otherwise rock-solid movie, it's an example of choosing a quick laugh over character building, which isn't the best choice.

> **MISCONCEPTION:** Every member of an ensemble should be well rounded and three-dimensional.
>
> **AU CONTRAIRE:** It is equally valid to create a polarized ensemble.

I think that this is the biggest misconception about dialogue, so we'll spend some time on it.

It always baffled me when fans of *Star Trek: The Next Generation* criticized the original *Star Trek* for having one-dimensional characters. It seemed to me that any comparison between the two shows made it obvious why writers might *want* to create extreme characters: It was never meant to be a realistic show about outer space but rather a *symbolic* show about *inner* space.

Every overheated argument amongst the crew on that show is an externalized version of an internal debate, with the main characters representing polarized personifications of the voices we all carry around in our heads. Spock is all head, McCoy is all heart, and Kirk is all gut.

Essentially they are three divided parts of one human, and their debates are supposed to resemble the *internal* debates that occur within one person, not the external debates that happen between multiple people. And, of course, many of the planets they visit are metaphors for real-life emotional challenges, so each episode is a metaphor for the debate within a person when confronted with that moral dilemma.

Let's look at a typical episode that happens to be a favorite of mine, "A Taste of Armageddon": The Enterprise discovers two planets that regularly launch virtual attacks on each other, then march themselves into death chambers when their computer tells them they would have died in the attack had it been real. This obviously represents a basic human dilemma: Should we make warfare more or less civilized?

When Kirk, Spock, and McCoy discuss this very metaphorical situation, they do so from their extreme points of view. In doing so, they re-create the debate we all have in our heads about these sorts of dilemmas.

This is a perfectly valid form of drama. Those who look at a show like *Star Trek* and say, "That's bad dialogue because they're not three-dimensional!" are totally missing the point.

Even though some of them worked on both shows, it seems like the creators of *Star Trek: The Next Generation* were embarrassed by the original. They felt Kirk, Spock, and McCoy had personalities that were too extreme and unbecoming for the dignity of the mission. To remedy this, the later show has quiet, thoughtful career officers in charge. Sure enough, it's less embarrassing to watch with a nonfan in the room, but it's also far less memorable. We're almost certainly never going to see any attempts to relaunch this cast with new actors, as they did with the original trio.

The biggest problem is that the new show is far less *volatile*. The original polarized personalities of Kirk and Spock ensured a lot of explosive conflicts, but on the later show, Captain Picard and First Officer Riker rarely disagree on anything. The later show is lucky to have a wonderfully charismatic actor playing Picard (Patrick Stewart), but the actor playing Riker (Jonathan Frakes) never makes his limp rag doll of a character come alive, and the scripts do him no favors. Riker is simply too risk averse to create any sparks with Picard or anybody else.

As the show progresses, Riker gradually diminishes in importance in favor of two minor *polarized* characters: Data the android is all head, and Worf the Klingon is all gut. Scripts based around these characters are far more interesting than scripts featuring the first officer.

Clearly there are sometimes good reasons to create characters who are *not* three-dimensional, so let's dig deeper.

THREE-WAY HEAD-HEART-GUT POLARIZATION. The idea of dividing consciousness into three separate aspects is nothing new. Socrates called these divisions reason, spirit, and appetite; Freud called them ego, superego, and id. I prefer to use terms that make it clear these three parts make up one complete human being: head, heart, and gut.

Let's look at the elements often associated with each (though some of these are based on gender, regional, or ethnic stereotypes writers might prefer to avoid today):

- **HEAD:** These characters correspond to Plato's reason or Freud's ego. They often use phrases like "I think" and "This is a bad idea." They tend to be smart, analytical, and/or unemotional. They're often stick-in-the-muds who talk a lot and are overly focused on odds. They can be scientists, professors, or father figures and are frequently depicted as Jewish (Spock, Egon in *Ghostbusters*, etc.)
- **HEART:** These characters correspond to Plato's spirit and Freud's superego. They often use phrases such as "I feel" and "Who will get hurt?" They tend to be emotional, merciful, caring, sensitive, and worried about human consequences. They're often listeners, doctors, and mother figures and are frequently Southern and/or rural (Dr. McCoy, Kenneth on *30 Rock*, Woody on *Cheers*, etc.).
- **GUT:** These characters correspond to Plato's appetite, and Freud's id. They often use phrases such as "I want" and "Wouldn't it be fun?" They tend to be honest, impulsive, hungry, horny, boastful, sometimes cowardly, and self-interested. They're often "the child" of the group.

Once you see the natural phenomenon of head-heart-gut polarization, you'll start spotting it everywhere.

- In *Tintin* comics, Tintin is heart, Captain Haddock is gut, and Professor Calculus is head. Haddock and Calculus were each added for the purpose of individual stories, but once they are introduced, they clearly "complete" the character Tintin, and so writer/artist Hergé had to come up with excuses to add them to every story from that point on.
- *Law and Order* had constant cast changes, but if we take one sample season, we see that each half of the show divides accordingly: On the "Law" side, Van Buren is head, Briscoe is heart, and Logan is gut, and on the "Order" side, Schiff is head, Kincaid is heart, and McCoy is gut.

ONE-PLUS-THREE POLARIZATION: A THREE-DIMENSIONAL HERO WITH HEAD, HEART, AND GUT ADVISORS. There's an early *House* episode in which the titular doctor is stuck on a plane treating a very sick passenger, but he finds he can't think clearly anymore without the chatter of his assistants in the background. To crack the case, House demands that three of his fellow passengers act out the personalities of his three interns. He needs one to be skeptical, another to be morally outraged, and a third to be friendly. House is basically admitting that his interns have become the externalized versions of his own head, heart, and gut, and he can't function without them.

Dr. House had come to the same conclusion that many dramatists do—it's easier to work out a problem if you create a dialogue of extreme points of view.

But you'll notice that *House* is different from *Star Trek*. In *Star Trek*, all three heroes are polarized with no one to mediate between them. Dr. House, on the other hand, is more of a fully rounded character, capable of having head, heart, *and* gut, but his three assistants are polarized. He relies on them to give him extreme points of view so he can choose which will be more useful in a situation.

This sort of one-plus-three polarization is also quite common:

- The most classical example of this dynamic is found in *The Wizard of Oz*. Dorothy is three-dimensional, but she also has three advisors who are all head (the Scarecrow, although, like the others, he insists otherwise), all heart (the Tin Woodsman), and all gut (the Cowardly Lion).
- HBO has made the same show twice: a three-dimensional New York essayist writes about the post-feminist woes of her generation, taking her examples from her three friends: a naïve romantic, a promiscuous risk taker, and the smart, responsible one who gets frustrated by the boring men she gets stuck with. On *Sex and the City*, Carrie is three-dimensional, Miranda is head, Charlotte is heart, and Samantha is gut. On *Girls*, Hannah is three-dimensional, Marnie is head, Shoshanna is heart, and Jessa is gut.

FOUR- AND FIVE-WAY POLARIZATION. Gut usually combines stomach (gluttony), spleen (hostility), and cockiness (arrogance or lust), but these are sometimes broken down in four- or five-way polarization:

- The *Fantastic Four* comic has four-way polarization: Reed is head, Sue is heart, Ben is stomach, and Johnny is cocky. (Note that the foursome, the product of working-class Jewish creators, upsets the traditional ethnic stereotyping, with the Jewish character as a gut character for once, not the head.)
- *The Simpsons* also has four-way polarization (and shows that the usual family divisions don't always apply): Lisa is head, Marge is heart, Homer is stomach, and Bart is cocky.
- *Cheers* has five-way polarization: Diane is head (along with, to a lesser degree, Cliff and Frasier), Coach is heart (later replaced by Woody), but gut is split up further—Norm is stomach (obviously), Carla is spleen, and Sam is cocky.
- The original cast of *CSI* has the same split: Grissom is head, Willows is heart, Stokes is gut, Brass is spleen, and Warrick is cocky.

A DIFFERENT FOUR-WAY POLARIZATION: ADDING "SPIRIT" BACK IN. Some polarized foursomes have a character who doesn't fit into head, heart, *or* gut, sitting instead *above* those three subdivisions. I define these religious or spiritual individuals as "spirit" characters. Let's look at four of these quartets:

- *The Three Musketeers* (which is actually about *four* musketeers) is split up this way: Athos is head, D'Artagnan is heart, Porthos is gut, and Aramis is spirit.
- Likewise, in *Star Wars*, Leia is head, Luke is heart, Han is gut, and Obi-Wan is spirit.
- In *Ghostbusters*, the original trio is a classic head-heart-gut: Egon is head (on the DVD commentary, Harold Ramis says he envisioned the character as "a new-age Spock"), Ray is heart (the same commentary says that "Ray is really the heart of the group"), and Venkman is clearly gut. But when the group adds a fourth member, he fits in just fine because he steps into the role of spirit, forcing the others to consider the biblical implications of their predicament. (One wouldn't normally think of Winston as the Obi-Wan of the group, but here we are!)

PARTIAL HEAD-HEART-GUT POLARIZATION. Some ensembles feature characters who have two of these aspects but lack the third. On the brilliant cartoon *Avatar: The Last Airbender,* the ensemble eventually expanded to four and then five, but let's limit ourselves to the three core members: the young master of the elements, Aang, and the brother-sister team, Sokka and Katara, who help him find his destiny. These three are *partially* polarized:

- Aang is usually heart or gut but almost never head.
- Sokka is usually head or gut but almost never heart.
- Katara is usually head or heart but almost never gut.

The show had some of the benefits of a classically polarized ensemble, such as heightened conflict and philosophical meaning, but it also allowed the characters to be more complex, to shift positions dynamically as situations escalated, and to grow and change over time. If you can pull it off, this is perhaps the best of all possible worlds.

UNIQUE FORMS OF TWO-WAY POLARIZATION. Frequently, you'll have two-way polarization, in which two characters form two halves of one human being.

- Even though *The Honeymooners* has a four-member ensemble, it's really just a two-way split, with the neighboring Nortons relegated to sidekick roles. The main duo, Ralph and Alice Kramden, respectively represent optimistic ambition and pessimistic practicality: two halves of one whole human being.
- On the *X-Files*, Scully and Mulder personify the divide between skepticism and belief.

This form of polarization, like all of the others, should not be biased toward either side. You should avoid the "Goofus and Gallant" problem, wherein one hero does everything wrong and the other does everything right, like on *The Mentalist*, where poor Robin Tunney has to be proven wrong week after week by Simon Baker.

Are we supposed to side with Scully or Mulder? We don't choose but instead appreciate them both equally. And how could we do otherwise? They represent the split halves of the human psyche, so to choose one over the other would deny half of our own humanity.

When you can create two or more personalities, each with a radically polarized point of view, and yet still allow each point of view to be equally valid, then your writing will automatically improve. You have discovered the ability to be not just all-powerful but also all-loving, like a good god should be. The dichotomy (or trichotomy) you've created will be a perpetual-motion machine, churning out honest dilemmas and genuine conflict for as long as your story lasts. But if you simply have a Goofus and a Gallant, your story will be inert, your dilemmas will be no-brainers, and your finale will be a foregone conclusion.

QUESTIONS TO ASK ABOUT DIALOGUE

So far, we've cleared up a lot of misconceptions about writing dialogue. Now let's examine the basic rules of crafting a conversation.

Your dialogue must be:

- **EMPATHETIC:** Is the dialogue true to human nature?
- **SPECIFIC:** Is the dialogue specific to this world and each personality?
- **HEIGHTENED:** Is the dialogue more pointed and dynamic than real talk?
- **STRATEGIC:** Are certain dialogue scenes withheld until necessary?

Empathetic

☑ *Does the writing demonstrate empathy for all of the characters?*

When you get started, writing can be really fun. There's nothing like that moment when the rush first hits you: You can do *anything*. This is *your* world. You can rewrite your high school years, but this time your crush abandons the in crowd and insists on going out with you! But, hey, why stop there? You can create your own kingdom! You can rewrite the laws of physics! You are a *god*.

But you soon realize that there's one big drawback to being a god: It's a lot of work, especially if you want to be a *good* god.

It's not enough to be all-powerful; a good god is expected to be all-knowing. That's a whole lot harder, and a lot less fun, but you haven't gotten to the worst part yet: The *great* gods tend to be all-loving. That's where the *really* hard work begins.

Try to love your villain as much as your hero. Try to love the messenger boy as much as the main character. Try to love not only your geeky heroine but also the snide cheerleader who picks on her. Think about how much Shakespeare loves *Hamlet*'s lowly gravedigger and pompous Polonius.

As you walk down the street, *practice* loving everybody. That Wall Streeter with slicked-back hair? Love him. That skulking drug dealer? Love him. That lovey-dovey mom cheering on her toddler's tantrum? Love her.

Ask yourself, *How did they end up here? Is this what they wanted to be?* Like you and everybody else, these people probably had hopes and dreams that were quashed long ago. Look at what is lacking in these people and ask, *Who took it away from them? What would they do if they could have it back?*

☑ Does each character, including the hero, have a limited perspective?

To write dialogue, you must attempt to understand *every* character with a speaking part in the little universe you've created and genuinely feel her wants and needs. To do that, you must understand what each character can and can't see about her world.

As you write, you will always be aware of the wider perspective only you can see, but as you craft each character's dialogue, you must deny yourself that wider view to adopt the limited perspective of that character.

And as you do so, you can't resent or belittle that limited perspective: Characters only know what they know, and that's fine. You don't need to educate or enlighten them to turn them into good people. A limited perspective should make each character more sympathetic, not less.

We all want our heroes to be relatable and their actions to be logical, but you can't take that too far. A character who's too logical becomes *generic*. Rather than make her overly logical, you should give her the freedom to do things only she would do.

This is the danger of overmotivation. It's easy to get a character to act "believably" if she has ten different reasons compelling her to do everything she does. But audiences lose interest in such heroes. The trick is to allow your hero to have reactions that are surprising but still understandable.

If we understand how circumstances have limited the hero's perspective, then it is possible to intensely empathize with her, even if we know that *we* would react differently.

In *Rise of the Planet of the Apes*, Caesar, the superintelligent ape, becomes deeply sympathetic to the audience, even when he declares war on the humans, because the audience can relate to him. In some scenes, they relate to him because he's clever and makes the decisions they would make, but in other scenes, they relate even more because they see that he has a limited perspective and makes poor decisions as a result.

At first, Caesar is raised as a human, but as he gets older, he instinctively becomes more violent. Eventually, his kindly owner (James Franco) has no choice but to put him in an ape sanctuary. The writers could have had Caesar expelled from his human home as a result of a false accusation or an irrational prejudice, but no: He genuinely freaked out and acted overly violent. *He* sees his exile as unjust, but *the audience* doesn't. And once he's there, the filmmakers make it clear that, though one of his human keepers is cruel, it's really not an evil institution, just a much colder place than what he's used to.

Since Caesar's banishment is his own fault—Franco did everything in his power to forestall it—and the keepers aren't overly evil, Caesar's exaggerated feeling of betrayal is all the more tragic. And because it's tragic, it's *universal*.

The Secrets of Story

Though Caesar has a genius IQ, it doesn't stop him from feeling a child's illogical sense of betrayal when he discovers the outside world is harsher than his childhood home and not everyone will treat him as well as those who raised him. We identify with this because we've all felt that illogical sense of betrayal. If Caesar had been truly, *totally* betrayed—if, for instance, the nice playroom the keepers had shown Franco was just a bait and switch, and Caesar had never been allowed to play there—then he would have more motivation to lead a revolt, but we would identify with him less.

We can see Caesar's sense of betrayal by Franco is unfounded, but we understand his limited perspective (and remember feeling the same way as children), so we intensely sympathize, far more than if Caesar had suffered a more exaggerated betrayal.

☑ Do the characters consciously and unconsciously prioritize their own wants rather than the wants of others?

Anybody who has done any work in sales, community organizing, or political campaigning has heard the same piece of advice: "The only way to motivate people is to appeal to their self-interest." This is universally true for both "good people" and "bad people," and if you create a story in which this isn't true, it will ring false. You need to motivate your villains and your heroes around their own self-interest.

Good characters must not be motivated by benevolence, and bad characters must not be motivated by malevolence. Characters, just like real people, only want what they want. In a story, it works like this:

- **GOOD:** A self-interested goal we empathize *and* sympathize with.
- **EVIL:** A self-interested goal we empathize with but *don't* sympathize with.

The audience should empathize with the desires that drive *every* character. The difference is, while we merely feel for your villain, we feel *and root* for your hero.

So why do we root for your heroes? Because we think they're the right people at the right time in the right place to bring about our desired outcome for this story, even if they're doing this for entirely self-ish reasons, which is fine. The fact is that, good or bad, people only want what they want.

Each episode of *Mad Men* on DVD has a fantastic commentary, usually featuring creator Matt Weiner, and they're all worth listening to. In one early episode, weaselly advertising executive Pete is stewing in his office, as usual, and boundary-breaking copywriter Peggy comes in to discuss a project. In his commentary, Weiner points out (paraphrasing here): "This is the point on most shows where she would ask, 'What's wrong?' as if people go around trying to solve each other's problems all the time."

But this isn't that sort of show. Peggy doesn't notice what's bothering Pete, even though she's probably the most sympathetic character on the show (and occasionally in love with him). People only want what they want, and that doesn't make them bad people. Unless your character is a parent or spouse (okay, let's get more specific, an *exceptionally caring* parent or spouse), she shouldn't become selflessly concerned with the emotional state of another character. Peggy isn't going to ask Pete what's wrong unless she *has* to act that way to get what *she* wants.

People only want what they want. That may sound terrible, but it's how life works—and it's probably for the best.

You, as the writer, know what every character's problem is, and so you want them to know it, too. The easiest way to do that is to have someone come into the room, size up the situation, and say, "Do you know what your problem is? Well, let me tell you. ..." But in real life, such conversations are not only uncommon, they're *unwelcome*.

On those rare occasions I do get armchair diagnoses from friends, they tend to be benign but unhelpful, because their friendship keeps them from perceiving my *true* faults. Ironically, the few times people have spontaneously told me what my problem was and actually got it *right*, they were people who hated my guts and never wanted to see me again. Needless to say, I wasn't happy to hear it, and I bit back each time. Only later did I sheepishly realize they had actually told me something I very much needed to hear.

Weiner's comment has ruined a lot of movies and TV shows for me. Every time someone walks into a room and helps the hero get to the heart of his problem, it now sets my teeth on edge. The ghostly voice of Weiner wafts up from the ether, providing a running commentary to everything I watch: "People only want what they want!"

This is true even in close relationships. Writers are often afraid to embrace this rule for fear that entirely self-interested characters will be unappealing, but the opposite is true. *Crazy Stupid Love* is a very appealing and good-natured romantic comedy, even though the characters could not be more self-motivated. The story centers on a divorcing couple, Cal and Tracy, but it's not just them: Their kids, their babysitter, their kids' teachers, *everybody* keeps getting walloped by their own unrequited, irrational desires, which they are helpless to ignore. Cal and Tracy have entire beautifully written conversations where each one *literally* doesn't listen to anything that the other says.

> **Cal:** Once I'm settled, I'll get the kids so they can see the place.
>
> **Tracy:** I think I'm having a midlife crisis maybe. Can women have midlife crises?
>
> **Cal:** Make sure the lawn gets enough water.
>
> **Tracy:** In the movies it's always men having them and buying ridiculous yellow Porsches, but I'm not a man and I really don't want a yellow Porsche—
>
> **Cal:** You have to fertilize once a month. Not twice a month, not once every two months.
>
> **Tracy:** We got married so young, Cal. And I'm forty-one. And that's so much older than I thought I'd be.
>
> **Cal:** The sprinklers turn off behind you.
>
> **Tracy:** And I got really upset with an umpire at Molly's T-ball game last month. ...

Tellingly, there are times when characters *try* to give each other selfless advice (such as the advice a local lothario gives Cal), but every time, it's hopelessly tainted by the advice giver's own frustrated desires and limited perspective.

For better or worse, the rule that "people only want what they want" applies even to friendships and relationships. If you and I are friends, it doesn't mean we want the same things from each other. I like you for certain reasons, and you like me for your own reasons. Sometimes our interests will actually be the same (we both love karaoke), but sometimes our interests will merely be *symbiotic*, and that can work, too. Maybe I like to talk and you like to listen, or I like to take and you like to give. Maybe I want a hunting buddy and you just want a drinking buddy. Or maybe we both expect things from each other the other won't give, and the friendship is ultimately doomed.

☑ *Are the characters resistant to openly admitting their feelings to others and even themselves?*

In chapter six, we talked about how characters are cagey about their feelings when pursuing their agenda. This should generally be true of all dialogue. We also established that it's far better to have characters accidentally betray their feelings (through behavior or protesting too much) than to tell anybody what's actually going on in their head or heart.

Resist the urge to have characters say they dislike each other. That generates some quick and easy conflict, but it dissipates more conflict than it creates. The longer you can keep that conflict suppressed, the more scenes it can fuel.

Likewise, resist the urge to have characters say, "I love you." Once you've got the audience rooting for the hero and heroine to get together, you might assume they now want to see the characters start gushing about their true feelings, but you'd be wrong.

Audiences have major commitment issues. In the dark, we all crave emotionally withholding lovers. Sure, we want to see two people get together, but first we want them to *want to* get together for a good long while. After all, *wanting* love is a far more universal emotion than *having* it.

Ideally the hero and heroine will never say, "I love you," because it's so much more appealing to watch them dance around the issue. But if they have to, the key thing is to make sure there's a healthy delay. Getting hit with the *L*-bomb too soon in a story feels just as alienating and manipulative as it does in real life.

Of course, the exception is when heroes suddenly blurt out, "I love you," as soon as they meet somebody special—and then start kicking themselves, which is endearing because the entire point is to highlight that it's a mistake.

Some examples:

- Patrick Swayze's character in *Ghost* almost loses Demi Moore because he doesn't realize she finds "ditto" more convincing than an actual "I love you."
- Harrison Ford, in *The Empire Strikes Back*, is smart enough to realize that the way to make both Leia and the audience melt is to answer her "I love you" with "I know" rather than the scripted line.
- Likewise, we love it when Shirley MacLaine simply responds to "I love you" by saying, "Shut up and deal" at the end of *The Apartment*.

Call us masochists, but we demand that our fictional lovers leave us wanting more.

☑ Do the characters avoid saying things they wouldn't say and doing things they wouldn't do?

If you've done a good job creating your characters, they will speak to you. Instead of handcrafting their dialogue, it's always better to just listen to what they *want* to say. But this can be a problem. Sometimes, they refuse to push the plot in the direction you want it to go.

When characters suddenly say, "I won't do that," what do you do? You have five options:

1. **IGNORE THEIR PROTESTS, AND MAKE THEM DO IT ANYWAY.** The problem is, they may never speak to you again, which means from then on, you'll need to put every word in their mouths, and they'll stop being real characters and become mere plot devices.

2. **ASK THEM WHAT THEY WANT TO DO INSTEAD, AND LET THEM DO THAT.** This requires saying goodbye to the rest of your perfect outline and letting your character lead you blindly forward. The problem here is, if left to their own devices, most characters will play it safe and minimize conflict.
3. **GIVE THAT ACTION TO A DIFFERENT CHARACTER WHO *IS* WILLING TO DO IT.** The problem here is that taking the focus off the hero too often might weaken the audience's identification.
4. **ARRANGE PLOT CONTRIVANCES THAT TAKE AWAY ALL OF THEIR OTHER OPTIONS** until they *choose* to do exactly what you want them to do. This is usually the best option.
5. **FUNDAMENTALLY RECONCEIVE THE CHARACTER** when all else fails.

Let's look at the part in Mark Twain's *The Adventures of Huckleberry Finn* where Huck and runaway slave Jim accidentally drift past Cairo and realize they can no longer head back north on the river. Twain's outline said they were supposed to continue south anyway, but to his surprise Jim objected and, quite sensibly, said that he wouldn't stay on that raft no matter how strongly Twain ordered him to. Twain gave up and abandoned the novel for seven years. Finally he decided to simply overrule Jim and force him to do it anyway. Sure enough, Jim refused to speak much after that, so Twain had to move the story away from him, which severely compromised this otherwise great novel.

You *have* to listen to your characters and let them object. When I write thrillers, this is a constant problem. My characters always want to call the police and shut down the entire story. This is especially tricky when I'm doing an adaptation for hire, where the producers and I carefully construct a very specific outline before I start writing. When my heroes object, I can't let them take the story in a new direction, so instead, I go back and preemptively preclude all of the safe options until the characters are forced to step down the dangerous path the producers have demanded.

But never forget this is a sign you're doing it right. Don't force your characters to create the drama by acting stupid. Trap your characters into dramatic situations, and then let them fight their way out of it as logically as they can. Any time the characters create the problem by doing something stupid, the audience will be enraged.

The Kevin Spacey and Samuel L. Jackson thriller *The Negotiator* gets this all wrong. Seeing the trailer, I was suitably intrigued: How would a top hostage negotiator get backed into taking hostages—the one thing he knows not to do! But the actual movie is ludicrous: They are in so much of a hurry to get to the premise that taking hostages isn't the negotiator's last resort but his first.

Surely this was a case where the character was shouting in the writer's ear: "I WOULDN'T DO THIS!" Surely the character was dreaming up all sorts of other things to try first, but the writer chose to ignore his character and forced him to create the most exciting situation right away. As a result, a potentially interesting story is ruined. If the writers had methodically closed off every other option, it could have been thrilling.

When it comes to listening to your characters, it's also important not to make them say things they wouldn't say out loud. It's an eternal conundrum: You need to reveal background information to the audience through dialogue, but you don't want to force your characters to explain things they wouldn't actually explain, especially when it's something they really wouldn't want to talk about in the first place.

Spider-Man pulls this off well. The writers don't force Peter Parker to say, "By the way, I'm an orphan, and here's how my parents died …" because, in real life, orphans are reluctant to discuss it. Instead, when Norman Osborn tells him, "Your parents must be very proud," Peter looks a little pained when he responds, "Well, I live with my aunt and uncle, and they are proud."

This is how *actual* orphans talk. They dance around the issue. (Not coincidentally, this is how Peter can get away with being so mopey without losing our sympathy—because he has some self-respect. We only pity him because he doesn't ask for our pity.)

Likewise, people in the CIA don't say, "I'm in the CIA." They say, "I work for the government." People who go to Harvard often won't say,

"I go to Harvard," they'll say, "I go to college in Boston." For various reasons, there are certain things people are reluctant to come right out and say, so don't make them.

These evasions make for good dialogue, because one of two things will happen: Either the other person pushes for a straight-up answer, which creates conflict, or the other person figures it out and accepts it, which clues in the audience that we're supposed to figure it out, too. Luckily, audiences love the moment when they get to figure out something unsaid.

☑ Do the characters interrupt each other often?

I was talking to a big-time screenwriter who spent years writing and rewriting dozens of different drafts of his first hit script before it finally made it to the screen. In that time, he learned that screenwriters get completely different types of notes at each level of development.

1. First, junior execs give you nothing but plot logic and structure notes.
2. If you make it past them, you get to the studio heads, who only want it to be "tight," with a lot of setup and payoff.
3. If you make it past them, you get to the directors, who only care about tone and set pieces.
4. If you make it past them, you get to the true seat of power: the actors, who are the first and only people who care about the dialogue. First, they insist you cut out all the exposition. Then they want you to eliminate all that setup and payoff, which sounds phony. Then they want to eliminate not just the *complex* sentences but all the *complete* sentences.

Writers tend to get annoyed by this. Actors insist that no one they know speaks in complete sentences. Writers respond, "Oh yeah, maybe that's because all the people you know are *actors*. *My* friends speak in complete sentences all the time!" Of course, the actors can shoot right back, "That's because everybody *you* know is a *writer*. *Normal* people don't talk that way!"

Alas, I hate to betray my own side, but the actors are right. People, as a rule, don't listen to each other. Even when we try, we frequently hear only what we want to hear, not what the other person is actually saying. But the truth is, we rarely even *try* to listen carefully. Instead we generally do one of two things:

- Listen just long enough to guess at the gist of what the other person is saying and jump in to interrupt and push the conversation forward.
- Simply ignore what the other person is saying and wait for a chance to jump back in and continue what we were saying before *we* got interrupted.

When characters listen too much, it always rings false, unless they're exceptionally polite. Let them be human.

Specific

☑ *Does the dialogue capture the jargon and tradecraft of the profession and/or setting?*

As we discussed before, "write what you know" really means "write the emotions you know." But if you're *not* writing about a world you already understand, then you've got a lot of work to do before you start writing.

If you're not going to write about a brilliant but unappreciated writer (and please don't), then you're going to be writing about people who do things you don't do. You'll need to learn as much as you can about these people—how to talk like them, think like them, party like them, and curse like them.

It's one thing to learn what a world is like, whether it's spies, cops, ballet dancers, or stock brokers, but it's another thing entirely to learn and reproduce the *jargon*. Read the pilots for *House*, *CSI*, and *The West Wing*, and the number one thing that stands out is how much *jargon* they contain, to the extent that the average reader can't understand a huge amount of the dialogue. Wouldn't that alienate the audience? Nope, it turns out audiences *love* jargon. It makes them feel like the characters (and the writers) know what they're talking about.

So how do you learn all this stuff? My first step is always to read some memoirs by people in the specific profession, but be forewarned that the language in memoirs gets cleaned up. It's great to find a reality show or documentary about these sorts of people and transcribe how they talk in the heat of the moment, when they've forgotten the cameras are on.

Another aspect of jargon is the need to understand the *subcultures* within the world you're writing about and the internecine conflicts between them. Every world has subcultures that feud with other subcultures. If you're researching this world, you'll need to really dig to uncover such things, because these squabbles are, for the most part, *not* in the memoirs, or they simply get glossed over. If they are mentioned at all, it's usually in passing, as the author will say something like, "I don't want to get sucked into the old X versus X debate, so ..."

That's the part to seize on and say, "Aha! That's the big divide nobody's talking about! I need to learn more about that!" Once you have the terms, you can simply Google them and discover uncensored message boards where they're actively debating this stuff amongst themselves, saying the things that they'd never say in their books, because they falsely perceive these boards to be private discussions with nobody listening in.

This is true of every profession or hobby I've ever researched. For stock brokers it was "the sell side versus the buy side." For rock climbers, it was "sport versus trad." For skaters it was "vertical versus street." For spies it was "analysis versus operations." For Afghanistan officers, it was "carnivores versus COINdinistas." Just dive in and don't come up for air until you've got a handle on it. Don't write a war story unless you know what sergeants tend to presume about captains, and vice versa.

In *The Departed*, the feds, the city cops, and the "Staties" all spew delightful fountains of contemptuous profanity at each other. I still have no idea what a "Statie" is (I can only infer that Massachusetts has some sort of statewide police force), but I don't have to. We don't understand *exactly* what's going on, but we can tell these people, like *all* people, have internecine conflicts that drive them crazy. And, paradoxically, because we've never heard this jargon before, it makes this world feel more real.

You can also go one step beyond jargon and learn the *tradecraft* of the profession. Mastering tradecraft dialogue is actually one of the most valuable and underrated skills a writer can have.

For writers-for-hire, this is the skill that gets you consistent adaptation/rewrite/ghostwriting work: If you're *the* writer who knows how to write about a particular world, then you get the first crack at *all* the projects set in that world. Aaron Sorkin can write politics in entertaining ways, so he's the go-to guy for a movie about a congressman, like *Charlie Wilson's War*.

This is one of the big reasons why networks love to hire show runners who learned their trade firsthand rather than spending their time getting writing degrees. *L.A. Law* creator David E. Kelley was a lawyer. The creator of the spy show *The Americans* is an ex-CIA officer. TV producers sometimes seem to assume that anyone can learn to write but that learning the tradecraft takes a lifetime.

Obviously, that's not true. Any writer can learn this stuff, but it does take a *lot* of work. Not only should you learn the details of your world inside and out (read the memoirs, watch the reality shows, hang out with the actual people), but you should also figure out how to package that tradecraft for an audience in an appealing way.

Screenwriter Ted Griffin was presumably never a con man, but he mastered the lingo and wrote a fantastic screenplay for the remake of *Ocean's Eleven* (and then became the go-to con/heist guy, so he was hired to adapt the novel *Matchstick Men* and rewrite *Tower Heist*). The secret of *Ocean's Eleven* is that it deftly moves back and forth amongst the following three different types of tradecraft writing:

COLORFUL BUT INCOMPREHENSIBLE CON MAN JARGON THAT'S NEVER EXPLAINED: "You'll need a Boesky, a Jim Brown, a Miss Daisy, two Jethros, a Leon Spinx, not to mention the biggest Ella Fitzgerald ever." Is this jargon real? Who cares? It sounds convincing, and that's all that matters. We're happy to be baffled, pressing our noses against the glass as we peek into the bizarre world.

NITTY-GRITTY DETAILS ABOUT THIS WORLD THAT *DO* GET EXPLAINED, such as the specific roles of each of the con men: "the bank," "the grease man," etc. These details open the doors and let us into this world, so we feel like we're really learning the inside dope.

INSIDE TIPS ABOUT THIS WORLD THAT ARE ALSO APPLICABLE TO THE LIFE OF THE VIEWER: This is the best kind of all. Audiences go crazy for it:

> Don't look up, they'll know you're lying. Don't look down, they'll know you have something to hide. Don't use three words when one will do. Don't shift your eyes. Look always at your mark, but don't stare. Be specific but not memorable. Be funny but don't make him laugh. He's gotta like you, and then forget you the moment you've left his sight.

Hearing this sort of tradecraft makes us feel like we can solve our own problems using the clandestine secrets we're learning.

Whether you're writing about cops, lawyers, spies, pirates, reporters, butchers, bakers, or candlestick makers, you should learn how to write all three types of tradecraft: pleasantly incomprehensible stuff, stuff that's fun to explain, and stuff that makes the audience feel smarter. Again, you want to read memoirs of those with similar worlds to your hero and look for neat little tricks that belong in each of these three categories.

☑ Are there additional characters with distinct metaphor families, default personality traits, and default argument strategies distinct from the hero's?

To review, chapter four establishes three key elements for giving your hero a distinct voice:

- **METAPHOR FAMILY:** the aspect of your characters' lives that determines which metaphors, curses, and exclamations they use. The source of this is usually their job, their home region, or their psychological state. More rarely, it's their career ambition or a hidden proclivity.
- **DEFAULT PERSONALITY TRAIT:** Characters grow and change throughout a story, and their moods can fluctuate wildly, even within each

scene, but whether they're happy or sad or regressed or enlightened, some aspects of their personalities will never change.

- **DEFAULT ARGUMENT TACTIC:** Characters should also have hardwired approaches to problem solving that they keep going back to, no matter how much smarter they get over the course of solving this problem.

This brings us to a tough question: How many members of your ensemble will have this level of definition? Just the top five characters? The top ten? The answer is, as many as you need to make it all seem real.

Even your minor characters need to have distinctive voices, or at least voices that are distinct from each other. In one episode of *Law and Order: Criminal Intent*, Detective Logan shows up at the scene of a bombing. A street cop tells him that the victim had a controversial past: "He was blackmailing a local newscaster." Logan nods sagely and asks, "Gay sex?" The cop responds, "Nope, call girl. Think Spitzer, not McGreevy."

Then, just two scenes later: Logan is in the lab talking to an explosives expert who points out that a bomb was both old-fashioned and cutting edge. The expert sums up by saying, "Think Tony Bennett, not Steve and Eydie."

These are two completely different characters in different places, using the same turn of phrase! That was a pretty ridiculous example, and somebody should have caught it and cut it (the show runner? the editor? the composer, even?). But it's actually very easy for writers to make this mistake. If you don't have time to give all of your characters their own personalities, then they're all going to have *your* personality. You should constantly reread your work and police for this.

Heightened

☑ *Is the dialogue more concise than real talk?*

Dialogue should be as realistic as possible, with two big exceptions: It should be more succinct and have more personality. The danger, of course, is that you'll accomplish this by giving every character the gift of sparkling, sophisticated banter, but that's not what I mean at all.

Instead, consider this exchange from the first *X-Men* movie, after Wolverine returns from fighting a shape-shifting villain:

> **Wolverine:** Easy, it's me.
>
> **Cyclops:** Prove it.
>
> **Wolverine:** (*thinks, then* …) You're a dick.
>
> **Cyclops:** (*thinks, then* …) Okay.

That is one of the few memorable moments in the movie, but the off-hand delivery of these three little words is enough to make Hugh Jackman a star and launch a franchise—and it's the opposite of sophisticated banter. Never write a page of banter when three words will do.

This also works for deeper dialogue in novels. Nobody was more famous for economy than Ernest Hemingway, and this abrupt exchange from *The Sun Also Rises* proves it:

> "Oh Jake," Brett said, "we could have had such a damned good time together."
>
> "Yes," I said. "Isn't it pretty to think so?"

☑ Does the dialogue have more personality than real talk?

I don't know about you, but I don't have enough personality to be a fictional character. For one thing, I have no pet names for my wife. On those rare occasions I feel it would be appropriate to tack an endearment onto the end of a sentence, I fall back on the old standbys like *sweetheart*, *darling*, or *baby*. But I'm not a fictional character. And the one thing you need to understand about fictional characters is that they have more personality than us.

When your characters use endearments, that's one more chance for you to give them a little more personality. Use something specific, something no one else in the story would say. Sometimes you can even find language that amplifies the keynotes of their personalities:

- Vince Vaughn in *Swingers* doesn't say, "You're awesome, dude!" like he probably would in real life. Instead, he says, "You're so money, and you don't even know it!" That's wonderfully specific, and it speaks to his predatory tendency to value people according to what they can do for him.
- In the great film noir *Scarlet Street*, when the sleazy lowlife played by Dan Duryea calls his girlfriend "lazy legs" and she loves it, we pretty much know everything we need to about both of them.

On the other hand, language quirks can also be a great way to cut *against* the grain of the other characteristics you've established and round out a character. When I wrote a script in which the villain was a hedge-fund asshole, my first instinct was to have him call his wife something crude like *sweet cheeks*, but then I decided I'd already rung that bell too often. But *sweetheart* was too generic, so I had him lovingly call his wife *sweet potato*. After all, this guy was a Wall Street shark now, but he'd worked his way up from a small town, so he should still have some of that cultural baggage.

In real life, we frequently converse in lazy clichés, but you must hold your characters to a higher standard because clichéd dialogue *disengages* your audience. When they read the line "I'll be home soon, Sweetheart," their eyes glaze over, but when the line is "I'll be home soon, Sharkface," then they have to stop and think about this person and this relationship.

Obviously, you can easily take this too far. Some writers tack a nickname onto the end of every sentence just to give their dialogue a feeling of rootin'-tootin' fun. But for those moments when you would *naturally* feel the need to use an endearment, don't be afraid to let your character show a little personality.

☑ Are there minimal commas in the dialogue?

To be far more concise *and* have more personality at the same time, cut out everything before or after your commas.

The fact is, almost all dialogue with commas sounds weaselly. Characters shouldn't preface things; they should just say them. So when characters answer questions, cut out every "yes" and "no." Compare these exchanges:

> "Are you going to the picnic?"
>> "No, I'm going to the bar."

> "Are you going to the picnic?"
>> "I'm going to the bar."

> "Do you love me?"
>> "No, but I need you."

> "Do you love me?"
>> "I need you."

> "Did you hear the news?"
>> "Yes, I'm so sorry."

> "Did you hear the news?"
>> "I'm so sorry."

> "Are you visiting Iowa?"
>> "Yes, we need the rural vote."

> "Are you visiting Iowa?"
>> "We need the rural vote."

Just lop off anything before a comma. I've gotten pretty good at this, but I still overuse "Well, I ..." and "Look, I ..." These are "change gear" words that allow characters to deflect or transition the conversation in the direction they want it to go, but you don't need them. Just let the character shift on the fly, even if it results in a little grinding of the gears.

For each of these, you may be thinking, *But then things might not be clear!* Good! Life isn't clear. Your goal should be to write dialogue with maximum personality and the minimum amount of clarity that you can get away with. The audience doesn't want you to hold their hand. They'd rather catch up. They want you to play hard to get so they can have the thrill of the chase.

☑ Do characters (excluding professors) speak without dependent clauses, conditionals, or parallel construction?

There are three types of sentences writers love but should never use in dialogue (unless the character is a professor or writer): dependent clauses, conditionals, and parallel construction. Let's tackle those one by one.

Real people avoid using dependent clauses when they speak, for good reasons:

- Our minds aren't quite fast enough to nest clauses on the fly.
- We know we're always about to be interrupted, so we lay out our thoughts one at a time, in case we don't get to finish. We do this to others, and we know they'll do it to us, so we speak with the *assumption* that we'll be interrupted. We know if we're interrupted in the middle of a dependent clause, our entire sentence will be meaningless.
- Even when we know for certain we *won't* be interrupted, such as when we're giving a speech, it sounds awkward to use dependent clauses. Rather than extemporaneous talk, it sounds like a prepared text.

Writers are used to seeing their words on a page, where dependent clauses can nest comfortably, which is why we're often shocked to hear how mealymouthed and wishy-washy our dialogue sounds when spoken out loud.

In the 2004 presidential race, linguists criticized John Kerry for using too many dependent clauses and praised George W. Bush for speaking simply, even though his faux-folksy speech patterns greatly annoyed the American intelligentsia. Kerry also got in trouble for speaking with too many conditionals. When speaking aloud, these sound like prevarication, which is inherently unsympathetic. If you say "If A and B, then C," that sounds weaselly. If, on the other hand you say, "C! Because A! Because B! C!" then you've basically said the same thing but sound more like a leader.

A third sentence structure that works well when written but not when spoken is parallel construction. On one episode of *The Blacklist*, James Spader is tracking down a killer using a dog hair from a crime scene, and he muses aloud to his henchman, "Dogs are not our whole life, but they do make some lives whole." Ugh.

It's a lot of fun to use that sort of parallel construction when you're writing something down, and it's fun to read. It creates a bit of additional meaning to take a turn of phrase and then turn it on its head, creating a "compare and contrast" moment and giving your language a little poetic lilt, but people just don't say that sort of thing out loud.

Once again, we don't set up elaborate constructions because of the fear that we won't be able to finish them. In real life, that exchange between Spader and his henchman would have gone something like this:

> **Spader:** Dogs are not our whole life, but—
>
> **Henchman:** —Yes they are. I love my dog.
>
> **Spader:** I know you do, but—
>
> **Henchman:** —There's no 'but' about it. He's my huggums-wuggums.
>
> **Spader:** I know, I know. He's a great dog. That was my whole point, asshole! If you hadn't *interrupted* me, I would have said, "But they do make some lives whole."
>
> **Henchman:** Oh, I see what you were trying to do: "whole life/life whole." That's cute. You should write greeting cards.
>
> **Spader:** Go to hell.

It's even worse when characters turn *each other's* phrases. On an episode of *Agents of SHIELD*, the "hacker" character confronts one of her fellow ex-revolutionaries who has betrayed the cause, and they have this exchange:

> **Hacker:** You've changed.

Ex-revolutionary: Good.

Hacker: I mean, you're not who you used to be.

Ex-revolutionary: You're not who I thought you were.

After that third line, I thought, *Why would he rephrase what he just said?* Then she said her line, and I just rolled my eyes: *Oh, he did it to set up her line.* One reason this sort of thing doesn't work is that people have different syntax. We build our sentences differently. It may be cute to turn someone's phrase, but it would come out all wrong if we actually tried it because we're not used to phrasing things that way.

While we're at it, let's tackle a similar problem: Never let characters extend *each other's* metaphors, either. In real life, when a husband and wife are extremely like-minded, we say they "finish each other's sentences." Why is this such a remarkable trait? *Because it's hard to do.* But you wouldn't know that from watching bad action movies, where people do it all the time.

I only saw the trailer of the action movie *Faster*, but it was all I needed to see. The trailer ends with a moment that's clearly from the end of the movie, when the revenge-seeker, played by Dwayne "The Rock" Johnson, has caught up to the slimy villain, played by Billy Bob Thornton. Looking defeated, Thornton laments, "I created my own hell." Johnson looms over him, growling back, "And I'm the demon that crawled up out of it."

How many things are wrong with this exchange?

- We'll overlook the first one—people don't tend to converse while beating each other up—because that's a well-established convention of the genre.
- But I still can't accept it when one character extends another character's metaphor. Sure, I'll buy that these characters may shout angry things at each other, but they're not going to listen closely to the other's figure of speech, accept that metaphor as a good way to sum up the situation, think of a way to twist that metaphor to address their own concerns, and then continue the other person's sentence, using the same general language and tone.

When you're confronting someone about something and he sums up the situation metaphorically, you're more likely to respond, "No, it's not like that at all, asshole." If he's speaking figuratively at a time like that, you'll be all the more tempted to respond in a more literal fashion, or, perhaps, nonverbally. Alas, there's only one language we all speak, and that's chin music.

You only have one brain, so it's natural to write each line as a continuation of the previous one, using the same language and continuing the same train of thought. But your characters all have different brains, and they have no interest in finishing each other's sentences— and they couldn't, even if they wanted to.

☑ Are the non-three-dimensional characters impartially polarized into head, heart, and gut?

I've already had a lot to say about the pros and cons of polarization in the misconceptions section of this chapter, but let's look at one final case study to see how you can use polarization without sacrificing realistic elements.

The book (and later movie) *Deliverance* is based on a real canoe trip the author James Dickey took with three other businessmen from Atlanta, with one big difference: In real life, the mountain folks who found the lost canoeists just gave them a nice meal and a lift back to town. (No good deed goes unpunished!) I know the true story because one of the men involved was a family friend. His name was Lewis, and he was the basis for the character Lew, played in the movie by Burt Reynolds.

In the first scene of the movie, Lew finds out that Bobby (Ned Beatty) is an insurance agent and snaps, "I've never been insured in my life. I don't believe in insurance. There's no risk!" When the real Lewis passed away recently, it turned out this was actually true: He owned a lot of property, but he had no insurance on any of it, to the chagrin of his family, who had to scramble to insure it all.

Anyone who knew the real Lewis and watches the movie can see that Dickey copied his friend's persona very faithfully. But the actor

Ronnie Cox, who played the character Drew, had this to say about Dickey:

> We used to joke about it, because the four characters are all these four aspects of Jim Dickey. There's a lot about him as that sort of "outdoors macho-man challenging everybody, and everything's a competition" in Burt's character. And there's the thoughtful, almost timid advertising man, the everyman that was Jon Voight's character at the beginning of the film. And then there's the buffoonish, klutzy Bobby. But then Jim Dickey was also a poet and a guitar player who loved to play music, and all of his artistic aspects were in Drew.

So which is it? Is Lew based on the real Lewis or on Dickey himself? There's no contradiction: It's both. It's always a good idea to base a character on someone you know, but that character must also be based on yourself, because you can look much deeper into your own heart. Lewis had the sort of larger-than-life personality that writers love to appropriate, but Dickey could not have written him well without finding part of Lewis in himself.

Deliverance has a classic, four-part polarization: head (Ed, played in the movie by Jon Voight), heart (Drew), stomach (Bobby), and cockiness (Lew). When you add them up, you get a complete human being, as Cox observed, but each character is *also* a believable human being in his own right, partially because each is *also* based on a real person.

The final product works as both an *inter*personal drama, creating a harrowing conflict between four believable characters, and an *intra*personal drama, dramatizing the internal debate a person goes through when faced with a traumatic situation. To do so, Dickey combined specific details from the lives of his friends (such as the real-life Lewis's adversity to buying insurance) with the polarized aspects of his own personality.

The results are tremendously powerful: We utterly believe in the reality of this situation, and yet we also feel the work has invaded our psyche and exposed our innermost fears and insecurities.

Strategic

☑ **Does the hero have at least one big "I understand you" moment with a love interest or primary emotional partner?**

We've all had the experience. You're sure you've met your perfect match. You rhapsodize for hours about everything that made you fall head over heels, but at the end, your friend just shrugs and says, "Are you kidding me?"

The problem, of course, is that your hormonal response is distorting your reality, and your cool-eyed friends are evaluating the shelf life of this new relationship dispassionately, asking, "Do these two have enough in common? Will they treat each other well? Do they need each other?"

It's great to capture the subjective experience of falling in love, of course, though novelists have a much better chance of doing that than screenwriters.

Screenwriters can try to cheat, like *West Side Story* did, by using subjective camera effects to capture Tony's besotted vision of Maria, but even back then, viewers just rolled their eyes. The camera eye is not the hero's eye, and we will always see more than he sees, no matter how much Vaseline you smear on the lens.

But in some ways, the screenwriter has the advantage, because a well-written story *in any medium* will capture both the subjective experience and an *objective* perspective on this relationship. Allow the audience to be both the besotted hero and the dubious friend.

So this is one case where you *don't* want to "write what you know." Don't trust your own distorted memories of love and/or heartbreak. Instead think back to your *friends'* relationships. Which relationships did you root for, and which infuriated you? Which ones endangered your friends, and which saved them? Most important, how did *you* know they were right for each other, maybe even before *they* did?

Whether your first draft is one huge love story or the romance is a minor element, once you've gotten some notes, you may be shocked to discover that nobody sees what you see in the love interest.

The reason so many love stories fail, and so many lame love interests drag stories down, is that the writers have failed to add "I understand you" scenes. I'm a huge Harry Potter fan, but the series has a big flaw: Nowhere in the course of these seven massive books does Rowling ever put in a single "I understand you" scene between *either* of the main couples: Harry/Ginny or Ron/Hermione! Ginny is especially thin; she's basically just "the girlfriend." Hermione is the one who understands Harry, and they should have ended up together. Finally, years later, Rowling acknowledged her mistake in an interview with *Wonderland* magazine.

> I wrote the Hermione/Ron relationship as a form of wish fulfillment. That's how it was conceived, really. For reasons that have very little to do with literature and far more to do with me clinging to the plot as I first imagined it, Hermione ended up with Ron.

Of course, given that your hero starts with a false goal and a false statement of philosophy, it's tempting to make the love interest the character who lectures your hero from the start. But then you risk drifting into *another* category of alienating character: Just as you don't want a hero who just says no, likewise you don't want a stick-in-the-mud love interest, such as the kind you find in *Old School* and many other man-child comedies.

Better "I understand you" moments don't have anything to do with wanting to change the other person and everything to do with accepting: We don't root for *Beauty and the Beast* to get together until the beast gives Belle his library.

Sometimes the hero finally meets someone who sees the world his way: In *1984*, Winston truly falls in love with Julia when he's feeling sympathy for the beaten-down old cleaning lady and Julia surprises him by saying that she finds the woman beautiful. She sees what he sees.

Sometimes you can establish that the two characters understand each other before they even meet. We know in advance that the heroes in *Friends with Benefits* will bond because we see they have an ironically shared dislike of relationships. And what could be more romantic than the song that drifts from Maurice Chavalier in the city out to Jeanette MacDonald in the country in *Love Me Tonight*, uniting their hearts before either knows the other exists?

Just as you must occasionally check with your friends to make sure you're not blinded by love in real life, you must get notes to find out how well your fictional romance is playing with your readers. Don't be surprised if you need to give it a firmer foundation.

☑ Is exposition withheld until the hero and the audience are both demanding to know it?

Writers hate exposition (long scenes where someone sits down and explains the plot). Not only is exposition clunky, dull, and uninvolving, but it's just so … so … uncool. Cool writers are those who come up with elegant ways to include exposition and still get the story across. Letting characters explain everything is admitting defeat.

The worst offenders of the dreaded "exposition dump" are supposedly the James Bond movies. (In the *Austin Powers* spoofs, for example, Bond's boss, M, is replaced by a character named Basil Exposition.) And indeed, in some of the more lazily plotted Bond movies, like *Tomorrow Never Dies*, the first we see of Bond is when he saunters into M's office for a new assignment and gets smothered in facts while he listens blandly, even though the audience has no reason to care at this point.

Distaste for this sort of thing has led some writers to try to do away with exposition entirely. Certainly, when I was a kid, we would fast-forward through all talking scenes in *Raiders of the Lost Ark* on VHS. Problem solved, right? But no, that doesn't work, either: We had no idea what was going on!

The modern equivalent of my nine-year-old mind-set can be found in the later Harry Potter movies, where they left all the boring "story" parts out. If you want to know what's going on, I sure hope you've read the books. Actually, I hope you've read them three times, because I've read them twice and *still* couldn't keep track of the characters onscreen or what's significant about each plot turn. It is like watching a three-hour trailer for an even longer movie: "Here's a bunch of creepy-looking suspense scenes! Don't they make you wish you knew what was going on?"

These movies prove there is such a thing as too little exposition. You can't just cut the entire story out. As we've already established, the audience can't care about the story until they care about the hero, but once they are invested in the hero's problem, then they're going to want to know everything the hero wants to know. Once we're firmly perched on the hero's shoulder, the audience will want, nay *demand*, to figure out everything at the same time.

This brings us back to a point that keeps popping up: A scene is not about something happening; it's about a character's *attitude* toward something happening. That's even more true for exposition. Audiences hate to listen to exposition if the hero isn't having an emotional reaction to the news, but, as with everything else, they will feel something if the hero feels something. When it comes to exposition, upsetting news is the best news.

If you look back at some of those James Bond movies, you might notice a few do a better job than others with all the dreaded exposition. In the best of the recent ones, like *Goldeneye* or *Casino Royale*, we first meet Bond on a mission, operating with little information, and it's only when things get bollixed up that he storms into M's office demanding to know the whole dirty story.

That makes the exposition a lot more interesting. Don't give the hero *or the audience* any information they aren't *demanding* to know.

Every scene should reverse an expectation, and exposition scenes are not exempt. If you need a scene in which the hero hears a five-minute speech revealing the nuts and bolts of his grandfather's corrupt business empire, then take some time first to roll that rock uphill before you release it. Let the hero brag in a previous scene about how proud he is to know our country was built by great philanthropists like his grandfather. Now when he hears the ugly truth, the audience will identify with the turmoil it causes within him as each painful word lands.

Here's another part of withholding exposition: A major character's backstory shouldn't be revealed in the same scene as that character's first appearance.

As we've already established, you shouldn't reveal a backstory unless it's ironic, and irony is defined as any meaningful gap between expectation and outcome. Without that *gap*, there's no meaning. You must first establish one aspect, then ironically reverse it once the audience has had some time to accept the original notion.

This gap can go either way: A character's ironic backstory can be revealed at least one scene *before* she appears, or at least one scene *later*. If the latter, it should ideally be revealed one or more scenes after someone asks about it to no avail. Audiences don't care about backstory unless they've been specifically *denied* it. Then they'll crave it.

Let's compare these three situations:

- **THE ALL-AT-ONE-TIME VERSION:** A guy shows up to volunteer and says, "Hi, I used to be a member of a gang, but now I'm trying to go straight, and I'm here to help."
- **THE BACKSTORY-FIRST VERSION:** At the volunteer center, community organizers hear a gang member who hassled them in the past is looking for them, and they're told to be on the lookout, but then he shows up and claims he wants to help.
- **THE BACKSTORY-A-FEW-SCENES-LATER VERSION:** Our point-of-view character sees a volunteer show up and say, "I'm here to help." The boss snorts and replies, "Sure you are. We don't need any trouble here," and the volunteer slinks away. Our point-of-view character asks, "What was that about?" "Nothing." Only later does the point-of-view character decide he really needs the extra help, leading him to ask around and find out about the volunteer's violent past.

The first version is terrible, but the next two work much better. Of course, the other two take more time, but it's worth it.

Audiences instinctively hate when a character is introduced along with an info packet. Trying to do it at the same time is like saying, "Here's who this person is, but wait … he's actually much more interesting than he seems if you'll just let me explain!" Nobody wants to hear that. As with everything else, if the character cares, then the audience will care.

☑ Is there one gut-punch scene where the subtext falls away and the characters really lay into each other?

A producer was giving me a long list of notes on a script, and then he tacked onto the end, as if it were self-explanatory, "Oh, yeah, and make sure you add one of those scenes that an actress will demand before she agrees to play the part." Huh? What scenes? "You know, one of those scenes where she takes a stand and then breaks down and cries." Um, okay ... I dutifully added such a scene.

Only months later did I really start to understand why. The *American Horror Story* pilot got a very mixed reaction, but one thing all the reviews had in common was a puzzlement that Connie Britton was willing to do such a cheesy show right after her acclaimed five-year stint on *Friday Night Lights*.

Watching the pilot, I wondered that, too, until I got to the gut-punch scene. Britton and husband, Dylan McDermott, have been ignoring their marriage problems throughout the episode, and then suddenly, unexpectedly, they finally let each other have it, and I finally understood that note. This one scene is so strong it would have lured anybody into the role.

If a story is all text and no subtext, it'll suck. On the other hand, if the subtext *never* erupts to the surface, that can be just as bad. Once and only once, let the emotions come roaring out without a filter. Let your characters hit each other with everything they have and tear each other apart. Again, the trick is to first roll the rock uphill as long as you can. The more scenes you have of sublimated emotion and indirect conflict, the more tension you will build. Stars like Connie Britton understand the power of those sublimated scenes, too, and they love to play them. But once they've created all that potential energy, they'll want to release it.

Yes, you should have as few direct confrontations as possible and let your characters trick and trap each other instead. But eventually all the tricks and traps are for naught, and the characters have no choice but to rip into each other directly. When all else fails, let them go for the gut punch.

After these five skills, of course, you'll still find that your audience is reacting in ways you never could have expected, which is tremendously frustrating. If only there were a way to control those expectations …

MAINTAINING A METICULOUS TONE

WHAT IS TONE?

Tone is one of the least-discussed aspects of writing, but never doubt that it's one of the most important. Tone is how you control your audience's overall experience and enjoyment. In some ways, controlling your tone is even more important than having a compelling hero: If your audience loves your tone, you've got them where you want them—even if everything else about your story sucks.

Your audience wants to be reassured right away that this is the type of story they *like* (funny, poignant, badass, etc.), and if it's not, you have to subtly reset their expectations so they'll enjoy it anyway. You need to set the mood, then gratify the emotional expectations generated by that mood. And you have to predetermine the audience's questions to increase satisfaction each time one is answered.

Don't assume that manipulating your audience will upset them. Audiences *like* to be manipulated to a certain extent. They like to be teased and taunted and goosed by a master storyteller who cares about their expectations and takes the time to set out some puzzles for them to solve. The last thing they want is a meandering shaggy-dog story that doesn't pay off any of its promises.

MISCONCEPTIONS ABOUT TONE

> **MISCONCEPTION:** *Tone* merely refers to the general *mood* of the story, such as light, dark, satirical, etc.
>
> **AU CONTRAIRE:** Mood is only the most obvious aspect of tone, but there are many other ways for a story to set, reset, and upset audience expectations.

Often when people say they don't like your story's "tone," they are referring to what I would call "mood." But my personal definition of tone is more expansive, and it encompasses many methods in *addition* to mood that authors use to set and/or reset audience expectations.

These include ways to tap into expectations created by previous stories, such as genre, subgenre, and others, as well as ways to create and fulfill *new* expectations like:

- posing and answering a dramatic question
- establishing your own set of rules
- framing sequences
- using open questions and other forms of foreshadowing
- using reversible behavior
- using parallel characters

When all of these are used together, an author can achieve a remarkable amount of control over audience satisfaction.

> **MISCONCEPTION:** Writers should ignore everything that's gone before.
>
> **AU CONTRAIRE:** Audiences love old stories and fear new ones. If they can't have the comfort of an adaptation, remake, sequel, or reboot, then they at least crave the reassurance promised by familiar genre conventions. They want to know what expectations to bring to your story.

As long as people have told stories, they've tried to avoid starting from scratch to put their audience at ease. "Don't worry," they say, "my story is new, but I haven't cut the material out of whole cloth. I've just retailored last year's coat to fit you better."

While most writers have contempt for this audience preference, the urge to piggyback every story onto a previous one is older than you may realize:

- In ancient Greece, Homer adapted *The Iliad* from legends about the siege of Troy that occurred four hundred years before. It was a hit, so he then composed a sequel called *The Odyssey*. A hundred years later, Greek playwrights Aeschylus, Sophocles, and Euripides wrote plays with plots spun from the events of *The Iliad*, including *Agamemnon*, *Ajax*, and *Electra*.

- A few centuries later, many miles away, the Roman author Virgil was hired to create a founding epic for the Roman Empire. He decided it should *also* be tied to *The Iliad*, so he wrote Homer's character Aeneas into a new epic, *The Aeneid*, in which he survives the fall of Troy and gradually makes his way to Italy.

- And a few centuries *later*, the Venerable Bede decided to transform English history into yet another spin-off of *The Iliad*. His *Historia Brittonum* created an imaginary past in which "Brutus of Troy" made his way farther west and founded his own nation, renaming it "Britain" in honor of himself.

It's always comforting for a writer to start with characters people already love, and there's no reason that a spin-off, sequel, or reboot can't use those characters to create a new artistic statement … *if* you're willing to create a new work that's as different from the original as *The Odyssey* is from the *The Iliad*.

These days, every genre of writing has succumbed to a fever of sequelitis. This sucks for successful writers who are tired of being asked to write sequels to other people's stories, but it's even worse for beginning writers. Beginners don't have the proven track record required to write sequels, and they can't establish that track record because no one is willing to buy their original stories anymore.

But let's say you haven't been hired to adapt a licensed property. There are still a lot of ways to take advantage of this craving:

- **BORROW PROPERTIES FROM THE PUBLIC DOMAIN.** There is no shortage of new books and movies based on aspects of *Oz* and *Alice's Adventures in Wonderland*.
- **BORROW FROM THE PUBLIC IMAGINATION.** A popular conspiracy theory became the comic, and later the movie, *Men in Black*; rumors about the JFK assassination become novels and movies such as *Winter Kills* and *The Parallax View*.
- **PUT OLD STORIES IN NEW SETTINGS.** The Theseus myth becomes *The Hunger Games*.

But let's say you want to tell a completely original story. That's fine—in fact, that's great. We all need some brave souls to plant new seeds, even if it's so more derivative writers can harvest them later!

But there's still a powerful way to put your audience at ease: the magic of *genre*. Genre allows an author to say, "Don't worry, you may not have seen this before, but you've seen something like it, and I'm going to play by those same rules." This may seem limiting, but in practice, it's liberating. If you want to do something wild and new, then this is a powerful tool. First, reassure the audience that what you're doing will be *somewhat* like something they've seen before to put them at ease long enough to commit. Then, and only after a while, will they say, "Hey, wait a second. This isn't really like *anything* I've seen before … and I think I love it!"

> **MISCONCEPTION:** *Genre* refers primarily to a story's setting (or type of action, mood, etc.)
>
> **AU CONTRAIRE:** First and foremost, a genre is a set of pre-established *expectations*.

So what is genre, and what are the pros and cons of aligning your story with one or the other? Unfortunately, like everything else having to do with tone, the definition is fuzzy.

"Genre" can be defined by a story's setting (western), type of action (kung fu), concept (science fiction), situation (thriller), presence of a certain type of scene (musical), or overall feeling (comedy and drama). As a result, almost every story falls into more than one genre, and yet the fine folks at Blockbuster Video, back in the day, had no problem sorting each movie into only one slot. How did they do that?

When thinking about genre, you need to put yourself in the shoes of that Blockbuster clerk to remind yourself that genre is all about *marketing*. It's a way to connect to the customers who are already interested in the story you want to tell.

A genre is a set of pre-established *expectations* that lives in the head of an audience. When you choose to associate your story with a certain genre (and you probably should), then you're implicitly promising you will fulfill most of those expectations.

Beginning writers falsely assume that the audience always wants a story where "anything can happen," but audiences actually fear and shun those stories. We select a genre for the same reason we select a type of restaurant: to limit the menu. We want to be reassured that only a certain number of things can happen.

Curry upsets my stomach, so I have to order very carefully at Indian restaurants, but at every *other* type of restaurant, I don't worry at all. I can simply presume that my favorite Italian place will never use curry and order without fear. Likewise, if you don't like musical numbers, then you'll carefully avoid musicals, but you won't even worry when you watch a thriller, because you'll feel reassured that nobody's going to break into a big song and dance.

You can still insert that random musical number into the second half of your thriller, of course, but you have to hope your audacity will win you enough new fans to replace all the audience members you piss off.

> **MISCONCEPTION:** The audience loves it when they're unable to guess what's going to happen next.
>
> **AU CONTRAIRE:** Your audience will demand to know all the rules so they can *try their best* to guess what might happen next. This is a huge part of enjoying any story. Once they've hazarded their guesses, they want to be proven right some of the time and proven wrong the rest of the time.

I once wrote a spec script in which a character had evil psychic powers, but I was a little sloppy about the rules. The powers worked slightly differently from scene to scene, depending on what sort of danger I wanted to create. My managers loved the script but insisted that I nail down *exactly* how the powers worked in the next draft. I thought this was silly. The audience doesn't care about a bunch of rules, and the powers are just a metaphor anyway. Why not bend the rules as I go along?

Finally, I got it: The rules of your world should be perfectly clear so your audience can try to anticipate what might happen *next*. Audiences engage with stories by playing a guessing game: "How will the hero solve the problem? What would I do in this situation? Will I spot the heroes' solution before they do, or will they come up with something that astonishes me?" But the audience can't play that game if the rules are constantly changing. And if they can't play, they just want to take their ball and bat and go home.

That is why they need to know the exact powers of your superhero, and exactly how physics works on your fantasy world, and exactly what's threatening the family farm in your drama. The heroic finale, the surprising twist, and the solution to the mystery all need to be things the audience *could* have anticipated, or they won't be satisfied.

If you've created a world where *anything* can happen, you've messed up. You should create a world in which one of *five* things might happen, and readers can't decide which of those five it will be, and then they're shocked when they find out which one happens. Or maybe a sixth thing happens that they *didn't* suspect, but they instantly realize they *should* have considered that possibility.

Let's go back to the distinction we mentioned before between the 2001 version of *Ocean's Eleven* and its sequel, *Ocean's Twelve*. Although few moviegoers guessed what was really going on in *Ocean's Eleven*, it still felt fair when all was revealed. The audience realized they *had* seen enough to guess, and now they were kicking themselves for failing to pick up on the important clues ("Oh yeah, I guess we did see them build a replica of the vault, didn't we?")

People walked out of that movie feeling dazzled, so of course the studio made a sequel, but in the sequel they just cheated. In the final twist, they revealed that the gang had *secretly* achieved their goal *off-screen* and that everything after that was just an elaborate con pulled on the mark *and* on the audience. The audience was *furious*. They had been tricked into playing a rigged game.

The audience is your opponent on the other side of the chessboard, trying to figure out what you'll do two moves ahead. Even if you win that game, they'll be happy to get a pleasant mental workout. But if you cheat and change the rules halfway through, they'll never want to play with you again.

> **MISCONCEPTION:** *Every* type of irony multiplies the meaning of a story.
>
> **AU CONTRAIRE:** There is one aspect of writing that usually should *not* be ironic: tone. You can choose to have an ironic tone, but it will make your story *less* meaningful unless you've used it very skillfully.

The more ironic you can make your concept, characters, scene work, dialogue, and theme, the better. Structure is a little trickier: For the most part, you want your structure to resonate with your audience's expectations rather than subvert them, but you do ultimately want your story to climax in an ironic way.

That leaves tone, which is the one aspect of writing that should *not* be ironic in most stories. There *is* such a thing as an **ironic tone**, and it can be a powerful tool, but it can only be used at great risk.

Every type of irony we've discussed contrasts some aspect of your story with an expectation *you* created. Ironic tone works differently: It contrasts the nature of the current story with expectations the audience has presumably brought with it from *previous* stories.

When people call the nineties the "Ironic Decade," they're sometimes referring to the characters' sarcasm, but more often they are referring to the fact that many of these works had an ironic tone:

- *Seinfeld* played on our expectations that sitcom characters had to grow and change, then shocked us by having them learn nothing.
- Bands like Nirvana played on our expectations that rockers had to be earnest badasses by treating the entire thing as a farce.

Both of these nineties' phenomena set up a playfully antagonistic relationship with their audience: It was as if they were saying, "We know what you want, and we're not going to give it to you, or at least not in the manner that you're expecting it." In each of those cases, the risk paid off. Both *Seinfeld* and Nirvana alienated casual audiences at first, but they also attracted a more intense audience of fans who "got it," and soon the general masses of people came along, wanting to know what the fuss was about.

By encouraging your audience to step out of your story and be aware of their own expectations, you are, by definition, alienating them. The hope is, after they realize you are refusing to suck them into your story, they will appreciate the respect you have shown for their feelings and knock on your door voluntarily.

Seinfeld eventually became one of the most popular television shows of all time, but it was on the verge of cancellation throughout its first few seasons because most viewers found the show off-putting and didn't stick with it. It was only when the early episodes went into syndication that the casual viewers were able to watch enough episodes in a row to finally get it. This is a show that is *trying* to upset (and reset) expectations about what a sitcom could or should be, and the resulting *tension* on the part of the viewer is precisely what makes it so *funny*.

If you're willing to take that kind of risk, and you succeed, then you can reap a great reward. The mental friction that comes from having one's notion of story warped into a new shape can itself be a source of meaning, but you need to be aware that it's only possible to create this type of meaning by sacrificing most other types of meaning. Viewers come to care deeply about *Seinfeld*, but they never care about Jerry. When he goes to jail for two years at the end of the finale, we don't feel strongly about it. That is the trade-off the show's writers chose to make.

Most subsequent attempts to create self-aware "shows about nothing" failed because they were excruciating for viewers. It's bad enough when a story asks the audience to care and then fails to earn their sympathy, but it's far worse when a story intentionally alienates them in the hopes of creating a greater meaning that never materializes. The creators of *Seinfeld* did something amazing, but it's no easy feat.

Finally, there are also other types of ironic presentation:

- **LOW CAMP** refers to works that the audience can enjoy ironically but were intended to be enjoyed in the opposite way, such as the movies featured on *Mystery Science Theatre 3000*.
- **HIGH CAMP** refers to stories that "wink" at the audience, such as the sixties *Batman* TV show, which worked on two levels: over-the-top fun for kids and sly satire for adults.
- **MELODRAMA** found in the films of Douglas Sirk, such as *Magnificent Obsession*, sometimes refers to stories that are so earnest they become absurd, forcing us to feel genuine emotion and yet, at the same time, forcing us to be aware of the absurdity of those feelings.

Once again, there have been examples of works that have used these techniques magnificently, but they did so at a huge risk, since most fail miserably.

Most stories should *not* use an ironic tone, which is only to be used if you are willing to sacrifice identification and suspension of disbelief in favor of uncomfortable but pleasant self-awareness on the part of your audience.

QUESTIONS TO ASK ABOUT TONE

So how do you set the tone? There are a variety of tools writers use to manipulate and then fulfill audience expectations. Let's group these tools into two categories:

- **GENRE:** Are you tapping into expectations that have been pre-established by other stories?
- **FRAMING:** Does the story set, reset, upset, and ultimately exceed its own expectations?

Genre

☑ *Is the story limited to one genre (or multiple, merged genres) introduced from the beginning?*

So let's leap back into the shoes of that long-lost Blockbuster Video clerk of yesteryear. He has been ordered to sort every single videotape by genre so people who want that type of movie will find it. As a writer, you must put yourself in that same position. To find your audience, you must choose a pre-established genre for your story.

But be careful, because each genre comes with a large set of expectations.

Most genres lend themselves to certain pre-established thematic dilemmas: westerns tend to be about individualism versus societal needs, science fiction is often about innovation versus tradition, comedies are about fun versus responsibility, and dramas pit two incompatible adult responsibilities against each other.

Genres also establish how the characters will be expected to act. In most genres, we expect the behavior of the characters to reflect human nature, but there are exceptions. Nobody in the real world has ever said, "A serial killer is obsessed with me, so I'll kill him myself without going to the cops," but it happens all the time in thrillers. At the end of the movie version of *Strangers on a Train*, it's ridiculous for Guy to go after Bruno himself, except for the fact that thriller fans would be disappointed if he didn't.

Mixing genres can be done, but there's always a danger that you'll mix or lose the metaphor, as we discovered before.

Choosing to write in a certain genre is always a trade-off: you agree to write within certain pre-established expectations, and in return you get a preselected audience that has accepted your inherent promise that you'll provide what they crave. It's a great power that comes with great responsibility.

But once you've chosen a genre, you're not done yet …

☑ Is the story limited to compatible subgenres, without mixing metaphors?

As with genre, subgenres can be defined by subject matter (time travel), point of view (satire), source material (docudrama), etc. Stories aren't strictly marketed by subgenre (subgenres never got their own sections at Blockbuster), but there are usually a lot of clues from the book cover, poster, trailer, or tagline to let you know which one you've got. Audiences don't limit their buying habits quite as strictly by subgenre, (most time travel fans also like space operas, and most fans of romantic comedies also like coming-of-age stories), but everybody has their preferences, which incline them more toward one than another.

Combining subgenres can be tricky. As with genres, you can mix one or two if you do it right from the beginning, but you can't switch back and forth at will, and you can't have it all.

Here are just some of the subgenres for major genres:

- **COMEDY**: romantic comedy, comedy of manners, farce, spoof, satire, dramedy, coming-of-age
- **DRAMA**: melodrama, soap opera, character study, slice of life, biopic, docudrama, ensemble, romance, coming-of-age
- **THRILLER**: noir, procedural, contained, detective, police, spy, revenge, manhunt
- **HORROR**: grindhouse, slasher, sexualized monster, gruesome monster, transformation, psychological, black comedy, zombie
- **ACTION**: superhero, historical adventure, superspy, supercop, martial arts
- **SCIENCE FICTION**: dystopian, space opera, space exploration, robot, one step beyond, alien invasion, time travel
- **FANTASY**: fairy tale, magical realism, sword and sorcery, medieval, crossover into fantasy world
- **WESTERN**: spaghetti, elegiac, modern day, cattle drive, lawless town, frontier, revenge
- **WAR**: biopic, black comedy, men on a mission, heist, docudrama, front lines, coming-of-age

You can find at least one story that has combined every possible pairing of these subgenres, but some work a lot better than others. It doesn't make much sense to do a zombie-romance movie (though they have tried it), but it doesn't make sense to do a zombie-slasher movie, either, since they tap into different fear centers in our brains.

One problem is, as with combined genres, you run into mixed metaphors. It would be ridiculous if, in the middle of *Terminator 6*, a wizard showed up or a vampire or a singing cowboy, but it would be almost as bad if an alien invasion occurred. That's a different subgenre, and, most important, a different *metaphor*, so what would it all mean?

Indeed, there have been several attempts to do World War II-zombie movies or western-zombie movies, with no commercial success. As a writer, these are very tempting: "I can't believe nobody has done this before! It writes itself! And everybody who hears about it says it sounds so cool!" But nobody is ever going to say, "Those two subgenres have different built-in metaphors, so that would be meaningless." Instead they'll just watch it and say, "Eh, this isn't as cool as I thought it was going to be, though I don't know why." Or, more likely, they won't watch it, because the advance word has been so lukewarm.

Each subgenre imposes some subtler restrictions as well. Let's look at high school movies that are representative of each *comedy* subgenre:

- **ROMANTIC COMEDY:** *Sixteen Candles*
- **COMEDY OF MANNERS:** *Clueless*
- **FARCE:** *American Pie*
- **SPOOF:** *Not Another Teen Movie*
- **SATIRE:** *Election*
- **COMING-OF-AGE:** *Gregory's Girl*
- **DRAMEDY:** *Fast Times at Ridgemont High*

These movies are all funny, and they have similar settings and characters, but it would be hard to move any scene from one to another. It would be jarring for *Fast Times at Ridgemont High* to have a scene that spoofs another movie, just as it wouldn't work for *Not Another Teen Movie* to have a sensitively observed moment of truth.

Another reason to stick to one subgenre is point of view. The audience sympathizes with Alicia Silverstone in *Clueless*, but they also look down on her as a tone-deaf exemplar of a certain type. The comedy of manners is a rather unique subgenre in that it allows the audience to have that sort of limited identification yet still root for the hero. On the other hand, they *fully* identify with Molly Ringwald in *Sixteen Candles*, who is on their level. Once you've chosen one of those two perspectives, it would be too jarring to jump back and forth between them.

☑ Does the ending satisfy most of the genre expectations and defy a few others?

> "The important thing in writing is the capacity to astonish. Not shock—shock is a worn-out word—but astonish."
> —*Terry Southern, writer of* Easy Rider

Everybody went into *Return of the Jedi* rooting for Luke Skywalker to kill Darth Vader. When the moviemakers chose to redeem Vader instead, the audience was happily astonished.

But what if, in addition to that, Luke had turned evil and Yoda had ended up with Leia?

If you defy *too many* expectations, then you'll lose the audience entirely. Shocks pile up until they become the new normal, leaving the audience just as bored as they would have been if you had stuck strictly to convention.

Kelly Reichardt makes super-small-scale independent films. Her first two movies, *Old Joy* and *Wendy and Lucy*, are amazing, but her third, the indie-western *Meek's Cutoff*, is so reliably iconoclastic that it became predictable. Halfway through, I figured out the movie is so in love with ambiguity that it could only end one way: cutting off abruptly just before the climactic reveal. The ending that was supposed to be shocking just got an eye roll.

Most jokes are composed according to the "rule of threes," in which a situation is repeated twice, then gets turned on its head the third time. Why three? Because you have to establish a pattern before you can break it. If you want to *surprise* your audience by defying a genre trope, then you need to first lower their guard by delivering a series of familiar payoffs, something that *Meek's Cutoff* wasn't willing to do.

So the question is, how can you deliver on classical genre tropes without resorting to old clichés? There are many groan-worthy clichés that persist for no good reason, such as "Let's blackmail a random guy into committing a crime." This tired story starter violates common sense, *and* we've seen it a million times. The same goes for anything involving world-weary assassins, nursery rhyme-spouting serial killers, or cool guys who don't look at explosions. But other clichés are harder to get rid of, because it just makes sense to tell a story that way:

- Why is every heist story about "one last job"? Because otherwise, if this heist doesn't work, there's always the next one, so who cares?
- Why is the hero always unexpectedly forced to work with an ex-spouse? Because it's a handy shortcut to add emotional complexity to a situation and turn obstacles into conflicts.
- Why is it always good cop/bad cop? Because it makes for good character contrast, and it also happens to be true to life. Cops really are trained to do that.

Not all clichés can be avoided. The trick is to pull off the clichés in new, exciting ways, which is why our job is so hard.

Once you've paid off a few expectations, then you're free to wallop the audience with something that breaks the rules. The more time you spend rolling the rock uphill, the more satisfying it is when you let it come crashing back down.

☑ Separate from genre, is a consistent mood established early and maintained throughout?

At this point, your genre has now added one set of limitations, and your subgenre another. So once you've accepted that, are you *now* free to tell any story you want *within* those limitations?

Your story also needs a *mood*, and that mood (light, dark, satirical, zany, postmodern, over-the-top, gentle, harsh, chaotic, intense, meditative, lurid, fairy tale, bittersweet, pulpy, etc.) also carries its *own* limitations.

Mood is one of the trickiest and most elusive parts of writing any story. No one ever compliments you on your mood but will savage you if you get it wrong. Mood problems are to blame when the audience assumes your story will maintain a certain emotional undercurrent but then feels betrayed when you veer off in a different direction.

Many writers fear mood. They want to be able to take the story anywhere, and they resent the fact that the audience might not be willing to follow along. But good writers can use mood to their advantage because it's an essential tool for managing expectations.

Let's go back to 1977 and change just one thing about the movie *Star Wars*. What if, instead of "A long time ago, in a galaxy far, far away …" the opening crawl had started with the line "It is the year 25,172!" Even if the rest of the movie had stayed the same, I doubt it would have been as big of a success.

Lucas's opening line is brilliant. It defangs the audience. It says, "Hold on there, buddy. This may *look* like science fiction, with spaceships and lasers and robots, but it's *really* a fairy tale. It's going to be about sword fights, magical hermits, and rescuing princesses, not supercomputers, air locks, and explosive decompression." George Lucas was *managing* our expectations. He was establishing a certain mood before we could start making false genre assumptions that would have left us frustrated.

The film *(500) Days of Summer* did something similar: An omniscient narrator openly states at the beginning, "This is not a love story," which preps the audience for the movie's melancholy ending.

In both cases, the audience is being directly addressed, but you needn't be so direct. On a more subtle level, your early scenes convey to an audience "This is going to be the kind of story where this sort of thing happens and has these sorts of consequences."

As a kid, I fell in love with *Back to the Future* as soon as Michael J. Fox grabbed onto the back of a Jeep while he was on his skateboard. Then, to up the ante, he switched to the back of a cop car!

This scene had nothing to do with the plot, but it had everything to do with setting the mood. In real life, skateboarding while hanging onto a car traveling at normal speed is recommended only for the suicidal, but this movie is set in a universe where the laws of physics are a little gentler, and rebellious teen misbehavior is all in good fun. No matter how much trouble is about to ensue, it's probably going to be okay. That's why Doc's last-minute resurrection feels like a satisfying payoff instead of a cop-out.

Framing

☑ *Is there a dramatic question posed early on that establishes which moment will mark the end of the story?*

As we established in chapter five, most stories are built around a hero's longstanding problem, which becomes acute in the first scene and eventually gets resolved in the last scene. In most of these stories, the hero's problem and the audience's "dramatic question" are essentially the same: Will the hero defeat the villain? Will the couple find true love? Who killed that person discovered in the first scene?

The end of the problem is obvious in *Jaws* (the shark gets blown up), but some problems aren't solved so definitively. If the hero doesn't know when his problem is going to end, the writer must establish a "dramatic question" in the minds of the *audience*, creating a subconscious expectation in *our* minds of when the story will end.

In the wonderful heist movie *Charley Varrick*, Walter Matthau robs a small-town bank only to discover that he's accidentally ended up with the mob's money, and now he's being hunted by some very bad guys. The reality is, even if he gets away, he's going to be on the run for the rest of his life, so how could the filmmakers keep the ending from seeming anticlimactic? They came up with a great solution:

Near the beginning, we see one of the mobsters announce, "He'll never make it out of Arizona alive!"

This is brilliant, because the audience subconsciously notes that "getting out of Arizona alive" has now become the official measure of success, so we'll stand up and cheer when Charley cleverly gets out of the state, even though we know he'll have to keep running for years after that.

Likewise, near the beginning of *Never Cry Wolf*, we see a bunch of grizzled Yukon mountain men laugh at nerdy newcomer Charles Martin Smith, who has come to study wolves. One of them declares, "He'll never make it through the winter!" Once again, we instantly accept that as the benchmark of success, even though his story will continue past the end of the movie.

Of course, in both of these cases, it still would have been fairly obvious that the movie was over, since each movie ends with the hero leaving town. In these cases, the question is intended to make a potentially anticlimactic ending seem more satisfying. But some stories truly *need* the dramatic question to be stated openly.

The Godfather is a long, sprawling story. Our hero Michael leaves town in the middle, hangs around in Sicily for a long time, and then comes back for the final stretch. The primary relationship, between Michael and his dad, ends halfway through when his dad dies. The secondary relationship, between Michael and his fiancée, Kay, seems to end a little later when Michael weds someone else in Sicily. So why does the story keep going? Why doesn't the audience get (overly) frustrated?

Here, too, the end date is planted in our mind subtly at the beginning of the story, when Michael tells Kay, "In five years, the Corleone family will be completely legitimate." So the dramatic question becomes, "Is that true?" No matter how many ups and down and beginnings and endings Michael experiences over those long five years, the ultimate question remains unanswered, so the audience is willing to go along for the ride toward that five-year deadline without saying, "Jeez, I thought this movie was done an hour ago!"

☑ *Does the story use framing devices to establish genre, mood, and expectations?*

When you know there's a chance your audience will be asking the wrong questions ("Whodunit?" instead of "Howdunit?" or "Will they survive?" rather than "*How* will they survive?") then you have to head them off at the pass.

There's no more effective way to do that than with a framing sequence and/or past-tense narration (as opposed to a present-tense narration, which has a different effect). A framing sequence establishes the outer bounds of the big picture, keeping some possibilities in the frame and cropping out others. Types of framing effects include the following:

A SCENE IN WHICH A CHARACTER IS TELLING THE STORY TO ANOTHER PERSON, so we see the entire thing as a flashback. This is most often seen in books, of course, but it's also used in a lot of movies. In *Stand By Me* and *Forrest Gump*, it's used to paint the scenes in a nostalgic hue they wouldn't otherwise have. It's used most often in crime thrillers (*Double Indemnity, Murder, My Sweet, D.O.A., The Usual Suspects*), where it serves many purposes:

- It allows us to sympathize more with the morally dubious heroes because we're getting the story through their skewed point of view.
- It allows their voice-over to establish a hard-boiled mood.
- It allows the story to move at a faster clip by using voice-over to bridge gaps.
- It can sometimes create a specific mystery: Why is Marlowe now blind in *Murder, My Sweet*? Why is the hero dying in *D.O.A.*? This gets us asking the question the writer wants us to ask rather than other questions that might come to mind.
- You can even deliberately mislead. A biopic I wrote ends with a suicide, but I begin the movie with a cryptic flash-forward that implies it was murder. Doing so tricks the audience into paying closer attention to the story, as they would with a whodunit. The hope is, by the time they get to the end, they'll enjoy the story enough that they won't mind being tricked.

BEGIN WITH A CRYPTIC FLASH-FORWARD, then cut back to the story in "the present." This can be used in novels, movies, or just about any form of writing, but it's become especially common in TV.

Alias and *Breaking Bad* are two (otherwise very different) shows about heroes who whip back and forth between quotidian domestic problems and international gunplay. Both shows often employ a structure in which the episode begins with a flash-forward where the hero is about to be tortured to death. Then it cuts to a "one week earlier" title card and shows the same hero dealing with some ho-hum domestic problem. This not only plays up the irony but also makes those domestic scenes hum with tension as the audience wonders when the danger will strike.

These can also be used to deliberately mislead. The flash-forwards throughout *Breaking Bad* season two imply that Walt's house is about to be blown up, which ratchets up the tension in each home scene. When the end of the season finally arrives, we discover we've been misled: We weren't watching the wreckage of Walt's blown-up house; we were watching the wreckage of a plane that blew up far above Walt's house (and was indirectly caused by his actions). This is far more bizarre than what we expected, but just as satisfying. (And it also tricked us into being more forgiving of Walt's actions, since we had falsely assumed all season that retribution was coming.)

A PAST-TENSE VOICE-OVER. This is the standard for most novels (although the past-tense narrator often seems to have no foreknowledge of the events she is narrating). It's possible but far less common in plays (where you need an onstage narrator, as in *The Glass Menagerie*, to pull it off). This type of framing is fairly common in movies (where you need voice-over narration) and sometimes even in TV.

Both *Sunset Boulevard* and *American Beauty* are narrated by heroes who explain right away that they're dead and this will be the story of how they died. Once again, this tricks the audience into paying much closer attention to the seemingly low-stakes domestic problems and being on the lookout for the one that will lead to the hero's death. Obviously, this is an extreme risk, since it gives away the ending. As

Hitchcock would say, the writers are sacrificing surprise in favor of suspense, hoping that the trade-off will make the entire movie crackle with tension.

These can also prepare us for difficult transitions. The young girl's voice-over in Terrence Malick's masterpiece *Days of Heaven* not only sets a powerful mood, but it also prepares us for the fact that she will become the main character late in the story.

In each of these cases, the writer is asking a certain question early on to keep the audience from asking others. The case of *American Beauty* is the most basic of all: If we didn't know Spacey was going to die, then our question would simply be, "So what?" Why would we care about some random shlub's midlife crisis, since those crises never have any real consequences? Writer Alan Ball knew that the only way to get us to care was to assure us up front that *this time* was different.

☑ Are there characters whose situations suggest possible fates for the hero?

Another way to create subconscious anticipation is to contrast the hero with parallel characters who face the same decisions. The fates of these characters automatically come to represent possible outcomes for the hero, either as cautionary tales or as potential role models.

In Billy Wilder's *Sunset Boulevard*, what happens if burnt-out screenwriter Joe Gillis stays with deranged ex-screen star Norma Desmond? He has his answer in the form of Max, her ex-husband who has now been reduced to the role of butler and chauffer, forced to watch her pursue younger men.

For that matter, when Joe first arrives, Norma is arranging the burial of her longtime pet monkey, insisting that he be buried on the grounds, even if it's against the law. This won't be the last time she's willing to break the law to keep one of her "pets" on the estate.

But wait, here's another: Norma is writing a screenplay about the biblical character Salome, who did the dance of the seven veils to get John the Baptist's head on a platter. Later, when Norma is dancing with Joe, she throws her own veil on the floor. Hmm …

And then there's the ultimate clone: Norma herself. Joe tells us his goal was always to be successful enough in Hollywood to get himself a pool, and then he meets a superstar who has one, but at what price? If he finds success, will he end up like her?

In *Sunset Boulevard*, the heavy hand of fate hangs over everything, but all stories benefit from the use of parallel characters as a subtle way to set audience expectations.

☑ **Does foreshadowing create anticipation and suspense (and refocus the audience's attention on what's important)?**

We've talked about several forms of foreshadowing already, from obvious methods like using a framing sequence, flash-forward, or voice-over to hint at what's coming, to more subtle methods like the creation of parallel characters that foreshadow the hero's fate.

But there are many more methods of foreshadowing. Here are just a few:

- **WHEN A SCENE CUTS AWAY RIGHT BEFORE A BIG REVEAL,** or when the story pointedly refuses to identify an important person in the room.
- **INTERRUPTED DIALOGUE:** Somebody sounds like she's about to say something important, but she's cut off, leaving the audience to perk up their ears in hopes of filling in the blanks.
- **WHENEVER WE ONLY HEAR ONE SIDE OF THE CONVERSATION,** or even when we hear both but something still doesn't add up, the audience assumes this is a big clue. (So let's hope it is!)
- **UNEXPLAINED CRYPTIC SCENES:** Who are these people having some secret meeting that seems to have nothing to do with the story? Why is the hero's ally dropping off a mysterious package somewhere?
- **DANGLING QUESTIONS:** Someone asks a leading question, such as "Why does this keep happening?" and nobody can answer.
- **UNPAID DEBTS** weigh heavily on an audience's mind. In both *Chinatown* and *The Godfather*, a debt is incurred in the first scene that gets called in at an ironic moment later in the movie.

- **THREATS OR VOWS OF REVENGE.** Use them to keep the audience on their toes until they finally forget about them. At that moment, deliver the payoff.

I used to think that foreshadowing was just showboating by writers: They know what's going to happen and we don't so they're rubbing it in our faces. But now I realize that there's a lot more going on. Fore-shadowing is a way to tie together a plot that might not otherwise come together. It's also a way to trick the audience into caring about things they might not have cared about. You tease the audience with details about the future, which makes them feel cheated, which makes them demand to know what you're not telling them. But if you hadn't teased them, they wouldn't care in the first place.

☑ *Are reversible behaviors used to foreshadow and then confirm change?*

In every type of writing, you must convey the hero's internal state to the audience. This is relatively easy in prose, but it's harder in drama-tized writing. Playwrights, screenwriters, and TV writers have three ways to achieve this:

- **PRESENT-TENSE VOICE-OVER** allows the hero to honestly and di-rectly tell the audience what's going on. The disadvantages, how-ever, are many. It's inherently uncinematic in that it's invisible, and it takes the audience out of the story by breaking the fourth wall.
- **DIALOGUE ABOUT THE CHARACTER'S INTERNAL STATE** is also prob-lematic. In real life, people don't like to honestly tell other people what they're thinking or feeling. Usually the other character has to trap the hero into revealing his thoughts.
- **BEHAVIOR** is the best way to detect the internal state of others, in movies and in real life.

Of course, scriptwriters know that most readers just skim the descrip-tion of behavior we write into our work, so it's tempting to just skip it. But that's a bad idea. Instead, you need to convince the reader to actually read your behavior descriptions by creating behaviors that, like good dialogue, are streamlined, deliberate, and packed with meaning.

Behavior, like dialogue, benefits from "setup and payoff." It allows you to create potential energy early on with the setup and then release that energy swiftly and efficiently when the payoff hits. The audience loves to see this happen. Because they saw the setup, they are in your secret club and know instantly what it means when they see the payoff, even though a casual observer wouldn't.

You can do this with physical actions by creating reversible behaviors. Rather than come up with new behavioral clues from scratch in every scene to convey emotional states, you can give a character a behavior that means one thing and then later have the character reverse that behavior, letting the audience know instantly that the internal state has flipped as well. This is why it's always good to look for behaviors that can do double duty by meaning one thing now and the opposite later on.

Several great examples are on display in the sensitively observed screenplay for *Rise of the Planet of the Apes*. When the audience first meets John Lithgow's character, he's attempting to play the piano but merely banging out discordant notes, letting them know instantly that he's losing his mind. When his son gives him an anti-Alzheimer's medication, he awakes the next morning to find his father playing the piano beautifully. The audience instantly understands what this means: The medication has worked.

Interestingly, the writers later have an opportunity to flip this again, but they don't use it. When the drug starts to wear off and Lithgow begins to lose his mind again, rather than put him at the piano a third time, the writers craft a heartbreaking moment where the two main characters silently notice that Lithgow is trying to chop up his eggs with the wrong end of his fork. Having used reversible behavior to good effect once, they decided to start fresh with a new behavior to indicate Lithgow's gradual return to senility.

The audience gets another powerful example of reversible behavior when Caesar, the human-like ape, is kicked out of his human home and sent to live in a concrete cell. At home in his attic loft, Caesar looked out on the world through a round window. In the cell, Caesar touchingly scratches a replica of the window onto his wall, showing his wish to return there. Later, once he realizes he can never trust humans, he violently erases the drawing. The audience knows all too well what that means.

Reversible behavior also allows you to create subtle character arcs, even in stories where character development is not the first priority, like *Ghostbusters*. Our hero, Bill Murray, has a muted and subtle character arc: He never has a midpoint disaster or a spiritual crisis, never seems to doubt himself or get humbled. He seems like the same cocky rogue all the way through … but is he?

He does in fact change quite a bit, and it's set up very nicely through reversible behavior. In the very first scene, Murray's paranormal researcher is sabotaging his own ESP experiment just so he can hit on the test subject. He doesn't truly believe in or care about the supernatural; he's just using it to get girls.

This scene is neatly reversed two-thirds of the way in, when the new object of Murray's affections, Sigourney Weaver, who has so far resisted his advances, suddenly throws herself at him. He's very tempted, but instead, he forces himself to admit she's possessed, and he now values solving her problem more than scoring with her.

It's not played like a big moment, nor should it be. By subtly contrasting this scene with the first, the movie allows us to notice the difference for ourselves, whether consciously or subconsciously.

☑ Is the dramatic question answered at the very end of the story?

Keeping a story going past the end of the dramatic question is exasperating for the audience, even if they're otherwise enjoying themselves. *The Big Sleep* is a wonderful movie, but the original mystery is solved two-thirds of the way through, leaving the audience baffled as to why the movie keeps going.

And the second half of *Gone with the Wind* never fails to exasperate me: The war ends, Tara is restored, the couple seems to break up definitively, then get back together definitively, and then marry, and then have a kid, then on and on and on. Even when Rhett leaves Scarlet for the "final time" at the end, I don't really buy that he's gone for good. What is the dramatic question here?

There isn't one. Unlike *The Godfather*, this sprawling epic saga doesn't seem to have a pre-established end point. No dramatic question unites the movie, and it limps to a finish two hours after it should have ended. (Seriously, folks, just quit watching at the intermission. You won't miss anything.)

So now we're done, right? Oh, wait, we forgot just one little thing: What does it all *mean*? That brings us to the final skill.

9

INTERWEAVING AN IRRECONCILABLE THEME

WHAT IS THEME?

Theme is often misunderstood and unfairly maligned. Some writers like to boast they *purposely* ignore it, because they don't want to impose an overriding moral judgment onto their stories. But a theme is not the same thing as a moral. In the end, every story *must* have a theme, but it shouldn't be artificially imposed on the story. Rather, it should arise *naturally* when irreconcilable values come into conflict.

Your audience doesn't want to reach the end of your story and ask, "So what's your point? Was this a meaningless series of events?" If your story is going to *resonate*, then you have to intrigue the audience with a thorny problem and draw them deeper into those thorns every step of the way. If they're going to fully identify with your hero, they must get drawn into your hero's painful dilemmas until they feel anxious and picture themselves in this situation. *That's* when they'll be totally engrossed.

MISCONCEPTIONS ABOUT THEME

MISCONCEPTION: Your theme is the moral of your story.

AU CONTRAIRE: It is better to deliver your theme in the form of an ironic, irreconcilable dilemma of good versus good (or evil versus evil). You are exploring this dilemma, not delivering a moral.

This brings us to two more types of irony that strengthen the meaning of all stories: a series of **ironic moral dilemmas** that culminates in one overall **ironic thematic dilemma**. If a theme can be stated in terms of "This is good and that is bad," then it won't be ironic or interesting. If your story, however, is about a contest between goods or between evils, then you will create a gap between expectation (good should always be pursued; evil should always be evaded) and reality (some goods must be rejected in favor of others; some evils must be accepted to reject others).

Your theme must take the form of an irreconcilable moral dilemma: a contest between two equally appealing or appalling ideas that come into conflict. We'll look at a lot of these in the questions section of this chapter.

> **MISCONCEPTION:** A hero is a character who chooses good over evil.
>
> **AU CONTRAIRE:** A hero who must choose between good and evil is always going to be boring. Your hero should be forced to choose between goods or between evils throughout your story.

As Robert McKee says in his book *Story*, a story cannot revolve around a choice between good and evil, or it will be a no-brainer and your hero will seem stupid for even considering it. Not only should your overall story have a good-versus-good (or evil-versus-evil) theme, but there should also be constant choices along the course of the hero's journey in which the hero is forced to choose between goods or between evils.

Modern audiences shun cautionary tales in which the author clearly feels one choice is the right one and the others are wrong. Your audience will not be engaged unless they, too, are stumped by the hero's choices and worried about the consequences either way.

MISCONCEPTION: You should state your theme.

AU CONTRAIRE: The audience should feel your theme, not hear it.

I've mentioned how important it is to "know more than you show." This is even more vital when it comes to theme. Once again, this can be hard to do: You've got something to say, and now you want to say it, but you have to stop yourself. You don't actually want your audience to *hear* what you have to say, but you do want them to *feel* it. And they'll only feel it if they've been allowed to draw their own conclusions. In this chapter, we'll explore how to *influence* rather than *dictate* those conclusions.

Let Hegel be your guide: Thesis plus antithesis creates synthesis. Your job is to slam a thesis up against an antithesis, then force the *audience* to create the synthesis for themselves.

MISCONCEPTION: It's a writer's job to "make a point."

AU CONTRAIRE: A fictional story belongs to its characters, not its author, and it's not *their* job to make *your* point.

When you tell a story to make a point, such as "don't use firecrackers," then that story will inevitably feature straw-man characters who exist only as bad or good examples: Goofus picks up the firecracker, and Gallant leaves it alone.

That's fine if your only goal is to keep your child from losing a finger, but that's not real writing. Strong writing features complex, volatile characters who sometimes act in ways the author doesn't expect. Once your characters start surprising you, then you can no longer count on them to make your point for you. In fact, you can no longer be certain of what the point of your story will be.

MISCONCEPTION: The ending of your story will create the meaning.

AU CONTRAIRE: The meaning of your story is created by the dilemma that drives every scene, not merely by its conclusion.

The meaning of your story will not be created by its final outcome. You are putting your characters in a situation that reflects a powerful and ironic emotional dilemma that will resonate with your audience. Watching your characters grapple with the dilemma scene by scene will create the meaning of your story *as you go*, regardless of the eventual outcome.

The endings of some great stories have been reconsidered and reversed. Most modern editions of *Great Expectations* include both published endings, one "happy" and one "unhappy." Does either one significantly change the meaning of the story? Of course not.

The classic crime drama *Chinatown* changed the ending on the set to be much more powerful: In the original, the villain is killed by the heroine, who is taken off to jail, despite the efforts of our hero to explain why she had to do it. In the final version, the heroine is killed by the cops, and the villain wins absolutely, *totally* devastating our hero (and the audience).

But would the movie have been rendered meaningless if they had gone with the original ending? Of course not. The ending would have had less punch, and a different "point" would have been made, but it was the total events of the story that created the meaning, not the final conclusion. The overall thematic dilemma (solidarity versus individual achievement) has already been driven home by every scene. By the time we get to the end, it doesn't really matter what the point is; we've already felt the theme in our bones.

> **MISCONCEPTION:** The best way to add meaning to your story is to have your characters say meaningful things.
>
> **AU CONTRAIRE:** Meaning comes not from propositions but from opposition. Far more meaning will be created by the clash of characters representing different values than by any "words of wisdom."

Audiences hate speeches. Speeches are the opposite of drama. "Great dialogue" doesn't have to be philosophical, flowery, or even articulate.

The job of dialogue should be to further each character's agenda, and that's it. If the character is witty, or pithy, or canny, it might be entertaining for the audience, but only if the character's goal (conscious or unconscious) motivates the character to speak like that—and it's believable in this situation. We don't want to hear any lofty talk in the middle of a life-and-death situation.

When discussing James Cameron films like *Titanic*, people will often say, "How can you say that was any good? The dialogue was just people yelling at each other!" But that's perfectly acceptable if the situation merits it. Cameron's movies get their meaning not from the wisdom the characters utter but from the clash of values that those characters embody.

QUESTIONS TO ASK ABOUT THEME

Now that we've dispelled misconceptions about theme, let's look at four important qualities your theme should possess. It should be:

- DIFFICULT: Is the meaning of the story derived from a fundamental moral dilemma?
- GROUNDED: Do the moral stakes ring true to the world of the audience?
- SUBTLE: Is the theme interwoven throughout so it doesn't have to be frequently discussed?
- UNTIDY: Is the dilemma ultimately irresolvable?

Difficult

☑ *Can the overall theme be stated in the form of an irreconcilable good-versus-good or evil-versus-evil dilemma?*

As stated in the Misconceptions section of this chapter, your theme should take the form of an irreconcilable moral dilemma: a contest between two equally appealing ideas that come into conflict. Usually these will be two "goods," both of which seem impossible to live without, like:

- solidarity versus individualism
- fun versus responsibility
- compromise versus integrity

These dilemmas need not dominate the story immediately. Slowly, over the course of the emerging conflict, it should become clear that there is an underlying fundamental human dilemma in the interpersonal conflict.

Some stories are focused not so much on good versus good but more on evil versus evil:

- death versus dishonor
- betraying a loved one versus betraying society
- societal control versus chaos

In your story, a conflict should eventually push one of these dilemmas to the crisis point and force your hero to confront this painful choice. This dilemma should seem totally irreconcilable for most of the story, and both the hero *and the audience* should feel torn and anguished over the decision.

Here are some dilemmas from the examples we looked at in chapter three:

- The movie *Casablanca*: love versus patriotism
- The novel and movie *Beloved*: death versus enslavement, self-forgiveness versus self-accountability
- The novel and movie *Silence of the Lambs*: dealing with one monster versus letting another go free
- The movie *Groundhog Day*: acceptance versus ambition
- The novel and movie *Harry Potter and the Philosopher's Stone*: justice (seeking out and confronting evil, even at the risk of innocent lives) versus peace (maintaining order by banishing evil from discussion)
- The novel and movie *Sideways*: delusional optimism versus clear-eyed cynicism

- The comic and movie *Iron Man*: societal responsibility versus individual innovation
- The memoir and movie *An Education*: living up to one's responsibilities versus having an interesting life

We'll revisit these examples again later in this chapter to see how they play out.

☑ Is a thematic question asked out loud or clearly implied in the first half and left open?

A good theme isn't a statement but a question the audience has to answer for themselves. The easiest way to plant this question in your audience's head is to have a character actually ask it aloud and receive no satisfactory answer. The entire story becomes a belated response to the dangling question.

The wickedly smart high school satire *Election* (both novel and movie) is a great example. At the beginning, a teacher asks his civics class, "What is the difference between morals and ethics?" but just then the bell rings, and the class leaves before they have to answer the question. Instead, each character is forced to confront this question in much more difficult ways. Ultimately, the teacher will choose to falsify the results of a student election when he decides the real winner is not a good person—with disastrous results.

Similarly, at the beginning of the backstage comedy *Bullets Over Broadway*, one character asks, "Let's say there was a burning building and you could rush in and you could save only one thing: either the last-known copy of Shakespeare's plays or some anonymous human being. What would you do?" In this case, the characters *do* get to discuss it, but they reach no satisfying answers, so the underlying question "Is great art worth more than any one life?" lingers on and colors every character's actions. In the end, one character will decide to kill for the sake of preserving art.

☑ *Do the characters consistently have to choose between goods or between evils instead of choosing between good and evil?*

Yes, the entire story should be driven by an overall irreconcilable moral dilemma, but the heroes should also face a long succession of additional dilemmas *throughout* the story. *Casablanca* is an excellent example of how such dilemmas can pile up and also of how the presence of these dilemmas need not sour the mood.

- Before we even meet Rick, we see the question that hangs over his employees' heads: As they try to run a nightclub in Nazi-occupied Morocco, is it worth accommodating the Nazis to keep the peace? How much interference in the club's affairs will be too much?
- Then we meet Rick, the suave club owner, just as Ugarte the criminal asks him to hide some letters. Should Rick risk his tricky peace with the Nazis to protect this man?
- When the police show up to arrest Ugarte, he begs Rick for help. Rick has already assured Renault, "I stick my neck out for no one," but it's hard to say no when Ugarte is clinging to him and begging as the Nazis drag him away. Unlike many "hero's flaw" scenes, Rick faces a genuinely hard choice. We don't know what *we* would do in Rick's position. We disapprove of Rick's callousness, but we've come to appreciate the impossibility of his position. We can't see any other feasible action he could have taken.
- Of course, we then arrive at the big question: If you suspect your ex-girlfriend still loves you, should you try to steal her away from her bland husband? This question will drive the main narrative, but others continue to pop up.
- This leads to a flashback where that girlfriend is torn by a similar question: Should you leave your new love if your husband turns up alive?
- And if you do, is it kinder to explain or slip away?
- Meanwhile, a subplot asks, "Should you sleep with a corrupt official to save your husband's life?"

- Later another tricky question is raised: Should you ask someone to attend a resistance meeting if you know it might get him killed?

These are all *tough* questions, and we dread the thought of having to face such dilemmas. And yet the mood of this movie remains sophisticated and effervescent, even though the painful emotional dilemmas faced by every character in every scene could not be more dire. The comedic elements are made that much sharper by scraping up against these cold, hard stones.

Grounded

☑ Does the story reflect the way the world works?

This is one of the toughest restrictions writers face: No matter how much meaning you pack into your stories, audiences won't be moved if they don't *buy it*. You need to make your world real to them if they're going to care about it. Pass the Holden Caulfield test: You can't be phony or they'll just roll their eyes.

For your story to be meaningful, it must ring true to the audience. It must resonate with their understanding of human nature. Most important, *every* story, even those not set in our world, needs to reflect "the way the world works."

Many of the criticisms of the *Star Wars* prequels boiled down to "That's not the way the world works." These attacks hit home, even though, if you think about it, these movies aren't set in "the world" at all. It's a different universe, so can't people act differently?

Nope. Audiences will happily accept different laws of physics before they accept screwy logic. In *Revenge of the Sith*, the villain convinces our hapless antihero that killing a bunch of kids will save his wife from dying in labor. Huh? He bought that? That's just not how things work—in any world, anywhere.

You need to know how human nature works on a universal level, and you also need to know how people tend to think differently within various subgroups: different time periods, different nationalities, different professions, etc.

For example, I once read a script about a bunch of small-town cops investigating the murder of the town beauty. When the town drunk is found with a bloody knife, he is arrested, even though he has no known connection to the girl. But then one cop finds a love letter from the girl to the drunk—so they determine he couldn't possibly be the killer.

Wait—what? That's not the way the world works! Every cop anywhere knows that love is the number-one motive for murder. If the cops find evidence that two people secretly loved each other, it would greatly *boost* the suspicion. Even if the audience somehow doesn't know this common wisdom, they'll be able to sense something is screwy about your cops.

Inception has the same problem. In the film, Leonardo DiCaprio plays Cobb, whose deranged wife killed herself and framed him for the murder. He wants to tell everybody she was mentally disturbed, but, alas, he explains:

> Her letter to the authorities refuted all the claims about her sanity that she knew I'd make. ... She'd had herself declared sane by three different psychiatrists. It was impossible for me to explain the nature of her madness. ...

Huh? On my planet, there are at least two things wrong with that logic:

1. No psychiatrist would ever declare anyone to be categorically sane. There's no blood test for sanity. Psychiatrists can declare a person legally competent to stand trial, but that's actually the opposite. It means the person is *capable* of doing a bad thing, not incapable.
2. In the eyes of your average jury, simply going to a psychiatrist is enough to prove you're nuts. Going to three psychiatrists and asking each for a little note that says you're sane is enough to prove you're *really* nuts.

People know how people are supposed to act. There is such a thing as human nature. That said, there are rare exceptions, depending on your genre. Certain literary conventions have become so ingrained that we now fail to see the problem. In fact, the realistic version would seem weird.

One of the most obvious ones is "The Mastermind Fallacy": In fiction, the cops always have a breezy contempt for dumb crooks, but they're terrified of criminal masterminds. When the phone rings and the cool voice of a master planner is on the other end, a cop's blood suddenly runs cold. But this isn't actually the way the world works. In real life, the exact opposite is true.

Real-life cops *love* smart crooks who have figured out all the angles. First, they tend to be nonviolent. Violence is always a dumb move, after all. Second, and even better, masterminds are actually rather easy to catch. Their actions are logical. They act in the most advantageous way, which is never that hard for the cops to guess.

On the other hand, cops tend to be terrified of dumb crooks, who are often violent and totally unpredictable, which makes them very hard to outmaneuver. In fact, cops are most afraid of criminals who are wacked out of their minds on drugs. Who knows what they're going to do? Who knows who they're going to hurt? Who knows what twisted logic will make sense to them?

So, if writers are always supposed to reflect the way the world works, why do they have a big blind spot here? Because mastermind-type stories, while totally inauthentic, are just too much fun to give up. And marauding meth heads are no fun at all. And this has been going on for so long it isn't likely to change.

So there are certain genre-specific exceptions to the "way the world works" rule, but don't let them go to your head. Never doubt that, even in these cases, the audience does know, deep down, that these stories violate common sense. They are giving you a pass for the same reason you're giving yourself a pass: These types of stories are just too juicy to pass up.

Never assume that because your audience has chosen to suspend disbelief about one aspect of your story you can now play fast and loose with other things. As one of my fellow students once wisely put it, "Just because we believe that *Superman* can fly doesn't mean that we'll believe it when he turns on the TV at the exact right moment to hear the news he needs to hear."

☑ Does the story have something authentic to say about this type of setting?

Obviously, you're going to have a huge leg up if your story is set in a place you know well. You're going to already know the syntax, the metaphor families, the jargon, the tradecraft, and the most common ethical dilemmas faced there. All of these things combine to greatly multiply the meaning of a story.

After all, this is a big part of having something to say: Do you have something to say about *this place* and *this time*? The more authentic details you add, the more believable your world will be, and the more your feelings about this world will ring true and resonate deeply with your audience.

If you don't have authentic firsthand knowledge of the place, then you've got a lot of research to do, as we've already discussed. Of course, some of you might be thinking right now that *you* get a free pass on this one, because your story is set on a fantasy world or a spaceship. I can hardly expect you to show any authentic knowledge of that setting, can I? Yes, I can. Sorry.

The writers of *Battlestar Galactica* could have been forgiven for just winging it. After all, their show was set on a deep-space warship many millennia ago, but they knew their story would be far more meaningful if they had something authentic to say, so they did a lot of research about what life is like on modern aircraft carriers. In the first season DVD commentaries, they point out several episodes that were drawn from interviews with modern naval officers, including an episode about deaths from a missile-loading accident. It turns out that every writer has to hit the books and do some research.

Of course, while research is great, there's no substitute for direct observation. But be warned: True observation is one of the hardest skills to learn because of preconceived notions or "big ideas."

I used to pride myself on being a "man of ideas." And that's one reason I became a writer: so I could spread those ideas to others. But now I realize that big ideas are actually poison for a writer.

A big idea is a set of self-satisfied certainties that allows you to stop looking, listening, and learning. Perpetual observation is the antidote to those certainties.

- Ideas are rigid; observations adapt.
- Ideas make you seem smart; observations actually make you smarter.
- But for a writer, the most important distinction is this: Ideas are generic, and observations are specific.

Journalists are trained to jot down ten observations every time they walk into a room. As a fiction writer, even if you don't have the huge asset of a journalistic background, it's never too late to start doing this. But watch out: Try to make sure that none of these observations carries the tainted whiff of your ideas. Write down what you *actually* see and hear, not what you *expected* to see and hear, and not what you *presume* is actually going on. This is really hard. At first, all you will see are things that confirm your preconceived notions. You have to force yourself to see past those preconceptions.

The hope is that eventually your observations will overwhelm your ideas, and you'll keep looking without the benefit of a "big idea" to contextualize what you're seeing.

But wait! Aren't I proposing an overly conservative worldview? After all, to have ideas is to be active, but to merely observe is to be passive and complacent, right?

When it comes to changing the world, nothing is more powerful than a truthful observation. If you want to take on the meat industry, you don't write a healthy-eating manifesto; you write *The Jungle*. If you want to say something meaningful about race, you don't pile up a bunch of high-minded, heavy-handed parables, like in the infamously bad 2005 Best Picture Oscar Winner, *Crash*. Instead, you should pile up a ton of true-to-life observations, as seen in *Homicide* or *The Wire*, both of which were created by longtime inner-city reporter David Simon.

Ideas are the true recipe for passivity, and observations are the true spur to action. But you can't observe anything if you're using your ideas as an excuse not to pay attention. The worst bias a writer can have is confirmation bias.

☑ Does the story include twinges of real-life national pain?

It was 1977, and America was depressed. We'd just lost a war, and, even worse, deep down where we wouldn't even admit it, we suspected that we had *deserved* to lose.

Then, an amazing thing happened. A great work of art came along that began the process of healing that wound, a movie called *Star Wars*.

In the movie, three American stars played scrappy young rebels taking on a massive empire. The empire kept using its advanced technology to track and slaughter the rebels, leaving smoking villages filled with charred corpses. But a ragtag band of farmers and outlaws won out by hiding in jungles, infiltrating the enemy army, striking fast, and scattering quickly, all the while drawing strength from a meditative, churchless spiritual force.

George Lucas was giving America a chance to empathize with our former enemies and refight the war on their side. As they watched *Star Wars*, Americans happily made that switch and felt their souls were a little bit cleaner.

Now let's jump ahead a few years: It was 1984 and America seemed to be on the edge of nuclear war. Few could imagine a bright future. In *The Terminator*, the Soviets became giant robots, and nuclear war became a robot apocalypse, but the implications were clear: We were caught in a closed loop that had only one end. There was nothing left to do but ride off into a sun-bleached desert to prepare.

Cut to eight years later, and writer/director James Cameron updated his fable in *Terminator 2*. The big, scary, deep-accented robot broke out of his programming, now determined to destroy his own side's weapons and break the loop, even if it meant destroying himself in the process. In the end, we're back on the highway, but now it's night, and we have no idea what awaits us down the road. We've been sure of the coming doom for so long; can we handle the freedom of not knowing what the future brings?

Nobody walked into these movies expecting any political content, and even afterward, most remained blissfully unaware of the movies' deeper implications. Audiences just knew that these movies had resonated with them on a much deeper level than many other blockbusters.

Those stories are science fiction, which is the most allegorical of genres, but all stories become more meaningful when they include twinges of real-life national pain. There's a myth that the movies of Hollywood's golden age ignored the Great Depression and created a fantasy world of glitz and glamour, but if you actually watch the movies, nothing could be further from the truth. The depression is a constant reality, and it's that pain that gives the movies their weight, even as they create a parallel glamorous reality for their characters (and audience) to aspire to.

You can't count on your audience to bring their sense of morality with them, but you can count on them to bring their fears, pain, and doubts. They don't want to think directly about those things, but you can add great resonance to an otherwise apolitical story by indirectly referencing them. This is true even for comedies: Great comedy always has an undercurrent of pain running through it, just under the surface.

If you want your story to be more meaningful, you should feel your country's pain, but you shouldn't *exploit* that pain. In other words …

☑ *Are these issues and the overall dilemma addressed in a way that avoids moral hypocrisy?*

Of course, if you're going to invoke real pain, the trick is to avoid hypocrisy. I can only guess that writer-director Joss Whedon got a note from the studio that said, "The Avengers are just tools of the government the entire time. They should show some independence!" So he added in a very awkward subplot in which the Avengers work together to uncover their boss's (Nick Fury) dirty secret: He wasn't just using the stolen alien artifact to create clean energy; he was building *weapons*! Gasp!

This tacked-on subplot not only goes nowhere, but it's also totally out of character. The Avengers *love* weapons. They're all *defined* by their weapons. Quick quiz—who's who? Shield. Hammer. Armor. Bow. Guns. Fists. Any questions? For that matter, they're also at war with a malevolent alien race. This is a movie that ends with Iron Man happily wiping out his enemies with a nuclear missile, and nobody bats an eye! Isn't he the same guy who was just lecturing Fury about not building any more weapons?

If they wanted to add a quick antiweapons-proliferation subplot in the middle of an intensely pro-weapon movie, then they should have figured out a way to have that issue resonate in the *second* half of the movie, as well, instead of being instantly forgotten and totally contradicted.

Of course, this hypocrisy is specific to *The Avengers*, but there's also the issue of the much bigger hypocrisy that hangs over almost *every* story about good and evil. Almost all heroic fiction is founded on the great hypocrisy.

See if you can spot the problem with this logic: "See that guy over there? He solves his problems by killing people! That makes him a problem! So let's kill him! Yay!" Explain to me again who the bad guy is here? In the real world, thankfully, meeting violence with violence is most often seen as a tragic last resort, but in fiction, we aren't satisfied until the villain has been turned into chopped liver. Watching people solve their problems through democratic action is *booo*ring.

When we watch movies about would-be peacemakers, like the lovable, pacifistic small-town sheriff Jimmy Stewart plays in *Destry Rides Again*, we root for him, but we don't *really* want to see him make peace with the town bully, because watching everybody put down their guns and go home would just be, you know, lame. We secretly long for the moment when he gets fed up and straps those guns on.

So how can you avoid the great hypocrisy and yet still have a satisfying ending? You can cheat. You can allow your heroes to make peace with the enemy army if you give that army a really evil, heretofore unrevealed boss. The most famous example of this is *Star Wars*. To redeem Vader, Lucas cleverly brought in the Emperor late in the game. Now they could team up against a greater enemy. Otherwise, the trilogy would have had to end on a hug and no fight.

I grew up on the Star Wars trilogy, and that pretty much ruined me for other sagas. That became my standard for greatness: Morally serious heroes should seek to redeem the villain, not kill him. Thus, I was inevitably disappointed with the endings of *The Lord of the Rings*, the Harry Potter series, *Lost*, and any other saga that gave lip service to complex moral dilemmas but, in the end, came down to happy ending = kill the villain.

This is one reason why I was so impressed by the movie *How to Train Your Dragon*. As I watched it, I was thinking, *Gee, they've been training all this time for a big dragon battle, but now they've got us rooting for our hero to make peace with the dragons instead. If that happens, it'll be admirable, sure, but won't that feel kinda unsatisfying?*

But then, halfway through, we find out the dragons have a big nasty boss, and I smiled. "They're going to make peace with every dragon except *that guy*." Is it a cheat? Sure. But it's a good way to satisfy both higher moral sensibilities and the need to still see just a little ass kicking.

☑ Do all of the actions have real consequences?

Lethal Weapon 2 is the most insulting movie I've ever seen. The villains are evil, snarling, Apartheid-loving South African drug dealers, but no matter how many people they kill, the police chief insists Mel and Danny let it alone: "Forget it, guys. They have diplomatic immunity. There's nothing we can do about it! If you touch a hair on their heads, I'll have your badge!" (Fun fact: This is not how diplomatic immunity works.)

What a predicament! How will our cops figure out a clever way around this conundrum? Well, they don't. They finally just get fed up and say, "Screw it!" They barge into the bad guys' place and begin a raging gun battle. Oh no, what will the consequences be for our heroes? Answer: nothing. They eventually call in backup, the police arrive to help, and then they all stand up and cheer together. All of those threatened consequences just disappear.

A similar recent example is *Taken*, in which Liam Neeson wants his daughter back so badly that he's willing to do *anything*. He even shoots a French official's wife and then refuses her treatment until the official helps him figure out the whereabouts of the bad guys! Wow, he's willing to throw his own freedom away to save his daughter!

Except not. Here's how naïve I was: I genuinely expected the movie to end with Neeson in prison, getting a visit from his daughter, and assuring her that it's all worth it if she's okay. Nope. It ends with Neeson happily flying home with his daughter without a care in the world. How does that work?

Now don't get me wrong. I realize that a lot of people love these movies just as they are, and they wouldn't be happy to see our heroes sitting in jail at the end, but nobody's *proud* of themselves for loving these movies. They get their adrenaline pumped, but when the credits roll, the taste of joy has already started to turn sour in their mouths. They know it doesn't really make any sense.

Two thrillers that have stood the test of time did a much better job with this: The town's economy gets wrecked because Brody closes the beaches in *Jaws*, and Lecter escapes as a result of helping Clarice in *Silence of the Lambs*. Our heroes make painful choices and must live with the grave consequences of the risks they take.

Of course, if actions require consequences, it's equally true that consequences require actions. There's nothing more ludicrous than a story with a lot of melodramatic *Sturm und Drang*, only to reveal at the end that there's no actual drama.

Movie producers tend to get skittish, and they often demand that writers tweak the heroes at the last minute so they become "more sympathetic." This can often result in ludicrous decisions. I saw two movies in 2003 that didn't work for precisely the same reason: Both were stories of husbands seeking redemption for cheating, even though, as it later turned out, they hadn't *actually* cheated!

Big Fish is all about a son's attempt to forgive his fabulist father, played by Albert Finney, for betraying the family. Finney's stories may be amusing, but they can't cover up the fact that he left the family for another woman. Finally, he has to stop lying and admit the truth—that he *didn't* cheat on his wife. Sure, Finney ran away and went to live with Helena Bonham Carter, but heavens no, he never actually slept with her—that would be unsympathetic! (The great irony here is we all know Burton had his *own* affair with Carter, and most of his fans forgave him, but heaven forbid they be allowed to forgive somebody onscreen for the same transgression!)

Shortly after, I saw *Phone Booth*, in which Colin Farrell plays a sleazy agent who stops in a phone booth to call a woman who isn't his wife. While he's there, a sniper who has bugged the booth starts shooting at him and threatens to kill him unless he calls his wife and comes clean. Finally, he has a tearful breakdown and calls his wife to admit the truth—that he *didn't* cheat on her. He just thought about it.

I highly suspect that, in the original scripts, the protagonists had actually cheated on their wives. But some producer said, "Hey, he can't do that. That's unsympathetic!" But this makes no sense. If a story is about a man's quest for redemption, then that quest will only have meaning if he's actually guilty. The audience doesn't want to sympathize with "goodness." The audience wants to empathize with difficult dilemmas—the more difficult the better. Redemption stories are about dealing with the consequences of mistakes. The bigger the mistake, the bigger the consequences, and the more engrossing the story will be.

Everybody loves *A Christmas Carol*, but that wouldn't be true if some publisher had insisted that Scrooge not be too mean to the Cratchits. He really needed redemption, which made the stakes sky high in this battle for his soul. That's the source of the story's meaning. Of course, that story also gains a lot of meaning from one of its most oft-quoted lines, which very much tapped into national pain: "Are there no workhouses?"

Subtle

☑ *Do many small details throughout subtly and/or ironically tie into the thematic dilemma?*

As you write your first draft, you can't worry very much about your theme. You have to simply assume that if the thematic question is linked to the dramatic question, and everything is sufficiently ironic, then meaning will accrue. However, when it's time to tackle later drafts, you may find your theme is so indistinct that it's barely detectable.

But wait, you say, isn't it good the theme is hard to spot? After all, you want your theme to resonate in the audience's bones, not rattle around in their skulls, so shouldn't you pitch it just below the frequency of human hearing? Yes, but like any good subaudible hum, it has to be *persistent*.

Once your story and characters are set, you can go back and second-guess every *minor* choice you made and change many of them to subtly reinforce your theme. When we write, we inevitably make a lot of choices at random, just to keep writing: What job does the hero's spouse have? Where are the heroes when they get the big news? Which blunt object is used for the killing? But now it's time to go back and make all of those choices more meaningful.

Enemy of the State is a fun little thriller about a labor lawyer who receives damning evidence about the National Security Agency from an old friend, then has to go on the run for his life. The movie has the "good versus good" theme of security versus privacy. This thematic dilemma is floated early on by a series of open questions posed by the hero's wife, who works for the American Civil Liberties Union, but it's also reinforced throughout in subtler ways.

- In the beginning, the lawyer is trying to win a labor law case by using a secret videotape against some gangsters. It's not admissible in court, but the gangsters don't want it exposed.
- Who got the lawyer the tape? A young woman he once had an affair with. The affair is over, but now he must hide the fact from his wife that he's still working with her.
- Where is he when he accidentally gets the item the NSA wants? A lingerie store, shopping for his wife, but because of his past affair, he's afraid she will assume he's buying for someone else.
- Why is he there? It's Christmastime, which means they're hiding presents from their son, and he's hiding the fact he's raided their gift stash, which complicates things later on.

All these things subtly make the point that we all do things we don't want exposed to scrutiny, even if they're perfectly legal.

I suspect that none of these details was in the first draft (since not one is essential to the story), and once the plot had been worked out, writer David Marconi went back and replaced whatever random choices he'd originally made with new details that tied into the theme. I've heard this referred to as making a "theme tree," or yoking every detail together into a vast system of root and branch that all feeds into an organic whole. Every choice is a chance to multiply the meaning.

In the surprisingly charming romantic comedy *Date Night*, every scene does more than one thing, on more than one level. The cleverly structured story allows every scene to be a plot, character, *and* theme scene, so the movie rarely has to stop to change gears or shift in tone. To save their lives, this couple must unravel a mystery, but the only way to do that is to adopt new identities that break them out of their ennui and force them to inadvertently reveal long-held secrets to each other.

It's no coincidence that they end up confronting a procession of bizarre *couples* mixed up in the mystery, with each representing an extreme example of what they wish they were or what they're afraid they'll become. These are parallel characters who act as cautionary tales and/or potential role models. Such characters not only help a story's tone by providing foreshadowing, but they also enrich a story's theme by ensuring every scene shows aspects of the central dilemma.

☑ Are one or more objects representing larger ideas that grow in meaning each time they're exchanged throughout the story?

Independent filmmakers Ted Hope and James Schamus had a great list of "No-Budget Commandments" when they ran their own production company. One was "Invest meaning in everyday commonplace things—make an orange a totemic object John Ford would be proud of."

You can't rely on character interactions to reveal all the emotions. When characters talk with each other, they have three different factors influencing them:

1. their current mood
2. what they want the other characters to do
3. how they feel about the other characters deep down

But when you establish their relationship to an object, they can express their *true* emotions, unfiltered by other baggage.

In *The Color of Money*, Paul Newman trains a naïve young pool phenomenon played by Tom Cruise. Together with Cruise's shady girlfriend (Mary Elizabeth Mastrantonio), they tool around the Northeast, hustling in dingy joints on their way to a big tournament in Atlantic City.

Sure enough, all of the characters have their own totem objects:

- First, Newman gives Cruise a fancy pool cue, on the condition he never use it because it would ruin the hustle. It becomes the object of all of Cruise's frustrations as he tries to learn the business.
- Mastrantonio wears a necklace she stole from Cruise's mother. She chuckles as she explains to Newman, "He says his mom had one just like it." As they compete to see who will get to exploit Cruise's talent, Newman keeps an eye on the necklace to remind himself of whom he's dealing with.

- Newman doesn't get his totem object until the end of the second act. It's what Joseph Campbell would call "the special weapon he finds in the cave." Newman finally admits he needs prescription glasses and uses them to compete with his former protégé.

Count how many glances and comments each one of these objects earns, and how they change meaning over the course of the movie— when they get taken out, put away, or change hands. The cagey characters can't say what they feel, but their interactions with these objects reveal all.

As Ted Hope points out, this is the sort of thing that creates easy value. Too many stories can be summed up as "people stand around in rooms and talk," but a story starts to come alive when the audience knows certain objects are fraught with meaning.

The acclaimed BBC series *Sherlock* updates the original Arthur Conan Doyle stories to modern day, with lots of texting and blogging added in, but show runner Stephen Moffat knows the art of adaptation is about more than technology. Even if his version had been set in 1887, Moffat is smart enough to know that some things must be changed simply because of the transition from prose to television.

The first episode adapts the novel that introduced Sherlock Holmes and his friend Watson: *A Study in Scarlet*. In the novel, our narrator, Watson, has survived a massacre in Afghanistan without injury, but he's plagued by depression (which modern readers recognize as posttraumatic stress disorder, though it was still unnamed at the time). Because this is first-person prose, Watson can tell the reader about his depression in the text. As he recounts his adventure with Sherlock Holmes, he explains how it gradually helps him break free of his malaise. This is what first-person prose does best: It allows us to directly commune with the thoughts and feelings of a person as he is changed by an experience.

But television's moving images are nowhere near as intimate as first-person prose. Sure, you can use a lot of narration or therapy scenes, but television is a visual medium, so the best way to convey a character's psychology is through his physical interactions. But a condition like PTSD is problematic because no one can see it. How do you show it? You *externalize* it.

Moffat does this very simply: He manifests Watson's PTSD as a psychosomatic limp. Watson walks with a cane, but as soon as he meets Holmes, Holmes instantly perceives he doesn't really need it, which both offends and intrigues Watson. Sure enough, after Watson has gotten thoroughly engrossed in Holmes's adventures, they find themselves caught up in a sudden chase. Only after the chase is over does Watson realize he's left his crutch behind, literally and figuratively.

Let's look at how nicely *Iron Man* showed the exchange of an object representing larger values: Tony's heart device.

- He, too, is ambushed in Afghanistan, and his heart is injured when a bomb sold by his own company pierces the armor provided by the army.
- Tony finds out the shrapnel is lodged in his chest, slowly making its way toward his heart, and can't be removed. He can only hold it back with magnets. The man explaining this to Tony understands because he's witnessed Tony's bombs kill children in his village the same way. (Tony is being literally and figuratively stabbed in the heart.)
- Tony and his new third-world friend devise a glowing device to keep his heart alive—and to fill a literal and figurative hole in his chest.
- His friend dies and tells Tony not to waste what he's given him: a heart.
- Tony gets home and invents a sleeker device using his superior technology. He doesn't trust doctors, so he gets his executive assistant, Pepper, to take out the old heart and put the new one in. She does so by reaching deep into his chest cavity and touching the heart. She asks about the old one, but he forcefully waves it away and says, "Destroy it. Incinerate it. I've been called many things, but never a sentimentalist." Nevertheless, she takes it with her.
- What do you get for the man who has everything? Pepper gives him back the device encased in glass, set in a metal ring that says "Proof that Tony Stark Has a Heart" (even if it is one he lost interest in).

- Stane, Tony's treacherous partner, builds his own armor, but he can't figure out how to build the heart of it, in more ways than one.
- So Stane ambushes Tony and rips the sleek new heart device out of his chest, leaving him to die.
- Tony crawls down to his lab and busts the glass on Pepper's gift at the last second. He gave his heart to the right person!
- The final battle can be seen as Pepper's heart versus Stane's heart, or as the authentic, third-world heart versus the stolen, first-world heart.

A lot of this sounds heavy-handed when I spell it out, but that's the beauty of it. The movie doesn't have to spell it out. We would reject these messages if we heard them, but we're simply feeling them instead.

Think of all the dialogue this object's exchange has replaced. Tony doesn't have to discuss at length how he feels about his weapons killing innocents, his feelings for Pepper, her feelings for him, how it feels to be betrayed, etc. It allows Tony to remain the happy-go-lucky guy we want him to be, because we have this object to tell us a lot of the things he doesn't want to say.

Untidy

☑ *Does the ending tip toward one side of the thematic dilemma without entirely resolving it?*

Your theme should take the form of an irresolvable dilemma, so you should give both sides equal weight for as long as possible until the climax. The trick is to come up with a finale that addresses the conflict and makes a concrete statement about it, without definitively declaring one side right and the other wrong.

Each of the first three seasons of *Lost* has a powerful overarching theme:

- **SEASON ONE:** our future is dictated by our past versus our future is a blank slate
- **SEASON TWO:** faith versus skepticism

- **SEASON THREE:** strict, safe order (the Others) versus chaotic, unsafe freedom (the crash survivors)

At the end of each season, the characters advocating one side of the debate are proven "right."

- **SEASON ONE:** The characters find ways to move on from the past, and even sing "Redemption Song" together on a boat.
- **SEASON TWO:** We find out Locke was right to have faith in the button, and Jack was wrong when he said it did nothing.
- **SEASON THREE:** The chaotic makeshift community of the crash survivors proves to be more sustainable than the cultlike Others.

But in each case, the victory is ironic and ambiguous. A statement is made about the dilemma, but it's not permanently settled.

You have something to say, but you don't have something *definitive* to say. You have a point, but your point is untidy. You're leaving room open for uncertainty and ambiguity, because that multiplies the meaning.

Let's return to the stories we looked at before. Each has an irreconcilable thematic dilemma, and five of them tip toward one side in the end, but not definitively:

- *Casablanca*: Patriotism is better than love, but it's a painful decision.
- *Beloved*: Sethe will never know whether enslavement was better than death for her daughter, but she warily accepts that self-forgiveness is better than self-accountability.
- *Harry Potter and the Philosopher's Stone*: Justice is better than peace, but it comes with dark consequences. (Harry not only kills Quirrell, but he condemns Dumbledore's friend Nicholas Flamel to death by destroying the stone.)
- *Iron Man*: Yes, societal responsibility is ultimately somewhat more important than individual achievement, but Tony still wants to be a badass all the time, not a do-gooder.
- *An Education*: Yes, living up to one's responsibilities is somewhat better than a life of excitement, but we sense she doesn't really re-

gret her dalliance and still longs to be more sophisticated than her parents.

But the other three have interesting variations:

- In *Groundhog Day*, one of the contrasting values in the thematic dilemma is clearly superior to the others. Phil concludes that acceptance is almost entirely better than ambition.
- *Silence of the Lambs* ends with its moral dilemma still totally unsettled. Neither Clarice nor the audience can decide at the end whether it was worth it to work with one monster to stop another.
- *Sideways* pits Jack's boundless optimism versus Miles's clear-eyed cynicism, but each man achieves his own goal by reverting to type at the end and fails to influence the other. Jack's outrageous, optimistic lies pay off for him, and Miles's cynical honesty pays off for him. The conclusion looks askance at both of their philosophies but refuses to privilege either one over the other.

So this rule isn't universal: You can resolve the dilemma definitively, tip to one side without resolving it, or leave it totally unresolved, but the middle option is the most common and usually the best bet. You have something to say, so say it, but you don't want to take away from the fundamental power of the irreconcilable dilemma.

☑ Does the story's outcome ironically contrast with the initial goal?

And so we arrive at our final irony: the ironic final outcome. Way back when we started, we discussed how the basic concept of your story should have a fundamental irony. That overriding irony should be apparent by a quarter of the way in, but it shouldn't be confused with the final irony that isn't clear until the end.

In chapter three, we explored why these story concepts are ironic. Now let's jump to the ending to see their ironic final outcomes:

1. *Casablanca*: Rick gets Ilsa back only so he can send her away.

2. *Beloved*: Sethe still thinks her daughter's vengeful ghost was "my best thing."
3. *Silence of the Lambs*: One killer is stopped, but the worse killer gets away in the process.
4. *Groundhog Day*: Phil finally figures out how to get out of the town he hates by deciding he wants to stay there forever.
5. *Harry Potter and the Philosopher's Stone*: The most scared teacher turns out to be most useful to the villain, rather than the mean teacher. Then Harry and his friends win the house cup by breaking all the rules.
6. *Sideways*: Miles discovers the way to get the girl is to have the courage to do nothing. He finds the book that failed to earn him the love of the world has ironically done its job after all, because it's moved the one heart he really needed to move.
7. *Iron Man*: Tony's own business partner turns out to be the villain.
8. *An Education*: At Oxford, Jenny gets the education she originally wanted, but she has to pretend she hasn't already received a far more worldly education.

Even stories that are already ironic can always benefit from another ironic bit at the very end. Because the Nazis are defeated by their own treasure, the ending of *Raiders of the Lost Ark* is already quite ironic, but it has one last kicker waiting for us. After all the action, suffering, and shouts of "It belongs in a museum!" Indiana and Marion finally bring this legendary artifact (and powerful weapon) home to the United States, where it gets dumped in a vast warehouse and forgotten.

It's ironic that Indiana's efforts have the opposite effect of his intentions, but even more ironically, the audience realizes this forgotten bureaucratic warehouse is probably the safest place possible for this dangerous artifact. The audience has seen Indiana's goal come to naught at the last possible second—and they love it. They actually enjoy a good ironic reversal more than a straightforward payoff.

We don't want to live in a clockwork universe, and we don't want clockwork stories. We don't want to watch authors plug numbers into a machine, pull the big lever, and get the expected result. We want irony because it's surprising, because it's clever, and, more than anything, because it's *realistic*. There are no straight lines in nature, and we don't want any in our stories, either. We love to see our heroes get what they want in the end—as long as they don't get it in quite the way they wanted.

☑ In the end, is the plot not entirely tidy?

I had the good fortune to teach a section of Andrew Sarris's Hitchcock course at Columbia. Mr. Sarris did more than anyone to cement Hitchcock's critical reputation in this country, and there was no better education than watching the films with him, hearing his lectures, and then facilitating a discussion with my half of the class the next day. My favorite student questions were those I never thought to ask. When we were discussing *Vertigo* followed by *North by Northwest*, I was asked an odd but interesting question. Allow me to paraphrase the student:

> Everybody pretty much agrees that *North by Northwest* is a perfectly constructed film. It fits together better than any other Hitchcock movie. And, yet, you say *Vertigo* is considered to be "greater" by almost every critic. How can *Vertigo*, which is really messy, be better than *North by Northwest*, which is perfect?

It was a good question. *Vertigo* has a very odd structure. It slows down to a crawl in places. It leaves plot threads dangling and forgets to pick them back up. The plot is untidy and so are the character arcs. We're left wondering at the end about everybody's motivation. We can guess, but we can't be *sure*. *North by Northwest*, on the other hand, builds and builds and then pays off seamlessly. We understand every beat of Cary Grant's journey, strategically and emotionally. It's an immensely satisfying movie to watch.

But depth is found in holes. A few unanswered questions and unresolved emotions are necessary to really have a profound effect on a viewer. Right at the beginning of *Vertigo*, we abruptly cut from Jimmy

Stewart, dangling from a building in terror, with no rescue in sight, to several months later, as he talks with a friend about leaving the police force. We can figure out what happened in between, but because we never see the rescue, we're left with the unresolved disturbance of his emotional reaction.

Similarly, I mentioned earlier that Madeleine's disappearance from the hotel room is never explained. Again, we can hazard guesses, but the refusal to tidy up this loose end gnaws at us on a subconscious level.

These aren't really plot holes; they're just holes, gaps in the story, and that's what makes *Vertigo* a greater film than *North by Northwest*. Great art shouldn't be *entirely* satisfying. It has to disquiet us a little—and have a few holes for us to get stuck in.

☑ Do the characters refuse or fail to synthesize the meaning of the story?

Meaning must be created in the minds of the audience, not on the page, the stage, or the screen. While it's tempting to preprocess your conflict and present your finalized synthesis to the audience (to control what their takeaway will be), there's no point, because they won't care.

Modern Family can be an entertaining sitcom—as long as you turn it off two minutes early. At the end of each episode, you have to watch a member of the family come onscreen, look right at you, and point out how all three of that week's storylines were really about the same big theme and how glad that person is to have learned so much. Any meaning the episode may have generated is quickly slaughtered by this clumsy exegesis.

Compare this to any of the far-superior, documentary-style sitcoms this show mimics, especially the American version of *The Office*. Boss Michael Scott frequently appears at the end to sum up what meaning has been created by that week's episode. But he gets it all spectacularly wrong and forces *us* to do the work.

You need to have the courage to let your audience draw their own meaning, even if that means they might not "get it," or they might even come to the opposite conclusion you intended.

What were Shakespeare's politics? In *Julius Caesar*, did he agree with Brutus or Marc Antony? Does he side with Prince Hal or Falstaff in *Henry IV*? No one knows. His plays are filled with huge ideological conflicts but few definitive statements. He gives us a thesis and antithesis and leaves the synthesis to us. That's why he's immortal.

So that's it! You're done! Ha. No. Not at all. Now it's time for the most important part of the process…

PART III

Getting from Good to
"Good Lord, This Is Amazing!"

So now we have an exhaustive (and, yes, exhausting) list of 122 questions in seven categories. This list will help you diagnose whatever problems you may have with your story or pitch, and suggest solutions.

Take the time now to download the list from SecretsofStory.com. We've put it there in a format that will allow you to fill in an answer to each question and check a box yes or no.

Let me once again clarify: Every story is unique and no story that I've evaluated has answered yes to all 122 questions, nor should it. I evaluated dozens of great movies using the checklist, and they've gotten a wide variety of scores. The highest score was for *Star Wars*, which isn't surprising, because it's a classically made movie. But a lot of equally great movies score much lower. The lowest score was *Groundhog Day*, which makes sense because it's an odder concept. You'll also find a spreadsheet that will allow you to scan by question and see how each movie got a yes or no, which should give you a greater understanding of what each question is really about and what it means to fulfill it or not.

Online, you'll also find a substantially different version of the checklist engineered for pilot stories: the first episode of a TV show, Web series, comic book, book series, etc. About half of the questions are the same. I've subjected a dozen TV pilots to this list in a spreadsheet all their own.

So what's your score? Are you happy with it? Has the checklist identified problem areas for you to focus on as you revise?

Well, I'm afraid I've got bad news for you: *You're not allowed to revise*. Not yet, anyway. This brings us to the first chapter of Part III.

10

DON'T REVISE, REWRITE!

WHAT IS REWRITING?

Before you revise, you have to rewrite! Rewriting is 90 percent of the writing process. If you don't believe me, download *The Adventures of Luke Starkiller as Taken from the Journal of the Whills*. That's what a first draft looks like. That's what *your* first draft looks like to any reader who's willing to be honest with you. That script improved a wee bit before all was said and done. Can you improve your story that much? Sure you can, but you've got a lot of work to do.

MISCONCEPTIONS ABOUT REWRITING

MISCONCEPTION: Now that you have The Ultimate Story Checklist, you can identify all of the flaws in your own manuscript.

AU CONTRAIRE: Now might be the time to demand a refund, because that just isn't true. You still need outside notes.

I've designed this checklist to be a powerful tool, and though it will remind you of many questions strangers will demand of your manuscript, it's still going to be *you* answering those questions about *your own* story, and you will always have blind spots about your work. This checklist is made to work in conjunction with outside notes.

MISCONCEPTION: People who care about you will give you great notes.

AU CONTRAIRE: If you can get notes from peers who are *not* friends or family, those notes will be *much* more reliable.

At first, only people who care about you will be willing to read your writing, and they will try to give you good notes, but (a) they are probably not trained writers who can identify the real problems, and (b) they will not want to hurt your feelings about the overall quality of your work. If you can somehow get notes from peers who are *not* friends or family, those notes will be *much* more reliable. But wait, you may still think that …

> **MISCONCEPTION:** Paid instructors will give you reliable notes.
>
> **AU CONTRAIRE:** Your instructors may seem tough, but they aren't tough enough.

There are two things you must keep in mind about your instructors:

- Their income depends on your tuition, so they have a strong financial incentive to overpraise you and keep you enrolled.
- They are evaluating your work against a platonic ideal that exists only in their heads, not on how successful your work will be with an audience. (In fact, they often have open disdain for audiences, because of an understandable bitterness about their own career setbacks.)

So we have a paradox: Free notes are far more valuable than paid notes. Luckily, getting free notes is easier than it's ever been before. There are a lot of online communities that will allow you to submit your work for group feedback, and if you want an in-person writing group, you can go to those same sites, tell them what city you live in, and say you want to form a meet-up group.

One way or another, you're going to need a lot of strangers to read your work and give you high-quality notes for free. So why on earth would they do this? There's only one reason: You have a reputation for giving great notes in return. (On the website, there's a section on how to give great notes so you can get great notes back on a regular basis!)

Of course, none of these notes will do you any good unless you've accepted a few things like …

MISCONCEPTION: Once you've perfected it, then it's done.

AU CONTRAIRE: It's not up to you to decide what's perfect. You need notes to know what you have and how to make it better.

Don't be precious. Don't be resistant to change. Don't defend your work against notes. Your peers, early readers, representatives, and editors and/or producers will hopefully all do a better job than you of determining what the story needs, so listen to them.

MISCONCEPTION: You don't want to mess it up.

AU CONTRAIRE: You do want to mess it up.

If any part of your story is fragile or delicate, then it won't survive the shipping process. Shake it up and chip away until everything left is rock solid.

MISCONCEPTION: You should revise your first draft.

AU CONTRAIRE: You should *rewrite* your first few drafts.

Let's face it: Revision is bullshit. You can tinker around the edges all you want, but you won't really improve your story until you tear it apart and rebuild it. You hope you can just tweak a few plot points or sweeten some dialogue without affecting any other scenes, but that's not going to get you anywhere. In fact, it'll just piss everybody off.

If someone reads your entire manuscript and is thoughtful enough to give you a ton of notes as to how you can improve it, then don't you *dare* ask them to read it again unless it's massively rewritten.

There's nothing more annoying than rereading something that's only been slightly revised since the first draft. That's true even when friends read each others' work, so imagine how infuriating it is when producers or reps devote more time to their reread than you did to your rewrite.

Rather than merely refining scenes or dialogue, your first rewrite should be focused on fundamentally transforming the characters' personalities—and this will then force you to change *everything* else. You should not attempt line-by-line revisions until you've totally reshaped your work according to the overarching feedback you've gotten.

> **MISCONCEPTION:** If you disagree with a note, you can just ignore it.

> **AU CONTRAIRE:** If you strongly disagree with a note, set it aside for now, but if you get the same note again from someone else, then I've got bad news for you: That's when the *Back to the Future* rule kicks in.

On the DVD commentary for *Back to the Future*, co-writer Bob Gale quotes his partner Robert Zemeckis as saying, "If one person says something, that's their opinion. If two people say the same thing, then there are probably *millions* of people that'll agree."

Indeed, Gale describes *years* of rewrites on that script, both before and after it sold. Let's start with the most basic: What does a time machine look like? Well, it's a big metal booth that you climb into, right? So if you needed to recharge one back in the fifties, what would you do? You'd hoist it up onto the back of a truck, throw a tarp over it, and drive out to New Mexico to steal some nuclear material. And in the first twenty or so versions of this script, that's exactly what happened.

Finally, after years of beating their heads up against the wall, one of them thought to ask, "Hey, what if we invented a time machine *on wheels*. Wouldn't that be more convenient? And what if he could stay in town and re-energize the time machine with *lightning*? But how would he know the exact moment that a lightning bolt would strike? Wait, that gives me an idea. ..."

That's hardcore, ground-floor rewriting right there. That's how great stories are painstakingly assembled over the course of many, many drafts.

That said, even if this rule *doesn't* kick in, be aware of another misconception.

> **MISCONCEPTION:** There's no point in paying attention to "bad notes."

> **AU CONTRAIRE:** Most bad notes have good notes hiding underneath, so you shouldn't ignore them.

In the end, there's really no such thing as a bad note. Every note is an indication of an unmet expectation, and that's always good to know. The problem is, most notes come in the form of suggestions for changes, and the changes they suggest are often *terrible*. The trick is to see past the bad suggestion to the good note underneath.

Here's a classic example. As I mentioned before, I developed a dark TV pilot about the CIA, and I showed it to an old mentor of mine. He read it and liked it, but he said I needed to add a scene at the beginning where our undercover hero planted a bomb and then calmly walked away while it blew up.

I was totally aghast: What a horrible note! Those scenes are so idiotic! To start with, let's just look at this from a tradecraft perspective: Failing to react to an explosion doesn't show that you're a cool, unflappable spy; it shows you're a bumbling amateur! Obviously, if you're the only one who doesn't act surprised by an explosion, then you're the one who set it, and everybody's going to instantly tackle you. And even if these scenes aren't silly to begin with, by now they've become painfully predictable clichés! I can't believe this guy wants me to add one of those stupid, stupid scenes!

But all he meant, I later realized, was I should include that *type* of scene: a bit of badass, exciting, I-wanna-be-that-guy spy action before I got to all the backstabbing, political infighting, and moral recriminations.

I could have blanched and said that wasn't the sort of show I wanted to do. After all, I wanted more of a John le Carré–type show about double-crosses and unexpected, real-world consequences, but I then realized this was *all the more* reason to begin with a scene that gets people to watch this type of show.

I wanted my show to be subversive, but if I started downbeat *and* finished downbeat, then I would merely be attracting downbeat viewers, and, in the end, fulfilling their expectations. Instead I wanted to take normal spy fans and subvert their expectations. This meant that first I had to create false expectations about the greatness of my heroes and the efficacy of spy work. That way, when it all unravels, the audience will feel shocked and unsettled. It's hard to subvert expectations you didn't create.

So how do you take the note but not the suggested fix? You replace the hoary old suggestion with something fresh, in this case, either a unique twist on a classic spy behavior or, even better, some real-life bit of badass tradecraft from a nonfiction book (as long as it's instantly cool without you having to explain).

> **MISCONCEPTION:** The problem with modern storytelling is that writers get too many notes.
>
> **AU CONTRAIRE:** That is sometimes the case, but the opposite can also be true. Writers need a lot of great notes to do their best work.

We've all felt oppressed by notes. If the process doesn't go well, they can make you doubt your instincts, get hopelessly lost in unwelcome rewrites, and turn your work into noxious slop concocted by too many cooks. But it's essential to remember that the alternative is even worse. Even if you self-publish, it's essential to hire an outside editor. But why, you may ask, would I subject myself to that willingly? Let's look at an example from the movies:

We all know producers can ruin a movie with too many notes, and without a doubt, the biggest problem in Hollywood right now is that movies take way too long to get made. But Clint Eastwood, to his credit, doesn't have either of these problems. In fact, he's gained a reputation as the only director in Hollywood who tends to shoot the first draft he's given, then brings in a beautiful-looking movie on time and under budget.

Great. So he's the solution, right? Well, not quite.

I love many of Eastwood's recent films, but his process has also resulted in some real stink bombs, and *J. Edgar* was pretty much rock bottom. This was especially disappointing because the writer was Dustin Lance Black, whose previous movie, *Milk*, was one of the best biopics of recent years.

If you put a great writer and a respectful director together, you should get magic, but the opposite often happens. Here's Black talking about the sheer terror he felt when he discovered Eastwood was going to shoot his first draft:

> When I found out Clint was interested it was both a blessing and bit of "Oh, boy … There are some things I'd like to change still." I'd heard Peter Morgan say that on [Eastwood's previous movie] *Hereafter*, he'd had that feeling … but they were already shooting! … But it is funny because I went to Rob Lorenz and I said, "Hey, we should probably cut a good chunk out of the first act. That's kind of everything and the kitchen sink." And he's like, "Well, we'll shoot it all and we'll see what turns out well."

As loathe as I am to admit it, *J. Edgar* was made too quickly and with too few notes. We screenwriters love to complain about how directors and producers mess up our work with their notes, and that can certainly happen in a situation where we aren't all working well together, but if we communicate well and learn to trust each other, then we can get the great notes we need to create a great final product.

MISCONCEPTION: There is one platonic ideal of what your story should be.

AU CONTRAIRE: There are a lot of great versions of every scene and sequence. Try them all out and see what you find.

If you keep trying out utterly different versions of each scene, you'll find surprising new angles that serve your story better. Even *after* you sell it, the buyers may demand that you spend *years* rewriting and revising your story. Do so happily and heartily. Make them tear it out of your hands when *they* think it's ready to go before an audience.

MISCONCEPTION: Peers who give you a lot of notes are picking on you.

AU CONTRAIRE: A note is a bighearted gift.

The only reason people will ever give you notes is because they want to improve your story. Peers who don't like a story just dismiss it, but notes mean that you've found someone who's willing to help that story improve. Even if the notes break your heart, and even if they're stated in a rude or insensitive way, thank the note giver.

> **MISCONCEPTION:** If potential buyers give you notes, that means they didn't like it.
>
> **AU CONTRAIRE:** If they didn't like it, they would ignore you or give vague noncommittal praise and *then* ignore you. Notes mean they're interested.

Notes prove they have engaged with your story and now feel invested in making it better. Notes are good. But you should be warned …

> **MISCONCEPTION:** Buyers who give you notes will be happy if you make half of the changes they ask for.
>
> **AU CONTRAIRE:** Buyers expect you to rewrite *everything* they had a problem with and much more.

Regardless of any assurances to the contrary, potential buyers do not regard their notes as optional requests or debatable opinions. Rather, they regard every one of their notes as sacrosanct and symptoms of even larger problems.

You must take every note potential buyers give you. This is fine: You can always save the current version just the way you want it and then open up a new copy and try it *their* way. There's no longer any danger of running out of space on a five-inch floppy disk. And guess what? You may like it better! Or both you and the buyers may hate the new version, but this still will be a valuable exercise, because it has encouraged you to re-approach your story from an outside point of view, which is a useful way of re-evaluating your story and an important skill for every writer to hone.

> **MISCONCEPTION:** If they *didn't* give you a note about it, they *don't* want you to change it.
>
> **AU CONTRAIRE:** Don't assume they're in love with the stuff they didn't mention. They want the notes they give you to spark a larger transformation.

Everybody hates reading a rewrite in which very little has changed. You still have the older version, and you can revert to it at any time, but for now, you should keep trying new things throughout your story, improving everything, not just the things they gave you notes about.

> **MISCONCEPTION:** You should focus your attention on those sections of your story people say aren't working.
>
> **AU CONTRAIRE:** Treat each problem like a polyp of an endemic disease.

If someone says you have "third-act problems" or you just need "a new first chapter," don't believe it. Note givers almost always misidentify the source of a problem. The person may be upset that your ending didn't pay off a false expectation, so instead of adding a payoff to the ending, you should go back to the earlier sections and remove the moment that created the false expectation.

HOW TO REWRITE (AND REWRITE, AND REWRITE ...)

So you can forget about "revising" for now. Forget about tweaking your dialogue or fixing a "third-act problem." You need to rethink your concept, reconceive your characters, and find an entirely new structure. If you're doing it right, your "second draft" will often be a page-one rewrite.

Step One: You Need to Fall out of Love

So let's say you've just finished your slick, shiny, pretty new manuscript. You're in love with it, and you're in love with yourself. You're open to making a few changes, of course, and you might be willing to get out your chrome polish and buff it to an even brighter shine, but it's hard to mess with perfection.

Wait. Stop yourself. Instead, put your manuscript in a drawer for a week. Better yet, leave it out in the backyard, exposed to the elements, to get dusty, rusty, and musty. *Unpolish* it. Then, a week later, look at it for what it really is: an unvarnished mess. Now you can strip it, sand it, deconstruct it, and rebuild it from scratch.

Rewriting is painful. You've already moved heaven and earth to get to "The End." You've avoided a million pitfalls that would have kept you from finishing. You've finally discovered a reasonable, if circuitous path that gets your hero all the way from innocence to experience, from failure to triumph, and you're now convinced this is the only path that could have led there.

You start to ask yourself some self-destructive questions:

- Why should I have to revise this?
- What about all the work I've already put into it? Shouldn't that count for something?
- Isn't this already better than something that recently sold for big money? Isn't it already better than *Transcendence*?

Alas, these are not productive questions. Here are some better questions to ask yourself:

- Would I be proud to see this go out to the world exactly the way it is? If not, why not?
- How many different ways can I make this better?
- What's the weakest scene? How can I transform it into the strongest scene?
- Are there writers doing work that's better than this? How can I surpass them?
- If a friend sent me this, would I tell her not to change a thing and send it out immediately? Or would I point out a dozen ways to make it better?

As with any job, the hope is not to merely impress your boss but to impress your boss's boss—not just to play by their rules but to beat them at their own game. You've written something that's good enough to send out to trusted friends, which is already a huge achievement, but now you need to write something that's amazing enough to win over complete strangers, which is a lot harder.

When the makers of *Anchorman* finished the first cut of the movie, they thought, *Gee, this is pretty good, but we can do a lot better*. They ended up cutting out and replacing so much material they were able to release both versions on DVD as separate movies!

Of course, while you're spending that time away from your manuscript, it's also an excellent time to send it out to your acquaintances for notes. By the time the last copy comes in, not only will you be ready to see your project with fresh eyes, but you'll be able to see it through the eyes of others as well.

Step Two: Heed the Notes You Get and the Notes You Don't Get

What does it *mean* to address a note? You have two choices: You can implement the specific change it asked for, or you can make a bigger change that addresses or eliminates the underlying problem. Here's the bad news: For every note you get, there will be two you didn't get that are even more important.

As you wrote, you presumably tried to police for problems, but many of them will be invisible to you unless someone else points them out. The problem is, note givers are much more inclined to point out some kinds of problems than others. For example, note givers are usually pretty good at pointing out **plot holes**:

> "This doesn't make any sense."

> "I didn't get what was happening here."

> "Didn't that character die two scenes ago?"

You're less likely to hear about **motivation holes**. These are moments where the hero does something without proper motivation, and they're far more problematic than plot holes. These alienate us on a subconscious level, but readers often fail to notice them as they happen. Instead of saying, "the hero needs more motivation," they're more likely to say things like:

> "I didn't buy it."

> "This feels too convenient."

Plot holes are bad, and motivation holes are worse, but the worst kinds of holes are **identification holes**. This refers to any moment where the audience says, "You know what? I just don't care about this hero anymore." Again, readers are bad at consciously noticing these moments. You'll almost never hear anything like "I didn't empathize with the hero enough," or "It wasn't emotional enough." People don't realize they *want* to be emotionally manipulated, so they're not going to ask you to do that. But *you* know they secretly love it.

If people aren't emotionally engaged enough, they tend to say things like:

> "It wasn't very interesting."

> "The middle was boring."

> "I wasn't sure what you were trying to say."

> "The story just kind of ends."

> "The villain was a lot more interesting than the hero."

> And the big one: "Sorry, I never finished reading it."

One reason your nice friends prefer to point out plot holes is because these holes can theoretically be fixed by just changing one scene. They're reluctant to say you have motivation or identification problems because then you might have to reconceive your entire story. Nevertheless, you need to reassure them that those are exactly the sort of notes you want to hear.

In *Indiana Jones and the Kingdom of the Crystal Skull*, there's a scene near the end where Indy and his crew survive an endless series of waterfalls and realize they've beaten the Soviets to the skull cave. Suddenly they stop and say, "Wait a minute. Now that we're here, what do we want to do? Do we even want these skulls or not? I dunno … I guess … maybe?" Wow! Biggest motivation hole ever!

This was a big-budget movie. Why did no one point out this giant sucking hole at the heart of the story? It's not hard to guess: There would have been no way to fix it without rewriting the entire story.

For Indy to go through all of that life-or-death struggle, he needed a strong motivation. He needed to either crave or despise the skulls. Instead he merely got roped into a fiasco he didn't really care about based on very weak motivation. This ruined the story, but nobody involved in the production wanted to pick at that scab since they knew the entire movie would hemorrhage and bleed out.

But identification notes are even *more* painful to deliver. After all, most writers base their heroes on themselves! If you say, "I hate your passive, petulant, self-righteous hero," you might as well say, "And you might want to fix your own personality while you're at it!" In the end, you either have to beat these notes out of people, or you can simply infer from them what they're *not* saying.

Step Three: Fill Each Hole Without Digging a New One

When building a house, it's not immediately obvious where the load-bearing walls are. If the client comes in and says, "I want to make this place a little airier. Why don't we take out that wall, that wall, and that wall?" then the architect has to jump in and say, "The first two walls are no problem, but that third wall is the only thing supporting the second floor."

This is what's so frustrating about getting notes. The fear is that some busybody might swoop in and say, "Oh, it's too hard to sympathize with the guy if he cheats on his wife, so take that out." And the writer can only stammer, "But it's a redemption story! If he doesn't cheat on his wife, he has no motivation to do any of the things he does to redeem himself!" In the case of *Phone Booth* and *Big Fish*, the writers presumably lost that battle, so the movies became simply inane.

So let's say you've written a book, movie, or TV pilot in which the hero fails to save a child, and that failure sparks a huge personal transformation, but your editor/producer/network says it's too unsympathetic to have the child die as a result of your hero's failure. Instead, they want your hero to save the child so we'll like her right away. You protest that the dead child is the entire reason for the hero's journey, but you lose that fight.

Your note givers feel that you have an empathy hole—she lets that kid die!—but to fill it, they want to dig a motivation hole. (If the kid doesn't die, the hero doesn't have strong enough motivation to go on her journey of personal transformation.)

Now, remember, you have to take *every* note you get from a buyer, so what do you do? The note givers think the solution is easy: Just have her save the kid and go on the journey anyway! But you know that won't work. So what do you do? You come up with a new situation. Believe your note givers when they say it's just too alienating to see the kid die, but don't give them the simple solution they asked for. Find an entirely new tragedy to motivate your hero that's less alienating to your audience.

Your note givers aren't idiots: They know that saving the kid is an imperfect solution. But it's the best solution they can come up with based on what you've given them. If you want a better solution, you just have to give them more to work with. They don't really want you to just parrot their note back to them. They want their notes to spark a larger transformation. They don't want to "win." They want to hear you say, "I tried something completely different. See if you like this better." They'll be delighted. If you keep rewriting, you'll come up with some clever solution that fills each hole without digging any new ones.

Step Four: Don't Paper Over the Problem

So now that we're more aware of our problems, let's take a tour of the various ways you can fix them, from the worst to the best:

1. The *worst* solution: Tack on an "explainer" afterward, letting your characters retroactively explain to the audience that what seemed

like a problem wasn't actually a problem. *Inception* does this over and over, like when they pause in the middle of a ski chase to retroactively explain the people they just killed aren't real people, so it's okay.

2. Set up foreshadowing of the problematic scene beforehand so the audience will be too busy making the connection to notice the problem. *Source Code* papered over several massive plot holes by distracting the audience with clever setups and payoffs.

3. For each problem, write a new scene that adds a missing element. If the character isn't sympathetic enough, then add a "save the cat" scene. If they don't have enough motivation, add a spouse in harm's way.

4. For each problem, remove the scene that sets up the unmet expectation. Instead of adding a payoff for a "problems at work" subplot that goes nowhere, simply eliminate the subplot altogether. The girlfriend's role was underwritten in *Michael Clayton*, and rather than add scenes to artificially "beef it up," they just cut it, and nobody missed it.

5. The *best* solution: Pair up the problems so every change eliminates more than one problem.

Remember, the goal of a rewrite should always be to *simplify* the story, not complicate it. The ultimate goal should be to have a simple story about complex characters, and not vice versa. With each draft, your characters should become deeper and richer, while the story becomes more streamlined and elegant.

Step Five: Pair Off Your Problems

It's important to get a lot of notes piled up before you start addressing any of them individually. The danger is that you'll deal with notes one by one, adding dozens of "fixes" to your story that don't integrate with each other or the story as a whole.

I have a series on my blog called "The Meddler" where I suggest fixes for problematic movies and books. In each case, I suggest ways to fix two huge problems with one simple change.

In the political thriller *The Ghost Writer*, we never get to see the supposed charm of Pierce Brosnan's Tony Blair–like character, and Ewan McGregor's hero is a passive protagonist who doesn't really care about the mystery. If we saw Brosnan charmingly win over McGregor to his cause, then the revelation of Brosnan's lies would feel like a personal betrayal *and* give McGregor a stronger motivation to investigate Brosnan's dark secret.

Likewise, Martin Scorsese's *Hugo* didn't work for me because of two big problems:

- First, the movie is founded on a huge motivation hole: Hugo has convinced himself that the automaton his father brought home will have a message for him, but this makes no sense. His father tells him up front that he just found it somewhere.
- Second, Hugo's missing father and uncle are both two-dimensional characters who serve overly similar roles in the narrative.

But this is a great example of how one change can solve multiple problems. If the saintly father and the dastardly uncle were combined into one complex character, then many problems would start to solve themselves:

- The backstory would be much simpler, because only one father figure would have to disappear instead of two.
- The drunken-but-loving dad could find the automaton, bring it home, and then *lie* to Hugo, idly boasting he built it himself. This way, after his father disappears and Hugo finds out the automaton was designed to write a message, his belief that it will give him a secret message from his dad would make perfect sense.
- The story would be more *touching*: Hugo would be especially unwilling to admit the automaton actually belonged to the old watchmaker because it would require Hugo to finally admit that his late father was a liar. That would make Hugo's actions in the movie hard *to want* to do, not just hard to do.

Don't just dive in and start fixing your problems one by one. First, make a list of every problem, and then brainstorm a list of dozens of possible solutions to each problem. Truly brainstorm: If you're trying to avoid the dumb solutions, you'll block up your mind. When you write down your worst ideas, you'll realize they're not so dumb, you'll spot ways to improve them, or you'll open up a blocked neural pathway and discover a better solution hidden behind the dumb one.

Now you have dozens of problems and dozens of possible solutions for each one. Scan through them all to find solutions that will eliminate multiple problems.

- What if your heroine's crush is her boss's boyfriend? That would explain why she has to hide the relationship and keep lying to the guy.
- What if the person trying to kill your heroes is changed from an angry postal worker to a corrupt cop? That would explain why they can't go to the police *and* how the killer is able to identify and track them down (using their fingerprints, etc.).

Now you've got a list of fixes doing double duty, but nevertheless, you're going to be making a lot of changes. How do you keep track of them all?

Step Six: Allow Your Changes to Snowball

Once you finally have a list of all the changes you want to make, you're still not quite ready to dive into the rewrite. Before you implement any of your changes, it's good to outline each one and figure out its cumulative impact.

I convert my first drafts back into a scene list, then plug that list into the left-hand column of a two-column chart. In the right-hand column, I note which scenes will be deleted and which will be majorly rewritten. Then I look at the rest of the scenes, the ones I *didn't* plan to change, and I figure out how each will be affected as my big changes ripple through the script.

Every change, for better or for worse, is like a snowball at the top of a ski lift: As soon as you start it rolling, it will get bigger and bigger. If you decide to eliminate one minor character, you'll be shocked to realize how many scenes he was in, and how many little contributions to the plot he made that must now be handed off to other characters.

Summer blockbusters always have a million cooks in the kitchen, so they tend to do a *terrible* job at this. Earlier I mentioned one aspect of *The Avengers* that feels tacked on and disappears after it's brought up: the opposition to using the alien artifact to create weapons. But this is just one of many plot holes, motivation holes, *and* identification holes in that movie. I'm guessing that many of these were caused by the writers' last-minute attempts to fill one hole without realizing they were digging another.

Here's another note poor Joss Whedon seemed to have gotten at the last minute: "Give Agent Coulson a more heroic death!" So Whedon had Coulson pull out a big-ass laser cannon and shoot down Loki with his dying breath. Loki seems to be down for the count! Yay! But the next time we see Loki, a few moments later in the same action sequence, he's happily completing his escape, none the worse for wear. They addressed the note but ignored the effect it would have on subsequent events.

When they made that change, they needed to let it snowball through the rest of the story. One change must be allowed to cause another, which causes two more, until your second half is inevitably transformed by the avalanche thundering downhill. The hope is that these reverberating changes will eventually stop *creating* problems and start *solving* them as they offer you more opportunities to pair off your problems and cross them all off in a few elegant moves.

As you fall out of love with your original manuscript, you will hopefully come to appreciate this radical transformation more and more. You should look forward to the day when you can shudder with disgust at that slimy caterpillar you used to love, barely able to believe your graceful new butterfly could ever have sprung from such humble beginnings.

11

WHEN IT'S FINALLY TIME TO FINE-TUNE

The second draft should almost always be a *complete rewrite* of the first, and this wisdom might easily apply to the third and fourth drafts as well. Nevertheless, though I'm reluctant to admit it, you do *eventually* get to a place where you're *finally* ready to start tweaking, and that's an entirely different set of skills. Now that the personality of the main characters and the general order of events are pretty much locked in, you can make changes that are less likely to snowball. Now you can start sharpening each plot point, punching up every line of dialogue, highlighting the theme, etc.

STEP ONE: RE-HUMANIZE YOUR CHARACTERS

The most important quality characters can have is to be organic. They must live and breathe both on and off the page and speak to you (and the audience) in their natural voices. You must strive to achieve full humanity in your first draft, even if you know you probably won't get there. You cannot begin with a formula or follow the checklist to get the perfect hero. Let your characters try to be human and natural.

But once your first draft is finished and you send it out for notes, you might discover that your characters, organic as they may be, aren't connecting with readers. Their language is insufficiently human, their motivations are murky, and they aren't worth rooting for.

So what do you do now? You crack your manuscript back open and start tinkering, using the checklist and whatever other tricks you have. Soon, you "fix" your heroes: They have a consistent metaphor family and default argument tactic, have a strong and simple motivation that tracks throughout, and earn a rousing "stand up and cheer" every time.

But there's just one problem: You now have a perfect paint-by-numbers masterpiece of a hero, but it no longer feels organic. Instead, you have a collection of well-considered traits without a heart and soul. It's time to get to know (and love) your new-and-improved heroes just as well as you knew your original heroes. Let *them* talk to you, and then rewrite their dialogue and actions according to what they *now* want to say.

This is also a good time to reconnect your characters with each other. Do a full memory wipe and forget all the missing sections of conversation you cut (and still secretly miss). Instead, listen to the final conversation to see if it makes sense on its own. Chop out fragments of the old dialogue that no longer make sense, and add more "I understand you" moments now that *you* really understand them.

STEP TWO: SET UP MORE OF YOUR PAYOFFS

Chapter four covered the need for "special skills" and listed several heroes who made use of skills from their day jobs to solve problems in unique ways. But often you'll find these job skills aren't enough to get the hero out of *every* scrape, and the hero suddenly needs a previously unmentioned skill to overcome a specific obstacle.

Each time this happens, you can either stop, go back, and pre-plant a reason these skills exist, or you can do what I do: Just keep going, and fix it later. You wrote your story by going forward, but now's your chance to rewrite it *backward*. Set up a plant for every payoff, so as the audience reaches each twist, they'll say, "Aha!" instead of "Yeah, right!"

The trick with pre-establishing special skills is to do it subtly and organically. Here are contrasting examples:

- I mentioned earlier the ridiculous example of *Salt*: Salt's husband is an expert on spider venom, which seems random and apropos of nothing. Only later, when Salt uses a very silly spider-venom bullet do we realize why the writers put that in there.
- But that doesn't mean that a skillful writer can't *organically* introduce skills that will be needed later. In *Aliens*, writer-director James Cameron establishes early on that Ripley can run the fork-lift exoskeleton, which will come in handy later. He hides the significance of this by turning the plant into a nice little stand-up-and-cheer moment, wherein Ripley proves her lowly dock-loading job can be useful in her new military setting. By giving the moment a meaning of its own, he hides the fact that he's really just setting up a special skill Ripley will later need.

You can also write backward to pre-establish things that will go wrong for your hero. A final-season episode of *Breaking Bad* begins with an odd little scene establishing that a young boy is motorbiking around the desert collecting tarantulas. The audience forgets all about it until he shows up later, at the worst possible time. (This also provides a nice visual thematic metaphor: You can't bottle up evil for long.)

This is why buyers and publishers are especially impressed if you have a lot of "plant and payoff": It shows that you *literally* know your stuff backward and forward, you've been circumspect, and you've tightened all the screws and battened down the hatches. This assures them the finished product won't fall apart under pressure.

STEP THREE: HAVE STEPHEN HAWKING READ YOUR WORK BACK TO YOU

So you've been rewriting and revising so long that your manuscript is just a blur. You see it in layers, each sentence haunted by the ghost of what it used to be. Worse, each sentence is unable to forget its fallen brothers—all of the surrounding material that's come and gone—and feels it must carry the fallen banner of that material: I will stand here eternally as the last memorial to a section that's been mostly cut!

The problem, of course, is that strangers who approach this material for the first time won't appreciate this noble duty. Instead, they'll just wonder why this sentence doesn't really fit in.

Of course, this is something outside readers can help with, but by now, you've probably run out of fresh eyes. Nobody is answering the phone anymore. If only you could give yourself a new perspective! Well, good news—you can.

We live in a technological utopia these days, and many don't realize which new and powerful tools are available. Yes, you have the ability to compose on a computer, but did you know that computers have also gotten much better at reading your work back to you? Your operating system probably has the ability to do this no matter what program you wrote in. Look for tools intended for those with disabilities.

Yes, the voice is a little robotic, but you get used to that pretty quickly, and then something amazing happens: You become a stranger to your own work. You hear it as if it's being read to you for the first time, and you become your own fresh audience.

This has huge benefits:

- First, there's no better way to identify typos. You probably can't see typos anymore because each word is now a symbol representing your thoughts, so you can't actually read the letters. But this method will reveal a lot of typos, and it's essential to find as many as possible before you send the manuscript out. You're going to need a lot of notes from friends, and then you're going to want a lot of professional readers to evaluate your work. Typos drive professional readers *crazy,* sending the message that you don't respect their time and quickly turning them against you.

- Second, it shines a bright light on redundancies. You're probably circling the rim several times before your ball falls into the net, and you can't see that when you read. But once you hear your work, all that repetition will annoy even you, and you can be assured it will annoy others.

- Third, it should become increasingly clear that too many of your characters have the same voice. You can identify and cut out in-

stances of multiple characters using the same turns of phrase, as in the example we examined from *Law and Order: Criminal Intent.*
- Finally, it highlights awkward sentence structure. I once saw a TV show that contained this line: "There are walls even a man as dexterous as you can't climb." No actor can deliver that line well! Even in prose, it rings false when characters utter awkward phrases like this.

Have your document open while the audio file reads so you can fix things as you go or mark them to be fixed at your leisure. By the time you're finished, you'll be deeply grateful you didn't send it out to anyone yet.

Revision is the perfect time to worry about these things. During your first draft and your major rewrites, you can't be bothered to create full personalities for every minor character, and there's no reason you should, since you're going to cut out and combine a lot of these characters as you move the large pieces around. It's only when things begin to settle that you'll see who's left, and you can make those minor characters come to life.

At this point, we've used the checklist, received notes from peers and/or buyers, rewritten, rewritten, rewritten, and finally fine-tuned. Are we finished? Nope, there's still one last thing.

NOW CUT ANOTHER 10 PERCENT

If you're anything like me, your first drafts will be far too long, and then, as you begin to rewrite them, they'll get even *longer* as you add the missing elements. It's only once you've rewritten and revised that you can go back and start cutting it down.

Professional readers are overburdened, and the shortest manuscripts get read first. Everything you send out has to be lean, lean, lean. Here's an infuriating thing that agents love to say: "I love it. Don't change a thing. Just make it 10 percent shorter!" But how on earth are you supposed to cut pages *without* changing the story?

STEP ONE: REPLACE SCENES THAT *GRADUALLY* INTRODUCE YOUR HERO WITH *ONE* GREAT SCENE

The hope is, once you've expanded your stories enough, they'll gradually begin to *contract*. After all, if you can create a new scene that makes the character's flaw poignantly palpable in half of a page, then you can eliminate ten pages that merely *implied* the flaw. As you sharpen everything, the less-clear pages will start to fall away.

Once again, this is an area where fiction writers can learn from nonfiction writers. When writing a work of narrative nonfiction, writers learn hundreds of facts about each of their subjects. But instead of dumping all those facts on us, they introduce each character with a *single* detail that immediately tells us all we need to know.

Here are some favorites:

- Shelby Foote in *The Civil War* describes Stonewall Jackson disdainfully watching his men dance polkas in camp: "Jackson sat on a rail fence, sucking thoughtfully at a lemon."
- The late, great Michael Hastings in *The Operators* describes General Stanley McChrystal's days at West Point: "He gets over one hundred demerits, earning the title of a 'century man,' wearing it as a badge of honor."
- Steve Coll in *Ghost Wars* describes CIA director George Tenet's childhood, saying he was the best stickball player on his block, "capable of knocking a Spaldeen two sewers from home."

Just look at how much specific detail is packed into that tiny description of Tenet: the stick, the Spaldeen, the street-level mind-set where distance is measured in sewer grates. You can practically feel Tenet's humble working-class determination and exuberance. Tenet doesn't necessarily come off as a hero in this book, but he does come off as a human being.

Can you carry over these skills to your made-up story? You know your hero a lot better now than you did when you started writing. You probably wrote several scenes that allowed you to find the character when you began. But now you don't need them anymore. You need the *one* iconic scene that hits with surgical precision.

STEP TWO: COMBINE BEATS, SCENES, OR SEQUENCES SO THEY HIT SIMULTANEOUSLY

One of the most unpleasant notes you can receive is "This story is just one damn thing after another." This can especially be a problem in the vast middle of your story. Your hero encounters an obstacle, resolves it, encounters another obstacle, resolves it, encounters another obstacle, resolves it, and again, and again, and again. And here's the kicker: These are all *good* scenes. Each obstacle is shocking, and each solution is thrilling. Nobody is asking you to cut any one scene, but the cumulative effect of all those episodic solutions becomes boring.

Most great stand-alone stories are ultimately about the solution of one big problem. That problem may have a dozen complications and permutations, but it's all headed toward the same climax. As a result, we don't want to spend the middle taking a rough ride over a speed bump–filled highway. We want one big emotional roller coaster, either lifting us up or plunging us down at all times. So what do you do with all those speed bumps? You pile them on top of each other until those ten molehills become a few big mountains and valleys.

As soon as your hero commits to pursuing this opportunity, you should have three of these problems hit simultaneously, with each compounding the other. Our hero busts out one big solution to all three, and the story shifts into high gear. But the hero then discovers this big solution was shortsighted, and it leads to a big collapse where several consequences come crashing down together. Now our hero needs a new set of solutions, but this time they'll be based on greater self-knowledge.

As you rewrite, look for places where three crises happen back to back to back and ask yourself, "What if these three crises hit *at the same time* in the *same scene*?" This is also a great way to keep the audience from getting ahead of the story. Even if they can figure out how to solve *one* of these problems, they still don't know which problem your hero will have to tackle first, so they're constantly surprised. They're playing checkers, so you have to play chess.

The movie *American Hustle* is based on an original screenplay called *American Bullshit* by a different writer, but writer-director David O. Russell totally rewrote the script, and every change made it better. If you can find the original script online, compare it to the finished film, and you'll note the original has a distinct air of "one damn thing after another."

In the original, the final twist is way too obvious, because the story is very linear and the twist directly follows from the events that precede it: The hero realizes he's being set up to take the fall for the scheme, and this is his way out. We may not know exactly what he'll do, but we know he'll do something.

That dynamic is still there in the final film, but there are also a lot of *other* crises hitting at the same time: The hero's wife is about to be killed by the Mafia, his mistress is falling in love with the FBI agent, and he feels duty bound to help the mayor he betrayed. All of these crises (none of which were in the original script) hit at the same time, so we are too busy to notice what the hero is pulling off in response, and we're utterly astounded when he suddenly fixes all of these problems in one brilliant masterstroke. The plodding one-thing-after-another screenplay is merely exhausting, but the rewritten final film is exhilarating.

STEP THREE: EMBRACE TELEPORTATION

As writers, we are unbound by space and time. Don't plod from moment to moment; leap forward as necessary, even within a small space.

How long does it take a TV or movie character to cross a room? Any video editor can tell you the answer: As long as it takes to register in the audience's mind that the character is crossing the room. Screen time is conceptual time. You show the *concept* that she is on one side, then the *concept* that she is crossing the room, then the *concept* that she is on the other side. Each shot will last only as long as it takes for the concept to register. Put together, the three shots will never take as long as it actually takes to cross a room.

First-time film or video editors feel the need to make every cut a "match," as if they were just cutting in real time between multiple cameras shooting a live event. They're shocked to discover the result is the most god-awful viewing experience they've ever had.

Even when they've accepted that, it's still physically painful the first time they *force* themselves to "teleport" a character from "just starting to cross a room" to "arriving at the other side." Their brains are screaming at them, "How can you do this? You're *literally* breaking the rules of space and time! *The universe will end!*" But it doesn't, and the editor quickly falls in love with the new, speedier cut.

A movie, like any story in any medium, is not a space-time continuum but a conceptual continuum. We don't move from inch to inch or second to second; we move from concept to concept. Of course, how long it takes a character to get across a room is not usually something a *writer* has to worry about, but once you learn to think conceptually, you can make your stories move a lot faster.

Stop asking yourself, "How do I get out of this scene?" or "How can I give the character a reason to leave the room?" Avoid this dreadful line of thinking: "Where does the character go next? Wouldn't he have some downtime before the next scene? Maybe he goes to McDonald's? I know—I'll make that scene interesting by making the clerk really quirky!" No. Stop. Please.

It's not your job to get your characters from place to place or to follow them around all day. You don't even need to get them into the scene or out of the scene. Just show enough of the scene to get the concept across ("She is increasingly embarrassed for her sister," or "He sees something odd while researching the shady land deal"). Your characters can get themselves from place to place, and into or out of scenes, without bothering the audience about it.

STEP FOUR: CUT OUT THE "FALLOUT," OR ANY OTHER TYPE OF UNSURPRISING SCENE

One of the all-time great seasons of TV was the first year of *Homeland*. This show had *a lot* of shocks for the audience, and the writers kept them coming at a breakneck pace. How did they keep it up? They simply skipped over every scene that wasn't surprising, even though many had a lot of dramatic potential.

At the beginning of episode seven, "The Weekend," the audience quickly realizes two huge developments have happened off camera since the end of episode six. The co-protagonist and his wife have agreed to take some time off from their marriage, and the CIA has discovered that the suspect they've been desperately tracking has been killed by his own people, revealing a wider problem than they'd suspected.

Both of the missing scenes might seem like slam dunks with potential for high drama and great acting, but nothing *surprising* happens in either one. We had already guessed that Brody and his wife would need some time apart, and we'd already seen the suspect get killed.

The two scenes that got skipped were "fallout" scenes, and actors love fallout, but it doesn't move the story forward. These scenes come right out. If we hear Brody say he and his wife agreed to spend some time apart, we can imagine how that conversation went. If we see that the CIA is now looking for who might have killed their suspect, then we obviously understand they found the suspect's body and freaked out.

Homeland quickly went off the rails, but in that scintillating first season, it was ripped-from-the-headlines television at its best, so it held itself to the same standards as a good newspaper: Keep it riveting, and only tell people what they don't already know.

In *The Fast and the Furious*, Paul Walker infiltrates Vin Diesel's gang and seduces his sister. Later, in the middle of a crisis, he has to dramatically confess to the sister that he's a cop. Sometime afterward, she clearly reveals the secret to Diesel and his gang, but we never see that scene, despite the fact that it was probably quite intense. For the audience, it would be a repeated beat, dramatic but not surprising.

What's even more remarkable is that even when Walker and Diesel finally confront each other, they never discuss Walker's betrayal! That would be fallout, and the script doesn't need it. The discussion at the end is entirely about whether Walker will arrest Diesel, without any "You betrayed me!" recriminations about the past. A great way to speed things up is to keep your characters arguing about what's *going* to happen, instead of what happened previously. The audience won't miss the fallout.

STEP FIVE: CUT OUT THE APOLOGIES

One time I gave a fellow student notes on his story outline. It was a family drama, with a lot of arguments back and forth. Just scanning down the list, I said, "Well, first of all, you need to cut out beat eight." Beat eight was "Everybody apologizes."

In our real families and relationships, we apologize all the time. That's why nothing really exciting happens to us. We defuse emotional situations before they get too big. Forget what they say in *Love Story*: In real life, love means you *always* have to say you're sorry. If we want to experience big cathartic emotions, we do it vicariously through fiction, where we see what would have happened if we *hadn't* apologized.

In most stories, people never get to apologize. Not until the very end, anyway. That doesn't mean everybody has to be a jerk. You can have a bunch of well-intentioned characters, but the fickle finger of fate intervenes to stop them from saying the right things to each other.

Never let up. In stories, things go from bad to worse, even if nobody wants them to. If she wants to apologize, interrupt her. Whenever anyone is about to release tension, interrupt them. Is the couple on the date about to kiss? Interrupt them. About to have sex? Pull them apart. You might think the audience will love you if you give them what they want. Not true. Make them want it, and then yank it away.

What's the real reason for all this *coitus interruptus*? Why not let your characters act like normal people and give the audience the release they're looking for? Because if you gave it to them easily, then they wouldn't want it. Audiences are like everybody else: They only want what they can't have.

Early on in *Black Swan*, Natalie Portman's character accidentally insults a fellow dancer, prematurely congratulating her on getting the role that Portman has actually won for herself. It looks like she did it on purpose to rub it in, even though it's just an honest mistake. But the movie doesn't give Portman the chance to apologize. In fact, we never see the ousted dancer again. Apology scenes are death. They reverse the momentum. Maybe Portman's character did apologize, but we don't see it, because the writers preferred to constantly tighten the screws without stopping to loosen any.

STEP SIX: ELIMINATE THE ORPHANS

This is a quick-and-dirty way screenwriters cut out a page: We go through and find every block of dialogue that has only one word hanging down onto the next line, and we pull a word out of each of those blocks.

Yes, this is a cheat, but it also gets you in the habit of looking for ways to streamline *every* sentence. Once you start, you'll hopefully find yourself cutting out stuff even if it *doesn't* save any space. You're not just trying to reduce the amount of paper in the reader's hand; you're also trying to speed up the reading experience.

This is something every type of writer should do: Trim down every paragraph until it takes up one less line. Try to cut a word out of every sentence and maybe even a sentence from every paragraph. Make it fly.

And let me reiterate the importance of removing most of the commas from your dialogue *and* prose. Commas are literally bumps in the flow of your text, and each one causes your audience to stumble for a second before resuming their regular flow. Take them out, even if each one only saves you one millimeter of space.

STEP SEVEN: CREATE A "TOO-SHORT VERSION" WHERE YOU SLIM DOWN EVEN MORE SCENES

As mentioned in chapter six, it's great to slice off the first two lines, last two lines, and even chunks of the middle of your scenes. It's good to try to do that as you write, but it's hard. You want to make sure your audience is with you every step of the way, and it's easy to feel panic at the thought of jumping ahead and leaving them behind.

But now, it's much easier to make those cuts. Try this:

- Save your current version with all of that connective tissue safely intact, and create a *new* copy called "The Too-Short Version." This will give you the mental freedom to make cuts that seem to be way too much.

- Go through and cut out all the lines that ramp up, ramp down, and string together your scenes.
- Then go back and reread it. Do you miss those lines? If so, put them back in. But I'll bet that you won't.

Soon I suspect that you'll rename "The Too-Short Version" as "Current Draft."

STEP EIGHT: SOMETIMES, YOU JUST HAVE TO SAY, "IT COMES RIGHT OUT"

These are all good reasons to cut stuff out of your story. But there's one we haven't gotten to yet: It comes out because it comes out.

Once I was talking to another writer about his sitcom development deal, and of course he was agonizing about the endless number of notes he was getting, even though he agreed with most of them and trusted the producers. At one point, they were suggesting about twenty jokes that could come out of the script. He thought they were all funny, and the producers generally agreed, but they had a different reason to cut each one: It contradicted character motivation, took the momentum out of a scene, muddied the tone, etc.

Then they got to another line that had gotten a big laugh at the read through and, upon reflection, suggested that he cut that one, too. "But why?" he asked. "Everybody loves that line!"

"Yeah," the producer said, "but it comes right out."

That's it. That was their reasoning. In the study of logic, this is known as a tautology: It comes out because it comes out, so it comes out. It drove him crazy! But after a day or so of frustration, he realized they were right. TV is relentlessly linear and relentlessly tight. Every moment needs to be part of the cascading chain of setup and payoff, or else it needs to go.

So that's it! You're done! Send it out to contests and your contacts, and blow everybody away. Oh, right, one last piece of advice ...

13

THE FINAL RULE

....

FORGET EVERYTHING I JUST SAID

I owe you one final caveat about all of this advice.

I've given you a tremendous number of tools for evaluating your manuscripts, but what do you do with the results? If the checklist convinces you that you have problem areas, you'll probably want to go through and fix them one by one, but I should warn you, adding a dozen spot fixes can be problematic. No matter how thoroughly I've convinced you that something about your story needs to be changed, there is always a risk that your fixes will feel externally imposed, unlike organic story developments. Your story might become "better" in a way that's cold and mechanical.

Well, okay, so what if you *start* with the checklist, applying it to your *beat sheet* before you begin, and then consciously apply the checklist questions at every step *as* you write? Well, again, I have to warn you: That's also risky. The danger is, if you're consciously applying the checklist at every step of the way, you'll be more focused on what you *don't* want to do than what you *do* want to do. To write well, you must find a way to enjoy (or at least *appreciate*) your own story as you're writing it, with a tingling sense of freedom and excitement about where it might go. You mustn't grimly proceed down a straight and narrow path, hemmed in by rules on every side.

So, why did you just read this book? You just wasted several hours of your life, only to discover these rules can't be followed! Forget it!

Well, guess what? You're right. Forget everything I just said. Rules are meant to be broken. Don't follow any writing rules ever. I really mean that.

Instead of having *rules* about writing, you need to have *beliefs* about writing. Rules are meant to be broken, but beliefs are sure to be followed. As long as these are rules to you, they won't do you much good, but if you *believe* these things, they'll work wonders.

If this advice is just "stuff that book said to do," then it's pretty easy to reject it. Even if you think of it as "really *clever* stuff that book said to do," then you still haven't internalized it, and it won't help very much. Instead, you need to reach the point where you say, "I don't remember if I read this somewhere or if I just made it up, but I've always found it works out if you let your hero ..." That's when this advice *really* becomes valuable.

This advice will only really help when it becomes second nature. It's hard to fix a passive hero retroactively, but it can be just as hard to police your heroes for signs of passivity in real time without blocking your creative process. The real goal is to get to the point where you're simply unable to create a passive hero, because it just seems intrinsically wrong. That's when you know you've internalized the advice.

My point is not to outlaw certain choices or insist on others. It's to point out that there are certain ways great stories tend to work. Once you learn those ways, you can use them to write a classically perfect story (like *North by Northwest*) or you can break some rules and take your audience out of their comfort zone (as with *Vertigo*), but either way, *you* should know exactly where that comfort zone is and how far you're from it at all times.

I highly recommend you now go check out SecretsofStory.com, where I frog-march several excellent new and old movies and TV pilots through the entire checklist and examine where they "broke the rules." For each deviation, I judge how well that departure works: Most of the time, this "mistake" is actually a good idea, because it's an exception that proves the rule, and stepping outside audience expectations is a key part of the story's statement. Indeed, these storytellers are *very aware* that they're pushing the audience outside of their comfort zone and skillfully using that discomfort to make the point more powerful.

For each question you're stuck on, go through the sample checklist and determine how each movie and TV show answers that question. You'll probably find 85 percent of the stories earn a yes, 5 percent earn a no in a problematic way, and the remaining 10 percent earn a no in a clever way, intentionally flouting audience expectations in a pointed and powerful way.

Fulfilling the steps of this checklist can be very powerful, and defying them can be even more powerful, *if* you know why you're doing it, what the risks are, and what effect your choice will have on your audience.

So go through the checklist, examine each question, *question* each question, *doubt* each question, and *reject* each question if you can. Decide for yourself if you really *believe* these nutty ideas.

If you find you don't believe any part of this book, just forget I said anything. And if you do believe it, just forget I was the one who said it.

CONCLUSION

....

TELL GREAT STORIES OR DIE!

This all started with George Clooney on *ER* and my frantic attempts to figure out why his saline-drip introduction was so compelling, until I finally made some progress by getting a saline drip of my own, unblocking my creative juices.

Over the course of this book, I hope I've assembled the vital tools you need to create volatile characters and stories at *any* time, on cue, with no hospital visits necessary.

As we wrap up, allow me to draw one last conclusion from my own story: Shortly after I began chemo, I got a chilling visit from an old college friend who had gone on to become a big-shot doctor (Mayo Clinic, Johns Hopkins, etc.). When I told him I was stage 4B, his face went pale and he started looking at me in the past tense.

He urgently took me aside and confided a terrible secret he felt I needed to hear: The most important thing I could do to stay alive was to make sure my doctors *remembered me*, even when I wasn't in their office, and the only way to do that was to make my story a lot more *compelling* than their other cases.

Doctors, he admitted, only allow themselves to get upset if certain heart-tugging patients die (new parents, for example), and they unintentionally reserve their best care for those patients. For the rest, they unconsciously decide that if this patient dies, it must just be their time.

Why should this be so? Doctors, after all, are paid to care about *everybody*. And the fact is, they *do* care, deeply, about their first forty or fifty patients. But after that, every patient starts to seem the same:

the same backstory, the same symptoms, the same complaints, the same prognosis. Worst of all, a sneaking suspicion comes over these doctors that they care about their patients more than those patients care about themselves. Patients won't change their lifestyles even when doctors tell them it's necessary to survive. So doctors stop investing in most individual cases to protect themselves emotionally.

Does this sound familiar? Doctors, it turns out, are a lot like professional manuscript readers, who are also supposed to care about every manuscript they get but quickly get fed up with generic stories about passive protagonists who can't even be bothered to care about themselves—so why should anyone else?

Ultimately both doctors and professional readers come to the same conclusion: "It hurts too much to care about these useless jerks, so I'm just going to go on autopilot until an especially compelling story wakes me up."

What I took away from this warning was, when you meet with your doctors, you can't just "seem sympathetic." You can't just tell your doctors about how many cats you saved this week. You have to *create a compelling character.*

Make it clear to them that there's more to you than whatever their first impression was—quirky and unique details that make you memorable. Describe your symptoms using shocking new metaphors they've never heard before, so they can really imagine the pain. Show them you have some big personal goals in sight so it'll be especially sad if you can't reach them. Prove to them you're motivated and resourceful, and they can trust you to take two steps for every one they take. And, most important, constantly remind them you're facing a very tight (and literal) deadline, so you need them to work with impassioned urgency.

In other words, tell a great story if you want to live.

I really believe this is the reason I'm alive today. Instead of presenting myself as a blandly generic "nice guy," I started doing whatever I could to let my doctors and nurses know I was a specific, flawed, compelling person. Rather than simply generate the same old earnest pathos, I did whatever I could to alert them to the oddly amusing *iro-*

nies of my unique situation, such as the saline-drip story. I tried my best to create a uniquely compelling character that would lodge in their minds and tug at their hearts.

This is why *everybody* needs to be able to tell a great story. Stories are powerful tools for achieving almost any objective, but only if you understand what your audience needs from you to *truly* care.

This book isn't your ticket to fame and fortune. I haven't attempted to teach you a secret handshake that will get you into an elite club of billionaires. I'm not your fairy godmother, and your writing career will not be a Cinderella story. Writing is a long struggle and a tough job that doesn't pay very well.

So why did I write this book? *Because writing is worth doing.* And I want everybody to try it and work at it and improve. The ability to make strangers care about a story is a vital skill, whether it's a fictional saga you're creating, a piece of nonfiction you're reporting, or just your *own* story you're telling, maybe in a speech you're giving, or a cover letter you're writing, or even in your first meeting with a jaded oncologist.

Wake your audience up. Wake publishers up. Wake producers up. Wake your doctors up. Let them know that, *this* time, it's safe for them to really care, because you have what it takes to compel them along to an emotionally satisfying conclusion. This time, they'll be moved. This time, there will be a satisfying payoff.

Doesn't that sound like it's worth doing? Doesn't that sound like something everyone should know how to do?

The evidence is overwhelming—clearly, obviously, definitively, your mission going forward, in fiction and in real life, must be this: *Tell great stories … or die!*

AFTERWORD

. . . .

Thanks for reading! For more advice, examples, and bonus material, please visit SecretsofStory.com. You'll find:

- Career advice, including sections on how to write every day, give and receive notes, launch your career, find representation, meet with buyers, and sell challenging material.
- Two dozen examples of films analyzed according to the Ultimate Story Checklist.
- A massive chart that helps clarify the difference between the goals, long-standing social problems, flaws, and the dramatic question for all of our examples.
- A chart that compares my proposed structure to those of other gurus.
- An in-depth series of articles on the fundamental differences between different media, especially books versus movies.
- A series of instructional articles that address how to write a pilot episode of an ongoing series.
- A supplemental version of the Ultimate Story Checklist specifically tailored to pilot stories.
- A dozen examples of popular TV pilots analyzed according to the pilot checklist.

APPENDIX
The Ultimate Story Checklist

CONCOCTING AN
INTRIGUING CONCEPT

The Elevator Pitch

1. Is the one-sentence description uniquely appealing?

2. Does the concept contain an intriguing ironic contradiction?

3. Is this a story anyone can identify with, projected onto a bigger canvas, with higher stakes?

Story Fundamentals

4. Is the concept simple enough to spend more time on character than plot?

5. Is there one character whom the audience will choose to be their hero?

6. Does the story follow the progress of the hero's problem, not the hero's daily life?

7. Does the story present a unique central relationship?

8. Is at least one actual human being opposed to what the hero is doing?

9. Does this challenge represent the hero's greatest hope and/or greatest fear and/or an ironic answer to the hero's question?

10. Does something inside the hero have a particularly volatile reaction to the challenge?

11. Does this challenge become something that's not just hard for the hero to do (an obstacle) but also hard for the hero to want to do (a conflict)?

12. In the end, is the hero the only one who can solve the problem?

13. Does the situation permanently transform the hero, and vice versa?

The Hook

14. Does the story satisfy the basic human urges that get people to buy and recommend this genre?

15. Does this story show us at least one image we haven't seen before (that can be used to promote the final product)?

16. Is there at least one "Holy Crap!" scene (to create word of mouth)?

17. Does the story contain a surprise that is not obvious from the beginning?

18. Is the story marketable without revealing the surprise?

19. Is the conflict compelling and ironic both before and after the surprise?

CREATING COMPELLING CHARACTERS

....

Believe

20. Does the hero have a moment of humanity early on?

21. Is the hero defined by ongoing actions and attitudes, not by backstory?

22. Does the hero have a well-defined public identity?

23. Does the surface characterization ironically contrast with a hidden interior self?

24. Does the hero have a consistent metaphor family?

25. Does the hero have a default personality trait?

26. Does the hero have a default argument tactic?

27. Is the hero's primary motivation for tackling this challenge strong, simple, and revealed early on?

Care

28. Does the hero start out with a shortsighted or wrongheaded philosophy (or accept a bad piece of advice early on)?

29. Does the hero have a false or shortsighted goal in the first half?

30. Does the hero have an open fear or anxiety about his future, as well as a hidden, private fear?

31. Is the hero physically and emotionally vulnerable?

32. Does the hero have at least one untenable great flaw we empathize with?

Invest

33. Is that great flaw (ironically) the natural flip side of a great strength we admire?

34. Is the hero curious?

35. Is the hero generally resourceful?

36. Does the hero have general rules for living that he clings to (either stated or implied)?

37. Is the hero surrounded by people who sorely lack his or her most valuable quality?

38. And is the hero willing to let them know that, subtly or directly?

39. Is the hero already doing something active when the story begins?

40. Does the hero have (or claim) decision-making authority?

41. Does the hero use pre-established special skills to solve problems?

SHAPING A RESONANT STRUCTURE

First Quarter: The Challenge

42. When the story begins, is the hero becoming increasingly irritated about her longstanding social problem (while still in denial about an internal flaw)?

43. Does this problem become undeniable due to a social humiliation at the beginning of the story?

44. Does the hero discover an intimidating opportunity to fix the problem?

45. Does the hero hesitate until the stakes are raised?

46. Does the hero commit to pursuing the opportunity by the end of the first quarter?

Second Quarter: The Easy Way

47. Does the hero's pursuit of the opportunity quickly lead to an unforeseen conflict with another person?

48. Does the hero try the easy way throughout the second quarter?

49. Does the hero have some fun and get excited about the possibility of success?

50. Does the easy way lead to a big crash around the midpoint, resulting in the loss of a safe space and/or sheltering relationship?

Third Quarter: The Hard Way

51. Does the hero try the hard way from this point on?

52. Does the hero find out who her real friends and enemies are?

53. Do the stakes, pace, and motivation all escalate at this point?

54. Does the hero learn from mistakes in a painful way?

55. Does a further setback lead to a spiritual crisis?

Fourth Quarter: The Climax

56. Does the hero adopt a corrected philosophy at this point?

57. After the crisis, does the hero finally commit to pursuing a corrected goal, which still seems far away?

58. By the time the final quarter of the story begins (if not long before), has your hero switched to being proactive instead of reactive?

59. Despite these proactive steps, is the time line unexpectedly moved up, forcing the hero to improvise for the finale?

60. Do all strands of the story and most of the characters come together for the climactic confrontation?

61. Does the hero's inner struggle climax shortly after (or possibly at the same time as) her outer struggle?

62. Is there an epilogue/aftermath/denouement in which the challenge is finally resolved (or succumbed to), and we see how much the hero has changed?

STAGING STRATEGIC SCENE WORK

Setup

63. Were tense and/or hopeful (and usually false) expectations for this interaction established beforehand?

64. Does the scene eliminate small talk and repeated beats by cutting out the beginning (or possibly even the middle)?

65. Is this an intimidating setting that keeps characters active?

66. Is one of the scene partners not planning to have this conversation (and quite possibly have something better to do)?

67. Is there at least one nonplot element complicating the scene?

68. Does the scene establish its own mini-ticking clock (if only through subconscious anticipation)?

Conflict

69. Does each scene both advance the plot and reveal character through emotional reactions?

70. Does the audience have (or develop) a rooting interest in this scene (which may sometimes shift)?

71. Are two agendas genuinely clashing (rather than merely two personalities)?

72. Does the scene have both a surface and a suppressed conflict?

73. Is the suppressed conflict (which may or may not come to the surface) implied through subtext (and/or called out by the other character)?

74. Are the characters cagey or in denial about their own feelings?

75. Do characters use verbal tricks and traps to get what they want, not just direct confrontation?

76. Is there re-blocking, including literal push and pull between the scene partners (that often results in just one touch)?

77. Are objects given or taken, representing larger values?

Outcome

78. As a result of this scene, does at least one of the scene partners end up doing something she didn't intend to do when the scene began?

79. Does the outcome of the scene ironically reverse and/or fulfill the original intention?

80. Are previously asked questions answered and new questions posed?

81. Does the scene cut out early on a question?

82. Is the audience left with a growing hope and/or fear of what might happen next?

DRAFTING ELECTRIC DIALOGUE

....

Empathetic

83. Does the writing demonstrate empathy for all of the characters?

84. Does each character, including the hero, have a limited perspective?

85. Do the characters consciously and unconsciously prioritize their own wants, rather than the wants of others?

86. Are the characters resistant to openly admitting their feelings to others and even themselves?

87. Do the characters avoid saying things they wouldn't say and doing things they wouldn't do?

88. Do the characters interrupt each other often?

Specific

89. Does the dialogue capture the jargon and tradecraft of the profession and/or setting?

90. Are there additional characters with distinct metaphor families, default personality traits, and default argument strategies distinct from the hero's?

Heightened

91. Is the dialogue more concise than real talk?

92. Does the dialogue have more personality than real talk?

93. Are there minimal commas in the dialogue?

94. Do characters (excluding professors) speak without dependent clauses, conditionals, or parallel construction?

95. Are the non-three-dimensional characters impartially polarized into head, heart, and gut?

Strategic

96. Does the hero have at least one big "I understand you" moment with a love interest or primary emotional partner?

97. Is exposition withheld until the hero and the audience are both demanding to know it?

98. Is there one gut-punch scene where the subtext falls away and the characters really lay into each other?

MAINTAINING A METICULOUS TONE

Genre

99. Is the story limited to one genre (or multiple, merged genres) introduced from the beginning?

100. Is the story limited to compatible subgenres, without mixing metaphors?

101. Does the ending satisfy most of the genre expectations and defy a few others?

102. Separate from genre, is a consistent mood established early and maintained throughout?

Framing

103. Is there a dramatic question posed early on that establishes which moment will mark the end of the story?

104. Does the story use framing devices to establish genre, mood, and expectations?

105. Are there characters whose situations suggest possible fates for the hero?

106. Does foreshadowing create anticipation and suspense (and refocus the audience's attention on what's important)?

107. Are reversible behaviors used to foreshadow and then confirm change?

108. Is the dramatic question answered at the very end of the story?

INTERWEAVING AN
IRRECONCILABLE THEME

Difficult

109. Can the overall theme be stated in the form of an irreconcilable good-versus-good or evil-versus-evil dilemma?

110. Is a thematic question asked out loud or clearly implied in the first half and left open?

111. Do the characters consistently have to choose between goods or between evils instead of choosing between good and evil?

Grounded

112. Does the story reflect the way the world works?

113. Does the story have something authentic to say about this type of setting?

114. Does the story include twinges of real-life national pain?

115. Are these issues and the overall dilemma addressed in a way that avoids moral hypocrisy?

116. Do all of the actions have real consequences?

Subtle

117. Do many small details throughout subtly and/or ironically tie into the thematic dilemma?

118. Are one or more objects representing larger ideas that grow in meaning each time they're exchanged throughout the story?

Untidy

119. Does the ending tip toward one side of the thematic dilemma without entirely resolving it?

120. Does the story's outcome ironically contrast with the initial goal?

121. In the end, is the plot not entirely tidy?

122. Do the characters refuse or fail to synthesize the meaning of the story?

INDEX

action, 122–23, 166, 167–70, 282–84

agenda, 179–80, 190

anticipation, 109, 116, 173–75, 260, 261–62

antiheroes, 25, 61, 82

apologies, 327–28

audience, 116

  and characters, 17–18, 20–21, 89, 176

  choice of hero, 18–20, 60–61, 116

  dramatic question, 256

  and empathy, 82, 84–86, 85, 89, 249, 284

  expectations of, 23–25, 33–35, 36, 241, 242–44, 274–76

  guessing what happens next, 245–47

  identification, 13, 26–28, 44, 45–48, 61, 82, 176–78, 310–11

  and plot, 20, 176

  rooting interest, 176–78, 213–14

  and story ending, 295

  and structure, 134–35

  and theme, 267–68

  writing for, 16–17

authenticity, 34, 162, 274–76, 277–79

background information, 219

backstory, 93–94, 238–39

behavior, 262–64

believability, 89, 90–106, 341

"big crash," 136, 137, 146

body language, 168

central idea, 52

challenges, hero's, 65–67, 137, 138–43, 343

change. *See* transformation

character arc, 71, 264

characterization, 36, 95–97

characters, 81. *See also* heroes

  action, 167–70

  and audience, 17–18, 20–21, 89, 176

  believable, 89, 90–106, 341

  caring about, 106–11, 341–42

  compelling, 81–127

  complexities of, 22

  creating, 23, 341–42

  and dialogue, 205–10

  and dilemmas, 268–69, 272–74

  emotional stakes, 59–60

  empathy for, 210–11

  expectations of, 90–91

  feelings of, 184–85, 216–17

goals, 180, 187, 269
identifying with, 45–48
inner life of, 95
introducing, 322–23
investing in, 89, 342
and irony, 200–201
listening to, 217–20
main (*See* heroes)
misconceptions about, 81–89
misunderstood, 28–29
parallel, 261
personality, 226–27
perspective, 211–13
and plot, 69, 71
polarized, 204–10
questions to ask about, 89–127
re-humanizing, 317–18
relationship between, 62–63, 234–36
revealing, 175–76
secondary, 22, 224–25, 232
self-image, 118–19
self-interest, 213–15
and story meaning, 295–96
transformation, 34, 58, 70–71, 131
verbal tricks, 185–87
clichés, 34, 69, 227, 254
cliff-hangers, 174, 194
climax, 138, 150–56, 173, 175, 177, 247, 290, 324, 344
commas, 227–29, 329
commitment, 143
compassion, 91
complexity, 59

complications, 171–73, 174
concept, 42–80, 325–26, 339–40
execution of, 50–52
ironic, 36, 56–58
misconceptions about, 42–52
questions about, 52–80
simple, 58–60
what it is, 42, 78
conditional statements, 229–32
conflict, 62–65, 67–68, 154–55, 164, 174
false, 192
importance through entire story, 79–80
increasing, 168
indirect, 157–58, 239
interpersonal, 271
and scene work, 175–90, 345–46
suppressed, 181–84
unforeseen, 132, 133, 137, 143–44
confrontation, 153–54, 184–87, 185
consequences, 58, 116, 282–84
contradictions, 95, 96–97
conversations, 170–71
counterpoint, 172
crisis, 138, 147, 149, 324–25
curiosity, 115–16
cutting, 166–67, 198, 322–30
deadlines, 152–53
decision-making, 123–24, 189
default argument tactic, 101–3, 224–25
default personality traits, 100–101, 224–25
dependent clauses, 229–32

details, 277, 285–86, 322–23

dialect, 197

dialogue, 47, 97–100, 196–240, 263, 347–48

  and characters, 205–10

  empathetic, 210–21, 347

  extreme points of view, 207

  heightened, 225–33, 348

  how to write, 197–200

  ironic, 37, 200–203

  listening to characters, 217–20

  misconceptions about, 196–210

  and personality, 225–27

  purpose of, 269

  questions to ask about, 210–40

  specificity, 221–25, 347

  strategic, 234–40, 348

  unnecessary, 194

  what it is, 196

dilemmas, 267–69, 270–74, 280–82, 290–92

discontentment, 131

distractions, 115–16, 172

dramatic question, 256–57, 264–65

"easy way," 136, 137, 143–46, 343–44

elevator pitch, 52, 53–58, 339

emotions, 24, 48–50, 58, 63, 87–89, 100–101, 168, 174, 175–76, 202, 287

empathy, 25–26, 82, 84–86, 89, 110–11, 141, 210–21, 284, 312, 347

ending, story, 153–54

  and characters, 295–96

  and dramatic question, 256–57, 264–65

and genre expectations, 253–54

  and plot, 294–95

  satisfying, 281–82

  and thematic dilemma, 290–92

epilogue, 155–56

ethics, 120

evil and good. *See* good and evil

expectations, 90–91, 165–66, 242–44

  audience's, 23–25, 33–35, 36, 241, 242–44

  and framing devices, 258–60

  and genre, 244–45, 250, 253

  hero's, 191–93

  and outcome, 36

  reversal of, 237

exposition, 236–37

failure, 146, 191

fallout scenes, 326–27

fear, 65–66, 108–9, 195

feedback. *See* notes

feelings, 184–85, 216–17

flashbacks, 258

flash-forwards, 259

flaws, 110–11, 112–15, 121, 138–40

foreshadowing, 164, 261–62, 262–64

framing, 249, 256–65, 349–50

friction, 161, 162–63, 248

fundamentals, story, 52, 58–71

genre, 242–44, 244–45, 249, 250–56, 258–60, 349

goals, 107–8, 149, 150–51, 180, 235, 269

good and evil, 266, 267, 271, 272–74, 281

gut-punch scenes, 239–40

"hard way," 136, 138, 147–49, 344

heroes, 18–20. *See also* characters

    active, 122–23, 133

    audience identification with, 26–28

    challenges, 65–67

    choices, 267, 271

    choosing, 18–20, 60–61, 116

    and conflict, 63–65, 67–68

    creating, 119–20

    curiosity, 115–16

    defined, 82

    empathy with (*See* empathy)

    fears, 108–9

    flaws, 110–11, 112–15, 121, 138–40

    identifying with (*See* identification)

    investing in, 112–27

    misunderstood, 96

    motivation, 103–6

    necessary qualities, 82

    personality, 100–101, 102

    philosophy, 86–87, 100–101, 106–7

    point of view, 21–23

    problem (*See* problem)

    public identity, 94–96

    relationship with other characters, 93–94, 260–61

    self-image, 118–19

    special skills, 318–19

    strengths and flaws, 112–15

    transformation of, 34, 58, 70–71, 131

    vulnerability of, 84, 89, 91, 109–10

    willfulness, 120–21

hesitation, 142

high-concept idea, 55

holes, 309–12

"holy crap!" scene, 75–76

hook, 52, 72–80, 340

hope, 65–66, 195

human nature, 33, 72–74, 131, 136, 250, 274–76

humanity, moment of, 90–93

humiliation, social, 138, 140–41

humor, 90, 92, 203

hypocrisy, moral, 280–82

"I understand you" moment, 234–36

ideas, 17, 50–52, 55, 78, 277–79

identification, 13, 26–28, 44, 45–48, 61, 82, 176–78, 310–11

imagery, 74–75, 159

improvisation, 133–34, 152–53

inciting incident, 131–33, 137

inner life, 95–97

instructors, writing, 300

internal conflict, 64–65, 154–55, 204

interruptions, 220–21, 328

irony, 35–37, 56–58, 94, 96–97, 112, 132, 164, 238

    concept, 36, 56–58

    dialogue, 37, 200–203

    moral dilemmas, 267

    and scene work, 37, 191–93

    story's outcome, 292–94

    and tone, 247–49

    unintentional, 200–202

jargon, 221–24

language, 98–100, 196–97, 197–200, 227

logline, 53–56

love interest, 160–61, 216–17, 234–36

marketing, 74–75, 78, 245

meaning, 36, 164, 166, 188–90, 268–70, 287–90, 295–96

metaphor family, 97–100, 224–25

metaphors, 204, 231–32, 251–53

mistakes, 149

misunderstandings, 192–93

momentum, 143

mood, 254–56, 258–60. *See also* tone

moral, 266–67

mortification, 35

motivation, 103–6, 131, 133, 148, 173, 212, 309–10, 312

national pain, 279–80

nonplot elements, 161–64, 171–73

notes, 299–300, 301, 302–7, 309–11, 312

objects, meaningful, 188–90, 287–90

observation, 277–79

obstacles, 67–68, 160, 168, 186

oddball moments, 91–92, 172

opportunity, 65, 132, 137, 138, 141–42

opposition. *See* conflict

orphans, 329

outcome, 35–36, 164, 165–66, 190–95, 260, 292–94, 346

out-of-character moment, 90–91

pace, 148

pain, national, 279–80

parallel construction, 229–32

partner, emotional, 234–36

past-tense narration, 258, 259–60

payoffs, 318–19

personality, 98–100, 100–101, 102, 196–97, 199, 225–27

perspective, 211–13

philosophy, statement of, 86–87, 100–101, 106–7, 138, 149, 150, 235

plot, 20, 59–60, 69, 71, 159–60, 175–76, 294–95, 309

point of view, 21–23, 253

polarization, 204–10, 232–33

present-tense narration, 258, 262

proactivity, 135, 138, 151–52

problem, 29–31, 47, 61–62, 69, 124–27, 129–30, 136–37, 138–40, 141, 214, 256, 324

promotion, 74–75

protagonist. *See* heroes

questions, 193–94, 272. *See also* dramatic question

reactivity, 151–52, 175–76

readers. *See* audience

real life, 274–76

re-blocking, 187–88

red herrings, 172

rejection, 11–12

resourcefulness, 116–18

reversal, 147–48, 165, 191–93, 237

revision, 11, 301–2

reward, 103, 142

rewriting, 12, 299–316. *See also* cutting; notes

  how to do it, 307–16

  misconceptions about, 299–307

  what it is, 299

risk and reward, 103, 142

sarcasm, 200–203

satire, 77

"save the cat" moment, 26, 91, 119

scene work, 157–95, 345–46

  conflict (*See* conflict)

  defined, 157

  ironic, 37, 191–93

  misconceptions about, 157–64

  outcome, 164, 190–95, 346

  questions to ask about, 164–95

  re-blocking, 187–88

  setup, 164, 165–75, 345

scenes

  gut-punch, 239–40

  ironic, 37

  replacing, 322–23

  rewriting, 323–25, 326–27, 329–30

  that create word of mouth, 75–76

secondary characters, 22, 224–25, 232

self-examination, 137, 138

self-interest, 213–15

sentences, 197, 229–32, 329

sequels, 243–44, 246–47

setback, 138, 149

setting, 47, 167–70, 277–79

setup, scene work, 164, 165–75, 345

"setup and payoff," 263

spin-offs, 243

spirit characters, 208

stakes, 59–60, 85, 106, 148

story

  fundamentals, 339

  making it meaningful, 274–76

  meaning of, 268–69

  writing lean and simple, 42–44

strength, 85, 112–15

structure, 31–33, 128–56, 343–44

  and audience, 134–35

  ironic, 36

  misconceptions about, 128–37

  questions to ask about, 137–56

  what it is, 128

struggle, 112, 154–55

subconscious, 174–75, 260, 295

subgenres, 251–53

subtext, 160–61, 169, 181–84, 189–90, 239–40

success, 145, 147, 191

superheroes, 85

surprise, 77–78

suspense, 261–62

sympathy, 120, 140, 141, 152, 178, 249, 284

syntax, 196–97

teleportation, 325–26

tension, dramatic, 112, 116, 239

texture, 162

thematic question, 272

theme, 266–96, 351–52

  and audience, 267–68

  difficult, 270–74, 351

  grounded, 274–84, 351

  ironic, 37

  misconceptions about, 266–70

  questions to ask about, 270–96

  subtle, 285–90, 352

  untidy, 290–96, 352

  what it is, 266

ticking clock, 173–75

title, ironic, 56–58

tone, 241–65, 349–50
    and irony, 37, 247–49
    misconceptions about, 242–49
    questions to ask about, 249–65
    what it is, 241
totem objects, 188–90, 287–90
tradecraft, 221–24
transformation, 262–64
transformation, character, 34, 58,
    70–71, 131
transitions, 194
trust, 116
turning points, 136–37
twist, 77–78, 159–60, 246–47
Ultimate Story Checklist, 38–296,
    298, 332–33, 338–52
undercurrent, 194
universal moments, 92–93
values, 108

verbal tricks, 185–87
verisimilitude, 161–64, 198
villains, 22, 177
voice, 47, 200, 225
vulnerability, 84, 85, 89, 91, 109–10
"way the world works" rule, 276
willfulness, 120–21
writing. *See also* rewriting
    beliefs about, 332–33
    cutting, 322–30
    essential laws of, 15–37
    fine-tuning, 317–21
    fixing problems, 312–16
    formulaic, 32, 33
    lean, 161–64
    reading out loud, 320–21
    skills and talent, 39–41
    "what you know," 48–50